uncomfortable

television

hunter

hargraves

D1526338

© 2023 DUKE UNIVERSITY PRESS. All rights reserved
Printed in the United States of America on acid-free paper ∞

Project Editor: Bird Williams
Designed by Aimee C. Harrison
Typeset in Minion Pro and Trade Gothic LT Std
by Westchester Publishing Services

Library of Congress Cataloging-in-Publication Data
Names: Hargraves, Hunter, 1983 author.
Title: Uncomfortable television / Hunter Hargraves.
Description: Durham : Duke University Press, 2023. | Includes
bibliographical references and index.
Identifiers: LCCN 2022035135 (print)
LCCN 2022035136 (ebook)
ISBN 9781478016939 (hardcover)
ISBN 9781478019572 (paperback)
ISBN 9781478024194 (ebook)
Subjects: LCSH: Television—United States—History—21st century. |
Television broadcasting—Social aspects—United States. | Television
programs—United States—Influence. | Television viewers—United
States. | BISAC: PERFORMING ARTS / Television / History & Criticism
Classification: LCC PN 1992.6 .H364 2023 (print)
LCC PN1992.6 (ebook)
DDC 791.450973/0905—dc23/eng/20221011
LC record available at https://lccn.loc.gov/2022035135
LC ebook record available at https://lccn.loc.gov/2022035136

Cover art: Adaptation of still from CSI, "King Baby," Season 5,
Episode 15.

uncomfortable

television

DUKE UNIVERSITY PRESS DURHAM AND LONDON 2023

For the Uglies

contents

acknowledgments

Like television, a first book is a collective enterprise, and I am deeply indebted to all of the scholars and extended family members who enjoy analyzing television with me. Television frequently centers itself around the image of a stable and close-knit family; like many queers of my generation, my relationship to such a concept has had to be negotiated and expanded. My parents, Marilyn and Sandy, instilled in me at a very early age a love for reading and thinking, for which I am very grateful. My sisters, Morgan and Hailey, have deeply etched their care onto this work: rescuing me from within my head and geeking out with me in the best of ways.

Lynne Joyrich's unflagging support and optimism are the primary reason this book exists today. She continues to be a genuinely kind and supportive mentor who makes everyone feel like intellectual peers, regardless of rank—and I aspire to her generosity always. Wendy Chun and Rebecca Schneider expanded and honed my views on affect in nuanced and intersectional ways, helping me understand the act of thinking polemically in solidarity with others. Laurie Ouellette has an uncanny ability to crystallize and sharpen my thoughts about television's often-hazy affective atmospheres—conversations with her always leave me feeling inspired. All of these brilliant scholars have challenged my ideas about television and popular culture while still welcoming and centering their weirdness, and this book is immensely richer for their imprint.

I thank Ellen Rooney, Barbara Herrnstein Smith, and Patricia Ybarra for their support while I was a graduate student at Brown. Elizabeth Weed, Suzanne Stewart-Steinberg, and Denise Davis married feminist rigor with friendship at the Pembroke Center and especially during its seminar on consent, in which I participated as a Graduate Student Fellow. Liza Hebert and Susan McNeil were indispensable to my graduate education, providing foundations of support beyond what I could have anticipated or asked. Of course, to survive in graduate school requires the networks of support offered by one's peers, many of whom influenced this project far beyond Providence: Peter Bussigel, Anna Watkins Fisher, Maggie Hennefeld, Brian Horton, Lydia Kelow-Bennett, Mike Litwack, Nathan Lee, Rijuta Mehta, Matt Noble-Olson, Coleman Nye, Pooja Rangan, Tim Syme, and, most importantly, Hans Vermy.

This book was drafted and completed while teaching at California State University, Fullerton (CSUF). I am lucky to have a department chair, Garry Hart, who consistently found ways to support my research within the under-funded state university system. Rebecca Sheehan is a fantastic colleague and friend who helped me refine this project's contours through conversations that made Orange County traffic jams strangely satisfying. Heather Osborne-Thompson and Martina Baldwin are similarly loyal interlocutors with whom I never tire of talking television and who never fail to make me smile. Other folks at CSUF who have energetically supported this book include Christina Ceisel, Vanessa Díaz, Tanis Fields, and Karyl Ketchum. Many thanks to all of my students who shared their intellectual enthusiasm about television in and out of the classroom; of these, Victoria Serafini, Micah Chambers, and Ad Loya stand out for their insights.

I would not remain in this profession without the warmth of colleagues and friends from across the humanities (many of whom generously read early drafts of various chapters): Miranda Banks, Cal Biruk, Michelle Cho, Aymar Christian, Ramzi Fawaz, Joseph Fischel, Hollis Griffin, Julia Himberg, Greta LaFleur, Julie Levin Russo, Taylor Nygaard, Don Romesburg, Poulomi Saha, and Jeff Scheible. The mentorship offered by Vicky Johnson, Misha Kavka, David Román, Nick Salvato, Karen Tongson (an early booster of this book), and Amy Villarejo has been crucial to my belonging within this vibrant and multifaceted intellectual community. Michael Warner's fingerprints are all over this book despite our vastly different archives; I am thankful to him for guiding many of my initial inquiries into the pleasurable dimensions of discomfort.

Several chapters were developed at conferences sponsored by the Society for Cinema and Media Studies, Console-ing Passions, and the American Studies Association, as well as at invited talks at Sonoma State University's Department of Women's and Gender Studies, Cornell University's Department of Performing and Media Arts, and the University of Michigan's Department of Communication and Media: I thank all of these audiences for their engagement and incisive questions. At Duke, Liz Ault has been indispensable, championing this book early on in ways that made its publication exciting: I could not ask for a better editor. Thanks to Benjamin Kossak, Liz Smith, Bird Williams, and Steph Attia for shepherding the book through production, Aimee Harrison for designing the perfect cover, and to the anonymous reviewers for their generative feedback, especially in pushing me to develop a more holistic conceptualization of affect.

Three names in particular have been instrumental to this project. Sanjay Hukku has been there from the very beginning, helping incite this book's origins through a combination of theoretical mastery, dark wit, and a shared love of mid-2000s *SVU*. He has taught me a specifically queer way to navigate this profession: a praxis of calling out and corrupting in the name of social and intellectual change. Lakshmi Padmanabhan does this as well through her trenchant questioning of what I assume and where I should go; I know now to follow her addictive laugh anywhere. Brandy Monk-Payton is the best coconspirator in the field, never failing to volley one of my ideas into different terrain. Whether hate watching or Deschanel-ing together at conferences, her very presence magnifies and enriches my thought.

I am extraordinarily fortunate to count a large number of powerful queers, storytellers, lovers, and fellow troublemakers as a chosen family that continuously nurtures and challenges me. Without them, I would be much poorer in spirit: Mike Albrecht, Daniela Aramayo, Joseph Barajas, Marke Bieschke, Sara Chang, Jacob Clifton, Emma Cunningham, David Davis, Mario Diaz, Joey Falcone, Stephan Ferris, Brian Freia, Isiam Friar, Ællen Freytag, Michael Friedman, Sindri Galván, Melissa Getreau, A.J. Goodrich, Corey Jiannalone, Aaron Kovalchik, Kyle Kupres, Kyndall Mason, Doug Mathern, Sam Moen, Chris Mourkabel, Luke Nagle, Popstar Nima, John Polly, Brontez Purnell, Jafri Rambeau, Corinne Rinehart, David Schnur, Malcom Gregory Scott, Tim Wood, Astor Yang, and Anna Zivarts. Jeff Carter's steadfast generosity and patience merit particular mention here, as do those of Joseph Nederveld, who had the uncomfortable pleasure of creating a home with me as this book came to fruition. And finally, to Aram, Ari, Beardoncé, Benwa, Blake, Carlos, Chè, Dami, Danimal, Dom, Ethan, Førge, Hex, HRO, Hush, Jiggles, Journey, Karis, Lapis, Matt, Major, Miss Louque, Mitchell, Nuh-uh, Oddly, Porkchop, Scooter, Spunk, Tangle, Texxx, and Tiger: your love is a restorative exercise in the deliberate ways one learns, and is made better from, navigating this fraught world and all of its discomfort. Thank you to all for showing me such joy.

introduction

TELEVISION *SCRIPTS*

This is a book about being made to feel uncomfortable by television. For most of the twentieth century, television—and especially American television, which structured the medium within a commercial context—pursued large audiences through typically family-friendly broadcasts, selling consumer comfort and narrative pleasure alongside broader cultural signifiers of postwar middle-class stability. Yet as television entered into the new millennium, it began to change on aesthetic, formal, generic, industrial, and technological grounds. While these changes to television have been extensively documented, little has been written about this television's affective texture: how these changes elicited different and often discordant responses from its spectators. *Uncomfortable Television* examines what I call postmillennial American television: television from roughly the early and mid-2000s until the mid-to-late 2010s, a period in which scenes and relations of discomfort became widely introduced into the spectatorial lexicon. Postmillennial television acculturated audiences to embrace discomfort in tandem with other changes to the medium, just as those same audiences were being asked to conform to the labors, rhythms, and social structures of late capitalism. It did so by marrying these changes in TV form, genre, industry, and technology to key affects of discomfort. Television thus began to normalize discomfort during this time as a strategy of governmentality, Michel Foucault's term for the way that the state governs and manages populations at a distance through various social institutions. By focusing on the changes that made postmillennial television a comparatively more exciting medium than what came before it, audiences learned how to transform feelings of discomfort into feelings of pleasure, a skill necessary to adjust fully into the systems of economic precarity and cultural instability brought on by the instantiation of neoliberalism into daily life.

Postmillennial television is a flexible category, referring to different viewing practices, technologies, genres, and narrative forms of television, all of which affect its content. Under this book's categorization, not all popular television programs broadcast from the 2000s to the early 2010s qualify as postmillennial television, insofar as many of that time span's most-watched series (for example, *Friends* and ER) had already been on the air for years. While the category is defined relationally to the television that came before it, the changes to TV addressed in this book include the following: the explosion of reality programming and the impact it has had on production processes, labor, and celebrity; the increased serialization across many genres of programming, but particularly within dramatic programming produced by cable networks; the legitimation of television as an art form, which translated to higher production budgets and expanded aesthetic effects; the widespread growth in platforms and technologies of distribution, which include subscription video on-demand (SVOD) services on streaming platforms; the increase in narrative adaptation across other media forms and global programming; and the expansive practice of reflexive commentary and criticism on TV (through think pieces, social media, and fan cultures, among others).

These changes have resulted in a television first considered to be "post-network" and "post–public service"—a television, according to one early scholarly anthology periodizing these changes, "after TV."[1] But these changes also have had concrete effects on the tone and topical matter of programming; far from the sanitized, family-friendly fare of its past, the television of the early twenty-first century bombarded viewers with unlikeable protagonists, widespread profanity, depictions of graphic violence and explicit sex, and the exploitation of cultural minorities. To give a few examples of this bombardment, many of which I explore in greater detail in later chapters: Police procedurals began to depict sexual assaults against women and children as quotidian events in metropolitan cities. Cheaply produced reality programs began to profile ordinary individuals and families as they engaged in decidedly excessive hobbies and behaviors, such as accumulating so much stuff as to make domestic life untenable or becoming addicted to life-threatening substances. Original dramatic programs exemplary of television's new "golden age" began to chronicle the violent lifestyles of individuals in the drug trade and the Mafia as well as those of several serial killers and white supremacists.[2] Comedy, too, began to embrace new norms revolving around cringeworthy interactions between coworkers, friends, and potential romantic partners and around character tropes such as the irritating or mentally unstable millennial.

To introduce the contradictory feelings of pleasure and discomfort that come from postmillennial television's rewriting of televisual conventions, consider two television episodes about masturbation. The episode "Come On, God," from the second season of the acclaimed comedy series *Louie* (FX, 2010–2015), opens on the televisual, specifically, the Fox News late-night program

LIVE

LOUIE C.K.
COMEDIAN/MASTURBATOR

I.1 Louie's appearance on Fox News late-night program *Red Eye with Greg Gutfeld*. *Louie*, "Come On, God," Season 2, Episode 8.

Red Eye with Greg Gutfeld, in which the episode's topic is masturbation.[3] Attacking the art of self-pleasure is Ellen Farber (Liz Holtan), an attractive Christian who believes that masturbation deprives young people of purity and grace. Defending masturbation is Ellen's foil, Louie (Louis C.K.), introduced by Gutfeld as "a man who is well-known for being a prolific masturbator, who even brags about it." In a roughly six-minute-long segment, Ellen asks Louie if he has ever attempted to stop masturbating (he responds negatively), and Louie asks Ellen if she has ever been married (she responds negatively). Ellen volleys next, asking Louie, "Have you ever been happy? Are you happy now?" As the camera zooms in on C.K., it emphasizes his discomfort, before alternating between shots of Gutfeld and of the full panel, all in an awkward silence.

Later, Louie masturbates, though not to completion, to a fantasy involving a woman with whom he shared an elevator. His fantasy devolves into a farcical attempt to place a literal "bag of dicks" into the object of his desire. He then attends one of Ellen's purity seminars, and afterward the two walk down the street while processing their respective relationships to sex. Louie reveals that during his first experience reaching orgasm with a woman, he farted, and this fateful act formed "the basis of [his] whole life sexually . . . just shame and cum and farts." A rapport established, Ellen invites Louie back to her hotel room for a drink, during which he attempts to kiss her. Assertively rejecting Louie's advances, Ellen voices her own desire for monogamous Christian love, in which both partners experience sex for the first time without shame or fear. Aroused by such a fantasy yet also entirely alienated from it, Louie

3

rushes to her hotel room's bathroom, furiously masturbating and climaxing with a long, drawn-out fart. The episode concludes with Louie at home, masturbating to digital stock images of *M*A*S*H* actress Loretta Swit until a BBC radio broadcast graphically describing Somalian genocide interrupts him, thwarting his attempts to orgasm.

In the episode, masturbation functions as an ontological characteristic of maleness: in Louie's stand-up routines that punctuate the narrative action, he self-deprecatingly argues that all (straight) men masturbate in order to deal with their presumably much worse perversions. The episode links masturbation visually and narratively to desperation, nihilism, and misogyny symptomatic of a perceived loss of White masculinity in a changing world. This treatment of masturbation resonates with twenty-first-century heteropessimism—evocatively defined by Asa Seresin as a set of performative disidentifications with heterosexuality that ultimately do not abandon heteropatriarchal desires, structures, and affects altogether—as an immutable and anesthetic condition.[4] Louie's attitudes toward masturbation stem, he suspects, from a disastrous high school hand job, and he subsequently reduces this root expression of male sexuality to affective responses of dissociation (shame) and markers of male physical and olfactory virility (cum and farts). "Come On, God" thus frames masturbation in line with Victorian scientific literature connecting the act to degeneracy and delinquency. While Louie justifies the act on *Red Eye* by saying, "It keeps me sane—I'm a good citizen, I'm a good father, I recycle, and I masturbate," the episode's use of awkward silences, compressed space, and narrative interruptions undermine this defense, as even Louie appears confused and chagrined by how exploitative his masturbatory fantasies have become and by how quickly he nonetheless embraces them. The episode represents a marked departure from scholarly attempts to link masturbation to the individual development of the modern subject, such as in Eve Sedgwick's description of the act as a "reservoir of potentially utopian metaphors and energies for independence, self-possession, and a rapture that may owe relatively little to political or interpersonal abjection."[5] The episode instead renders Louie's beliefs on masturbation as well as his constant desire to masturbate as deeply abject, always already inscribed by his failure to respect women fully. While the camera's frame is cropped carefully so as not to show genitalia, the episode presents masturbation in exhibitionistic and excessive terms, as in the exaggerated pouts of the woman in the elevator asking Louie to penetrate her with a "bag of dicks," or in the soft camera movements meant to represent the act itself. Rob King has argued that "in *Louie*, absurdist fantasy is the boomerang" in opposition to the lure of abjection, one of many dialectics central to the auteur's visual and narrative style.[6] For Louie, masturbation's explicitness (its permanence as a fact of male heterosexuality) as well as its mediation (its dependence on controlling women as objects of desire) advance the heteropessimistic thesis that all male fantasies must compulsively mistreat women.

Of course, this argument was corroborated by C.K.'s own predatory behavior. In November 2017, the *New York Times* published accusations of his sexual misconduct made by five women: C.K. masturbated in front of two women after a late-night show at the US Comedy Arts Festival; he masturbated during a phone call with another woman; and he asked another woman permission to masturbate in front of her.[7] The following day in a statement to the press, C.K. confirmed these accounts, and he quickly became one of the television industry's highest-profile casualties among that year's #MeToo scandals: his film *I Love You, Daddy*, then nearly ready for distribution, was canned, and both FX networks and Netflix cut all ties to him.[8]

Now contrast *Louie*'s commentary on masturbation with one that aired nearly twenty-two years earlier, the 1992 episode "The Contest," from the NBC comedy series *Seinfeld* (1989–1998). "The Contest" presents masturbation through its absence: network prohibitions prevented the word from being uttered in prime time, and thus the episode relies on euphemisms for comedic effect.[9] The plot revolves around a bet to see which of the series' four protagonists can go the longest without masturbating; importantly, the temptations each face in this challenge—a neighbor who walks around her apartment naked, an attractive nurse giving a patient a sponge bath, John F. Kennedy Jr.—are shown in silhouette or out-of-frame entirely. Masturbation is still a constant, a release required to maintain sanity, but neither *Seinfeld*'s characters nor its audience are exposed to the subject and object of masturbatory desire, which would force a confrontation with that desire's potential to offend audiences. In fact, most critics and fans view "The Contest" as completely *inoffensive*, insofar as network censorship facilitated a comedic expression of sexual desire that was light-hearted, with the characters more angry about losing money than about their relationship to self-pleasure.[10] Both *Seinfeld* and *Louie* feature straight, White male comedians (Jerry Seinfeld and C.K., respectively) who play somewhat fictionalized versions of themselves, like many noted TV comedians before them, and who integrate their stand-up routines into the structure of each episode. Both series have also been recognized for their writing within the logics of quality afforded to episodic comedy; "The Contest" earned *Seinfeld* cocreator Larry David the Emmy Award for Outstanding Writing in a Comedy Series, for example,

5

while C.K. was nominated for the same award during each year of *Louie*'s five-season run (winning twice). How, then, to explain the stark differences between these representations of masturbation, an act that—despite its habitual omnipresence—remained a rarity within the narratives of prime-time television for most of the medium's history?[11]

The surface-level differences between *Seinfeld* and *Louie*—network versus cable, multicamera versus single camera, episodic resolution versus narrative complexity—have been extensively documented in television criticism and scholarship. If *Seinfeld* represents one era of TV genre, *Louie* represents its next instantiation: serialized narratives that test formerly accepted boundaries of episode and season length. *Louie*'s episodes largely consist of vignettes shot handheld in cinema verité style, with camera angles in shot–reverse shot sequences slightly out of proportion, mapping imperfect lines of sight onto its characters. In their attempt at selecting the "greatest American shows of all time," critics Alan Sepinwall and Matt Zoller Seitz find *Louie*'s "revolutionary" formal innovation to be its legacy, asserting that the series "translated the thought processes of stand-up comedy into cinematic terms."[12] And *Louie* fits easily into FX's stable of adult-oriented and provocative programming; as critic Tim Goodman writes (in unapologetically masculinist prose): "Series on FX have balls, no question about it. They are aggro, not Zen."[13] Yet these aforementioned differences fail to account fully for this shift in tone. In hindsight, C.K. may have been attempting to confess to his own perversions through *Louie*, cloaking his collapse of the space between representation and reality through rough, amateur aesthetic techniques (a shallow depth of field, mostly handheld camera work, and little lighting) and loosely bound narrative form.[14] Functioning as a kind of script for actual episodes of misconduct, *Louie* communicates specific identity truths to its audience: that men are not capable of enacting romantic gestures toward women without also sexually demeaning them. Yet this script was rarely recognized as such by cultural critics and scholars, with *Louie*'s auteur-driven and formally innovative brand encouraging audiences to disinvest in the possibility that C.K. himself could be a sexual predator. The revelations of his misconduct force questions about how audiences should respond to episodes such as "Come On, God": Was C.K. trolling his audience all along, daring them to suspend their disbelief in his own capacity to assault women? How were audiences trained to disavow and, indeed, take pleasure from, the consequences of such a breakdown between representation and reality? Why is what is beloved about C.K.—his significance to the evolution of early twenty-first-century television comedy—also what makes him dangerous, irresponsible, and ultimately uncomfortable?

Sitting beside a TV "Gone Too Far"

As a historiography of television's formal relationship to pleasure, *Uncomfortable Television* describes a script for how audiences reconceptualize the boundaries of pleasure and discomfort, drawing from a number of schools of thought: television history and theory; feminist, anti-racist, and queer theories of affect; and cultural, political, and economic periodizations of late capitalism. This book places these bodies of knowledge *beside* each other, bearing witness to their many collisions while tracing the affective residue that subsequently lingers. The emphasis on the preposition is intentional, as the notion of the *beside* rejects binary critique, offering instead a critical practice that affirms instability, promiscuity, mobility, contingency, and circulation. Eve Sedgwick uses the term to describe a perceptual lens that allows us to think in terms of nondualistic modes of critique; she maintains that "the irreducibly spatial positionality of *beside* also seems to offer some useful resistance to the ease with which *beneath* and *beyond* turn from spatial descriptors into implicit narratives of, respectively, origin and telos."[15]

I find the term particularly rich for the study of television, a medium that historically defined spectatorship through configurations of domestic space. This book summons certain figures that affectively appear beside spectators and who in turn animate affective reactions within audiences—irritated millennials, addicts, and the urban poor, among others—who help them make sense of the present. As a medium of popular culture, television functions as one of the ideological state apparatuses famously outlined by Louis Althusser that interpellates individuals as constituted subjects. As Richard Dienst has observed of Althusser's canonical essay on ideology, however, ideology does not necessarily hail the subject in place but rather operates within a communicative context.[16] Even though television has historically replicated the status quo, buttressing key institutions such as the family and the nation, the "short circuit between the singular and the general" created by television allows for possibilities of rupture, and thus the medium has also been positioned as committed to incrementalism, often alluding to the disruptive forces of social change while concurrently containing those disruptions.[17] Television's ability to thrill from the safety of the domestic home implies that audiences are interpellated "at a distance" (as the *tele-* in television suggests), drawing attention to the significance of the affective conditions of interpellation. When these figures of discomfort trigger affective dispossessions—minor acknowledgments of discomfort—within the viewer, television provides viewers with pathways of rationalization and disavowal as a strategy of containment. That these

figures represent perverse but necessary forms of neoliberal subjectivity testifies to Jodi Dean's (here riffing off Slavoj Žižek's) framing of communicative
capitalism as "characterized by the prevalence of the superego injunction to
enjoy."[18] In describing both how new cultural forms and practices articulated
through discomfort emerged around the millennium as television's response
to late capitalism, and how audiences willingly embraced discomfort as a
way to gain pleasure from (and, at times, resist) these cultural logics, this book
employs discomfort as a reparative viewing practice.[19] Because television is a
medium fundamentally of the present, analyzing the moments of discomfort
that regularly punctuate postmillennial television allow us to view better
how television has disseminated new regulatory norms regarding American
cultural, economic, and political life.

Uncomfortable Television turns to affect as necessary to make sense of this
changed relationship to pleasure. As I explore in the next chapter, the renewed
interest in affect across the humanities and social sciences resonates with the
ascendancy of neoliberal culture. I thus consistently problematize distinctions
between the affective and the ideological throughout this book, believing
both analytical modes necessary for making sense of television, the dominant
entertainment medium of late capitalism. Following the work of scholars like
Amy Villarejo and Sara Ahmed, this is a rather ethereally *queer* book: queer
not only in that it demonstrates the entanglement of political-economic, aesthetic, technological, and formal concerns, but queer in that it thinks through
the rather queer feelings experienced by spectators who are confronted with
provocative material on their screens.[20] Indeed, a certain structural fluidity
undergirds many of the terms and concepts central to this book. *Discomfort*, for example, manifests as disgust, perversion, addiction, uncanniness,
disidentification, realism, and irritation. *Television* includes both broadcast
programs as well as those found on streaming platforms and transformative
works created by fans disseminated online. As free-floating, *affect* itself can
encompass a range of embodied responses. And *representation* can refer both
to processes of spectatorial identification (watching people who purport to
"represent" you demographically or visually) as well as to the acknowledged
staging of real-life situations ubiquitous to television programming. One of
my goals in this book is to trace the promiscuous encounters between and
beside all these terms, insisting on their promiscuity because of the affective
flexibility demanded by neoliberal culture.

The clash between affect (as presubjective or individual) and ideology
(as institutional or social) makes the act of identifying and categorizing uncomfortable television difficult. Who determines, for example, what counts

as uncomfortable, and for which audiences? In a seminal text of audience-reception theory, "Encoding/Decoding," Stuart Hall advanced a set of three possible ways that readers make meaning from texts: preferred readings (in which readers receive the dominant ideology of the status quo reflected in the text and by its creators), negotiated readings (in which readers may modify the preferred reading based on their own positions or experiences), and oppositional readings (in which the reader's social position places them in direct conflict with the preferred reading, and thus they reject it).[21] To find a text uncomfortable or disturbing may be a privileged reaction based on its position within this schema, in part because Hall assumes that social identities and experiences are key determinants in how audiences affectively respond to and make meaning from texts. This could partially explain, in the example of *Louie*, why male television critics generally lauded *Louie*'s gender politics as "complex" and "complicated" without attempting to derive many moral lessons from it, whereas female television critics consistently expressed troubling and conflicted feelings about *Louie*'s toxic masculinity well before the revelations about C.K.'s sexual misconduct surfaced.[22] These reactions are often influenced by *Louie*'s use of various mirroring and framing devices: episodes in the program's early seasons were often framed by stand-up, mirroring two smaller stories against one another. Such formal techniques allow for more contested readings to emerge, especially since Louie, in many of his stand-up routines, makes broad generalizations about the behavioral patterns of straight men and women. While the encounters with discomfort described in this book are not thought of as universal, they are informed by the representational practices of television and its attendant discursive apparatuses (such as television criticism or fan cultures). In many instances, like in *Louie*, metacomedic gags are deployed to provoke a confrontation with uncomfortable or offensive material; in this sense, *Louie* is no different from other television programs that self-referentially and mockingly announce their flaws—Louie's flaws, this argument goes, are simply more abject or perverse.

Even television critics have metatextually acknowledged similar provocations. One example is a March 2005 issue of *Time* that posed the question "Has TV Gone Too Far?" while announcing on its cover, "What's really at stake in the red-hot indecency war." The accompanying cover story by James Poniewozik takes up this question through an investigation into the Parents Television Council's (PTC) anti-indecency campaign, which was organized in the mid-2000s around instances of nudity and sexual content, profanity, and violence.[23] Poniewozik provides no close readings of the offensive material in question, framing his approach to indecency solely through the reactions of

9

activist viewers, itself a selective arrangement organizing spectatorship around discomfort that includes both political conservatives (on the grounds of decency) and liberals (on the grounds of speech). A 2005 episode of CSI: *Crime Scene Investigation* (CBS, 2000–2015) about infantilism is the most fleshed out example of indecency within the story, and Poniewozik focuses more on the PTC's highlighting of the episode's popularity (30.72 million household viewers) than on describing the plot, which he does in a single sentence. He notes how *CSI* opens up a set of questions about the conjunction of the popular and the perverse: "It is probably the most gruesome, explicit drama on broadcast TV—and it is the single most popular. Did all those people tune in by accident? When the greatest plurality of viewers chooses to watch a show they know to be graphic, can that show be beyond the pale? Or does [the PTC] simply not like where the pale is nowadays?" While I will return to this particular episode of *CSI* (and others like it) in a later chapter, it is important to note that the scope of his article precludes Poniewozik from considering *CSI*'s form (episodic procedural) or its primary narrative and aesthetic devices (omniscient forensic technologies). The importance he places on ratings as a barometer for the tolerance of content suggests a faith in a free-market approach to viewing pleasure, one reinforced by the industry: if viewers are truly offended by such content, he implies, they would change the channel.

Time magazine's cover image affirms this free-market logic: actress Teri Hatcher, the star of *Desperate Housewives* (ABC, 2004–2012), lies down on a bed, holding a remote control in her right hand and placing her left hand over her mouth in feigned shock. Light emanating from the television set illuminates Hatcher's face, positioning her as the spectator of TV "gone too far," with such a linguistic construction implying an acceptable amount of indecency.[24] Her mouth is slightly puckered in a vaguely sexual way, and she wears a night-robe that gestures both to television's private and domestic nature—it is not uncommon to find television in a bedroom—and to Hatcher's character in *Desperate Housewives*, Susan Mayer, who often found herself in steamy romances with the men of Wisteria Lane. Far from innocent, her exaggerated eyebrows make her appear to revel in her complicit position as both the instigator and recipient of indecency (tellingly, some reviews of *Desperate Housewives* found her guilty of overacting); she thus blurs the boundaries between representation and reality not unlike C.K., whose character Louie is similarly grossed out by what television depicts. Readers of *Time* can be inferred to share the same position as the TV set, a TV "gone too far"; but even indecent television, the cover implies, produces a viewer savvy to the medium's theatricality and intertextuality. *Time* thus scripts its readers to find

I.2 Teri Hatcher on the cover of *Time*, March 28, 2005.

an intimate comfort with an "indecency" that is tied to television's artistic value.[25] In other words, the savvy TV audience knows quite well how "far" content has gone and finds that content acceptable and even exciting.

Televisual Neoliberalism at the Millennium

A television "gone too far" represents redefinitions of the medium's technological, aesthetic, generic, industrial, and formal aspects; yet within many studies of contemporary television these redefinitions are rarely linked to the larger cultural and economic changes brought on by neoliberalism and felt within American popular culture during this same time period. (Importantly, the subfield of reality television studies has consistently thought through the

11

genre's neoliberal shape, as I later describe.)[26] Late capitalism here refers to the shift from a period marked by an emphasis on post-Fordist modes of production and consumption to one marked by the fluidity of capital, the movement of multinational media conglomerates, and the rise of management discourse; or the historical difference between what Luc Boltanski and Eve Chiapello frame as the second and third "spirits" of capitalism.[27] Driven by commercialization, privatization, and marketization, late capitalism—and, crucially, the television industry that late capitalism depends on in order to maintain its ideological hegemony—reshaped the dominant vector of consumption, changing it from one emphasizing the mass as a public to one emphasizing the individual as a unique, mobile, and diversified consumer. On television, this manifested through practices of narrowcasting, or targeting niche audiences through a menu of expanded cable channels and technologies such as DVRs and SVOD platforms that divorce the viewer from the live broadcasting schedule while giving them more options of series to watch. This fractured the once-dominant units of viewers such as the family into discrete and diffused audiences, resulting in broadcasting that now reflects, in the words of William Uricchio, "adaptive agent mediations of individual tastes."[28] It has also allowed for the expansion of the diegetic universe of a series and for the consolidation of authorship, as in when showrunners, directors, writers, and actors provide interviews and commentary across a series' paratexts. But this requires new logics of calculation to determine the new audience's individual tastes, and algorithms thus occupy an important space in organizing spectatorship and even the creative decisions behind production.[29]

Neoliberalism is generally used to describe an economic relationship between free markets, the state, and civil society. Historicizing neoliberalism is a difficult task, and one that is ultimately not my project here. Most accounts of neoliberalism place its ascendancy during the 1970s, starting from the implementation of free-market economic policy in Latin America to its de facto adoption as official state policy in the United States during the Reagan presidency.[30] Regardless, neoliberalism has been associated with a number of political, economic, and cultural discourses, namely an emphasis on individual rights, the privatization and deregulation of state assets (including the welfare state), and new global scales of production supervised by corporate conglomerates. These discourses are what interest me most in my study of a popular culture, which is partially indebted to neoliberal policy. Elizabeth Povinelli asserts that neoliberalism refers "not [to] an event, but [to] a set of uneven social struggles within the liberal diaspora."[31] Neoliberalism, we may say, takes as its project the promiscuity of late capitalism, allowing for a diffuse set of political and cultural actors to indulge in its applicability. It may make sense, in fact, to characterize the cultural consequences of neoliberal state and economic policy more as a *turn* than as an *-ism*: a neoliberal turning toward and beside individuation, privatization, global markets, and customization that plays out across a range of cultural texts.

Framing these shifts as a neoliberal *turn* allows for a different reading of popular entertainment cultures: while neoliberalism as an economic system has been implemented on both domestic and international scales since at least the 1970s, the average American citizen did not then immediately turn toward—or turn away from—its cultural effects. This book contends that neoliberalism's effects on popular culture and on everyday American life began to be felt throughout the 1990s and normalized as embodied feelings throughout the 2000s. As Wendy Brown has argued, the 1970s and 1980s saw the institutionalizing of neoliberal policy throughout the Americas and Western Europe, but these policies were often brought on by "fiat and force." Yet by the 1990s, neoliberal policy started to be implemented "through specific techniques of governance, through best practices and legal tweaks . . . through 'soft power' drawing on consensus and buy-in, [rather] than through violence, dictatorial command, or even overt political platforms."[32] The West turned to neoliberalism with certain affection throughout the 1990s. Once the Cold War could be declared officially over, multinational corporations—including, importantly, those within the media industries—began to consolidate a "new world order" thanks to advances in telecommunications technologies. The sale of the "Big Three" networks (ABC to Disney, for $18.28 billion in 1996, and CBS to Viacom, for $34.9 billion in 1999) gave Disney and Viacom a wide variety of network and cable platforms with which to target tailored audiences. Disney, in fact, was frequently invoked as a prime symbol of the customized standardization of cultural experiences brought on by neoliberal policies, becoming a metonym for globalization during this time, alongside other brands such as Starbucks and McDonald's.

Neoliberalism can best be summarized as a formula of economization: it gestures toward the transformation of human capital, energy, and rationality into economic capital, energy, and rationality. These transformations have resulted in the proliferation of neoliberal discourses into schemas of representation (such as television programming) and their concomitant decoding apparatuses (such as television criticism and even its scholarship). While neoliberalism has, within the humanities, acquired a distinctively unpleasant stench—in part because of its odorous ability to overdetermine economic life—I situate this scholarship to expose the fascinating and pervasive breadth

13

of neoliberal critique. Because of television's wide reach and centralized artistic structure—somewhat challenged throughout the 2000s by the evolution of a participatory culture, as this book's third chapter examines—it is impossible to imagine many postmillennial TV programs that have been developed and executed outside of neoliberal schemas. While I am skeptical of considering neoliberalism as a synonym for the *popular* (insofar as it is signified by popular cultural texts or representative of populist expressions of political culture), television has always exploited its position as the dominant mass medium of the late twentieth century as an asset: it may not have been the most culturally valued or legitimated art form, but at least it was popular among the masses. If neoliberalism turned to governing through common economic sense at the turn of the millennium, television became the most accessible medium to enact its project of governmentality and financialization.

With its emphasis on new technologies of distribution and on corporate hegemony of such markets via the mergers of multinational corporations, neoliberalism thus has a specific relevance to and resonance with postmillennial television. In writing about Latin America (the laboratory for experiments in neoliberal economic policy in the 1970s), Jon Beasley-Murray explains this connection through comparative analysis: "Replacing the theatricality of traditional liberalism," he asserts, "populism is cinematic; neoliberalism is televisual."[33] What might this curious set of alignments indicate? On the surface, his claim accurately pairs popular forms of entertainment and leisure with the prevailing economic movements of the time. Yet Beasley-Murray frames these comparisons not within proper objects (*the* theater, *the* cinema, *the* television) but instead within modalities of being (theatrical, cinematic, televisual), gesturing away from the material technologies themselves and toward the spectatorial atmospheres they generate. His insistence on medium specificity is therefore provocative yet also misleading, since late capitalism uses many styles, forms, and modes of address to maximize profit potential, even as these communicative and representational codes contradict or come into tension with one another. As my fourth chapter argues at greater length, the discursive intermediality of quality television—describing it as "cinematic" or "literary"—is a symptom of neoliberal culture's logic of valuation, which is often a proxy for talking about (while also *not* talking about) racial schemas of white supremacy.

Yet despite these critiques, I find there is something seductive in the phrase "televisual neoliberalism," in part because it is suggestive of how the cultural effects of specific economic policies can be perceived by the "complex of formal tendencies that shape television works and their reception." If, for

14

Beasley-Murray, populism "is incarnated bodily," then televisual neoliberalism explains not only the way the protocols of late capitalism become integrated into television but also, and more importantly, the way that these ideologies require the contextual—that is to say, affective—framework of television's form, aesthetics, technology, and genre. Even if consumed in private or semiprivate spaces, television spectators perform their pleasure and discomfort through their bodies, registering complicity with and resistance to the status quo.[34]

Television Scholarship and the Question of Postmodernism

If neoliberal policies began to take political and economic shape in the 1980s, why did they not begin to appear prominently on American television until the millennium? Some of the aforementioned changes studied in this book have roots in the television of the 1980s and 1990s: the DVR as the genealogical inheritor to the VCR, or the expectation of what Jason Mittell has identified as complex narratives within prime-time drama as the proliferation of the same techniques employed by *Dallas* (and daytime soap operas before that).[35] It was in the 2000s, however, that what this book calls postmillennial television began to be recognized as something different and unique within American popular culture. In a decade retrospective of the aughts, critic Emily Nussbaum has argued that this was the decade in which television "became art." Her glowing tribute to contemporary television echoes a sentiment felt not just by her fellow critics but by many consumers of American popular culture. Television's position in the American cultural imaginary—that is to say, its status within a hierarchy of artistic and entertainment mediums—no longer yielded mere contempt (Nussbaum even cites former FCC chair Newton Minow's notorious "vast wasteland" speech of 1961 to this effect) but instead elicited near-universal acclaim. In her words:

> You could easily memorialize the aughts as the Decade of Reality TV, that wild baby genre conceived in some orgy of soap opera, documentary, game shows, and vaudeville—it was reality, after all, that upended the industry's economic model and rewrote the nature of fame. Or you could mark this as the era of the legal procedural, or the age of Hulu and DVRs and TWOP [the fan website *Television Without Pity*]. But for anyone who loves television, who adores it with the possessive and defensive eyes of a fan, this was most centrally and importantly the first decade when television became recognizable as art, great art: collectible and life-changing and transformative

and lasting. As the sixties are to music and the seventies to movies, the aughts—which produced the best and worst shows in history—were to TV. It was a period of exhilarating craftsmanship and formal experimentation, accompanied by spurts of anxious grandiosity (for the first half of the decade, fans compared anything good to Dickens, Shakespeare, or Scorsese, because nothing so ambitious had existed in TV history).[36]

In their book *Legitimating Television*, Michael Newman and Elana Levine have critiqued Nussbaum for essentially writing "one long *auteurist* celebration" in which "great art" is equated with a single visionary who serves as the guarantor of high art. Thus, Nussbaum can compare the aughts to comparable decades in music and film, invoking Western canons of "ambitious" individual storytellers ("Dickens, Shakespeare, and Scorsese").[37] My goal in this book is to elaborate on Newman's and Levine's interpretation, contextualizing these discourses of taste and cultural value within the affective circuits of pleasure and discomfort surrounding TV spectatorship. What makes television "feel" like great art (or conversely, like bad art) is not solely a result of the success of a showrunner or *auteur* (or lack thereof); rather, it comes from an affective climate of "craftmanship" and "experimentation." This logic equates artistic value with the ability of *auteurs* to push the envelope with respect to formal and topical conventions. To recognize discomfort is thus to view a work of art.

So, what distinguishes the television of the millennium from that which came before it, the television of the 1980s and 1990s? 1980 represents a turning point in the medium's history, with the following decade's expansion of cable networks accelerating industry practices of courting market demographics through practices of narrowcasting. But the 1980s also saw the development of a new broadcasting network (Fox, in 1986), the widespread use of graphic and visual effects across all genres of television, and renewed interest in serialized storytelling—first through prime-time soaps, as well as the serialized arcs that governed romantic relationships in quality dramas such as *Hill Street Blues* and *St. Elsewhere*, and sitcoms such as *Cheers*—that constituted a second golden age to some critics.

Analyses of this era of television initially circulated within the emergent institutionalization of television studies during the late 1980s and throughout the 1990s, and these readings have shaped the discipline's understanding of its theoretical commitments to TV form, aesthetics, and representation. Much of this scholarship dissected the aesthetic codes, narrative logics, technological mirrorings, and modes of address of 1980s and early 1990s television, finding the television of that time to reflect a number of observations and critiques popularized in the ascendancy of postmodern inquiry within the humanities.[38] In *Televisuality*, John Caldwell maps out a stylistic methodology invested in excessive or intentionally citational style; TV's new stylistic exhibitionism, he claims, "is not adequately posed nor fully explained by reference to postmodernism," yet he maintains that both theorists and practitioners (workers in the media industries most concerned with aesthetics) have a problematized faith in televisual images.[39] In *Re-viewing Reception*, Lynne Joyrich also acknowledges the spread of postmodern representational devices in the television of the 1980s and early 1990s, although she cautions that many of these devices have been central to the medium from its inception as a domestic technology targeting housewives. Her critique is thus directed as much toward postmodern theory for omitting gender as a central analytical category as it is toward television studies, and she provides a useful feminist counterpoint to that offered by Richard Dienst, who provides not so much a unified argument about the medium as a number of interrelated theoretical observations about postmodern television (as evidenced by the subtitle to his book *Still Life in Real Time*, "theory after television"). And, while Jane Feuer draws some connections between postmodernism's obsession with destructuralizing simulacra and the presidency of Ronald Reagan, her interests in *Seeing Through the Eighties* lie more in how 1980s television serves as a formal and representational vehicle for Reaganism and its many ideological contradictions. Taken together (as all these monographs were published between 1994 and 1996), these works proffer four assumptions about so-called postmodern television's position as both a symptom of and a potential site of resistance to capitalism, central to both the Reagan presidency and postmodern lines of flight.

First, Caldwell, Joyrich, Dienst, and Feuer all assume that understanding television requires excavating contradictions and approaches from multiple perspectives: Dienst instructs us to "engage in creative speculation, combining and recombining all kinds of images," while Joyrich parenthetically notes that "the very omnipresence and multiplicity of discourses on and about TV contribute to the portrayal of television as *the* diffuse and enveloping medium of this (and our) time."[40] Second, this leads these authors to read television's intertextuality and self-conscious repertoires of performance as central to its formal and representational politics. Caldwell's excitement for the winking and nodding TV set is clear in his alignment of television with spectacle, "conceived of as a *presentational attitude*, a display of knowing *exhibitionism*."[41] His description of the medium's self-image as a consumer technology of entertainment and pleasure (much like the brands associated with advertising

17

television *scripts*

culture) fulfills Dienst's prescription that the televisual image functions as a "transformation in the capacities of capitalism through a new production of time."[42] Both Caldwell and Dienst argue that the value of televisual images lies in their persistence across television's cluttered and often ephemeral flow, a formal and aesthetic grammar that simultaneously democratizes and destabilizes the image.

Third, they all articulate how the medium's position as cultural "trash" or as the lowest common denominator of mass culture partially determines this investment in self-referentiality. For Feuer, one of Reaganism's more curious paradoxes was its yoking together of elitism with populism, creating a decade that advertised itself as a means to "avoid dealing with the economic and social realities of the times."[43] Such tension, moreover, highlights other binary framings of television as both complicit and critical, as both artistic object and commodity. As Joyrich points out, this could have only been accomplished because television produces the assumed feminization (and thus infantilization) of its audience, with its promotion of consumption positioned as both symptom of and resistant act to the threat of a feminized world.[44] Caldwell takes up this argument in a theoretical register, using the postscript of his book to invite readings that meld "low cultural practice" with "high theory," leading to the devaluation of the image.[45]

Fourth, and perhaps most important for my purposes here, these authors take television's capacity to structure affective transmission for granted, attempting to graph (without fully doing so) the temporal and spatial flows that enable constructions of affective spectatorship. In her first paragraph, Feuer figures television as capable of both dissecting and epitomizing "the aura of the eighties," and while she concedes that we should not read 1980s TV as "a reflection of an eighties Zeitgeist in any simple way," her project nevertheless remains committed to demystifying the various structures of feeling embedded within the television and its viewers (in particular, the yuppie audience of the 1980s).[46] Joyrich, in fact, opens her book through a close reading of Deanna Troi (Marina Sirtis), the empathic counselor in *Star Trek: the Next Generation* (syndicated, 1987–1994), as the exemplary "image of professionalized feminine receptivity" who is also illustrative of television's deployment of therapeutic discourse.[47] While Dienst anticipates her critiques in announcing his skepticism of "a conclusion in which television and 'the feminine' are alike reduced to a set of necessary affects associated with 'consumption,'" he does not question television's ability to be reduced to a set of affects, necessarily commercial or otherwise.[48] In "looking at television as if it were not already there," Dienst states, we produce "our own fields of visibility . . . the as-yet-unrealized, blocked, and diverted power of television," a delineative conceptualization both scaffolding and eroding affective potential.[49] Television generates affect, these studies intimate, because of television's power to construct intimacy.

In establishing these commonalities, my aim is to test if and how they apply to television's subsequent evolution: the assemblage of changes to television beginning at the turn of the millennium and extending until the mid-2010s. What comes after postmodern television, and how do these changes in turn transform our understanding of television? The late 1990s signaled a gradual departure from the television earlier on in the decade. Even if many of the cultural themes associated with the 1990s—its rejection of aesthetic glamour, its emphasis on multicultural diversity, and its use of sarcasm as a dominant form of comedy—were present in television throughout the decade's entirety, the decade contains radical differences between its earlier and later periods, particularly with respect to TV aesthetics, form, genre, and technology. These changes both build upon and contradict the shared assessments about the postmodern television of the 1980s. With the widespread adoption of narrowcasting and the rise of cult television throughout the 1990s, television amplified its commitment to multiplicity; recent emphases on algorithms as a metric for assessing audience response summon the logics of capture emblematic of control societies, with every series with a fan base eligible for consideration as a cult text. Television still deploys postmodern representational techniques in the service of self-conscious or acknowledged performance—but without one of its most theatrical capacities, as live television viewing and commercial breaks became relics of the past. Television is no longer thought of as merely trash, with critics noting its "novelistic" qualities as early as 1995, though reality television was exempted from this legitimation, and even still, it was not until the end of the 2000s that arguments were being made about a third golden age. And while Feuer's argument for the interpenetration of 1980s television and Reaganism helps us follow the political structures of feeling of the time, the decade-defining two-term presidencies following Reagan (Bill Clinton in the 1990s, George W. Bush in the 2000s, and Barack Obama in the 2010s) do not cohere under a specific political or economic ideology—unless, of course, one accepts the already disparate and ethereal rationalities of neoliberal culture.

Both postmodernism and neoliberalism share a certain investment in images—neoliberalism thrives on risking credit in the pursuit of new markets, with this credit consisting of an electronic currency that is simulacral—and each requires the diffuse infiltration and naturalization of market logics. Fredric

19

Jameson, in his seminal work on postmodernism, contends that "'the market is in human nature' is the proposition that cannot be allowed to stand unchallenged; in my opinion, it is the most crucial terrain of ideological struggle in our time," and he emphasizes that the postmodern schizophrenic subject is ultimately unable to "organize its past and future into coherent experience."[50] Yet while postmodernism may have signified the end of grand metanarratives used to explain human behavior (contributing to the fragmentation of the subject), late capitalism is rather invested in the metanarrative of free and unfettered access to global markets, with the individual focusing on maximizing investment potential in order to fulfill the functions of *Homo economicus.* Thus, one can trace the affective registers of this metanarrative as it has played out in the various genres, forms, and discourses surrounding television. As Patricia Ventura argues, "The end of the Cold War saw neoliberalism crystallize as a structure of feeling," so that "by 2003, at the start of the Iraq War, American neoliberal culture had reached a kind of maturation point."[51] With the consolidation of economic and political power, the cultural effects of neoliberalism can be found in the ways that it reorganized American citizenship, with various policies affecting welfare and immigration and restructuring the family as a target, an object, and an instrument of governmental power. And with technological change shifting the primary unit of economic organization from the family to the individual, television could introduce discomfort to its audiences more easily, as adult audiences increasingly viewed themselves as sophisticated consumers.

This Book's Script

Uncomfortable Television registers these spectatorial performances of pleasure and discomfort across key genres of postmillennial television: auteurist comedy, documentary reality, the police procedural, prestige drama, and fan-produced satire. This book organizes its objects primarily by genre for a few reasons. First, genre exists as a cultural category not only specific to a set of texts (genres are inherently organizational and thus contingent) but specific to practices across media industries and audiences as well.[52] Audiences classify and categorize texts as they consume them, and with the development of a participatory culture, fan communities have been able to assert their expertise in these acts of classification. Second, genre persists as a critical category despite the popularity of generic hybridity (e.g., dramedies, docusoaps, and mockumentary sitcoms) within television programming during this time. In part, this is because of increased quantities and accessibility of original programming enabled by cable networks and SVOD platforms. With so many series to watch, genre increasingly shapes audience attention and, more importantly, often determines or governs *what* gets watched. Third, because this book is making a historical claim, genre allows for more refined explanations of pleasure in popular culture. One question central to TV historiography is why certain genres are popular at certain historical times (science fiction, fantasy, and horror in the 1960s; prime-time soaps in the 1980s), and this book follows in this practice. Last, I have intentionally excluded some genres of television from this book not because they do not necessarily fit into a model of televisual discomfort but because of how those genres script their spectators' discomfort. Many series with uncomfortable elements do not appear in this book, and not just for a lack of space: fantasy and horror series such as *Game of Thrones* (HBO, 2011–2019) and *American Horror Story* (FX, 2011–present) appear to qualify as deeply uncomfortable, given their displays of sexual and racial violence, but I see their generic classifications as doing other work in governing the mechanisms of disavowal and critique by which uncomfortable affects become rerouted into viewer pleasure.[53] Such exclusions may strike some readers as being unfair or incorrect, but I do not mean to limit definitions or experiences of discomfort through erecting these parameters.

Genre is organizationally privileged because of what it does: in establishing a set of expectations for its viewer, it thus structures a viewer's affective engagement with a text or a set of texts. By expectation I mean not only the operational aesthetics that structure how viewers follow a program's narrative. Instead, I use the term to signify the ways in which popular discourses in both mainstream journalistic and academic criticism—and especially discourses anchored around a set of ideological assumptions about a series or network—script viewers' affective reactions to a series. Audiences have certain expectations about the representational messages these programs contain, so their negotiation of pleasure is always tempered by a disclaimer, occasionally one that expresses ambivalence or resistance to a particular ideological message. Such expectation is, of course, built into the larger viewing economy, an economy that requires those very expectations in order to market and brand programs for different viewing communities constructed through industrial practices of narrowcasting and franchising. This book thus utilizes practices of close reading of a single episode or a collection of episodes from a single series representative of these changed viewer expectations, in order to highlight the formal and industrial mechanisms that produce and script viewer affect.

Robin Bernstein uses the term "script" to describe the relational nature of material things and people (her examples range from museum exhibits to children's alphabet books). For her, the term equates neither directly to mimetic representation nor to the rigid dictation of performed action but instead carries additionally resistant, performative, and improvisational valence, making each engagement akin to a dance: "Dances with things, too, are performative in that they constitute actions: they *think,* or, more accurately, they *are the act of thinking.*"[54] Turning to characterizations of choreography, Bernstein situates affective expectation as interpellative, or what we might call here the viewer's coming into being, or subjectivation. The seductive light of the television, the lure of its abundance, and the accessibility of programming function, this book argues, as a sort of scriptive thing: "The scriptive thing hails a person by inviting her to dance. The person ritualistically engages the matter, and in that process, subjectivation—how one comes to 'matter'—occurs. Interpellation occurs not only through performative utterances but also through thing-based enscription into identifiable, historicized traditions of performance from both the stage and everyday life."[55] For Bernstein, the scriptive thing structures spectatorial behavior alongside cultural assumptions of identity and, notably and importantly, alongside racial violence. Following her lead, postmillennial television-as-scriptive-thing negotiates the construction of identity alongside the many violences central to early twenty-first-century culture, as in my opening example of *Louie.* The slippage between narrative and reality present in the audience's identification of Louie with C.K. are a regularly repeated and ritualized part of this script. Indeed, this can be traced to the technological and industrial imperatives of the medium itself, which are premised upon the false construction of boundaries between visibility and invisibility, public and private, and fiction and reality. As Dienst observes, television "allows us to imagine new values for the visible image and visual realm without resorting to the ultimate privilege, or the ultimate evasion, of the invisible."[56] *Uncomfortable Television,* then, recasts these "new values" into affective economies that pressure both the study of representation (how cultural taboos appear in postmillennial television) and the study of spectatorship (how viewers perform discomfort). Perhaps what makes viewers squeamish is neither the dramatic depiction (representation as re-presentation) of sexual assault, as in the case of *Louie,* nor the televisual homomorphism (representation as in a legislative context) symbolic of a larger "culture" of sexual assault, but instead the affective circulation of both: a creepy dance that spectators haphazardly consent to by turning on their televisions.

If for Bernstein the scriptive thing cannot be divorced from affective histories of racialized and sexual violence, *Uncomfortable Television* is particularly invested in documenting the ways in which depictions of discomfort allow for audiences to both embrace and disavow popular expressions of white supremacy and misogyny. Here, I acknowledge how my own spectatorial position as a queer White male will inevitably inform the following readings of postmillennial television presented. While my own intuitive perceptions of discomfort are certainly marked by my identifications, I combine them with discursive analyses of reviews, recaps, interviews, and other forms of television criticism and scholarship to pinpoint the uncomfortable structures of feeling present within these series and episodes. Many of the programs examined in this book cohere along a certain formation of audience that attracts a specific kind of viewer: one with a certain amount of class privilege to have access to cable or premium cable television, for example. This should come as no surprise to historians of television, many of whom have noted the ways that "quality" television and its synonyms reflect a desire to encourage audiences to identify as sophisticated and savvy spectators. This key branding strategy has been embraced by television executives going back to the 1970s, when the "rural purge" at CBS saw the premiere of several series branded as feminist and politically progressive that also targeted more urban and younger (yet still White) audience demographics.[57] At the same time, however, television's expansion to include profiles of "ordinary" individuals and families (in reality programming) and new forms of production (through fan cultures) somewhat challenges these demographic assumptions. On a metatextual level, then, this book is a commentary on the pervasiveness of televisual discourse—and of its popular misogyny and Whiteness—as much as it is a historicization of televisual affect.

The first chapter, "The Irritated Spectator: Affective Representation in (Post)millennial Comedy," provides this book's theoretical scaffolding, spelling out the relationship between discomfort and pleasure. Drawing from the theories of affect and embodiment that animate my methodology, I demonstrate how television encourages its audiences to perceive affects of discomfort through ideological frameworks despite changes to television aesthetics, form, and technology that suggest a more immersive experience. This chapter extrapolates from discomfort, ultimately advancing a central claim of this book: that under late capitalism, televisual affectivity depends on the fiction of meaningful representation. In developing this argument, I turn to irritation as a minor affect with which to approach the study of representation. Using the example of *Girls* (HBO, 2012–2017) and its polarizing series creator, Lena Dunham, I consider how irritation may be recouped as the form of neoliberal resistance par excellence, thus situating it as a fundamental way of studying (and coming to terms with) conflicting affects surrounding televisual representation.

The second chapter, "The Addicted Spectator: TV Junkies in Need of an *Intervention*," focuses on reality television, which exploded in popularity at the beginning of the millennium. If the genre of reality television has been linked to consumer technologies of self-improvement, this chapter examines instead the more stigmatized—yet equally necessary—form of citizenship embodied by the addict. It reads theories of narcoanalysis alongside episodes of recovery television, a subgenre of reality TV in which individuals with compulsive behaviors or addictions to unhealthy substances are profiled and reformed through a staged intervention. I argue that recovery television advances a form of addictive spectatorship, a concept that takes seriously the notion that television may act affectively as a drug. Recovery television thus helps viewers negotiate their own relationship to television consumption. Through an episode of the reality series *Intervention* (A&E, 2005–present), I demonstrate that reality television's structuring of affect provides its audiences with a motive to disidentify with its subjects in order to disavow their own addictions—including, importantly, their addiction to TV itself.

It is not just that the ordinary citizen becomes a larger character across TV during this time, but that the ordinary consumer does, too. Accompanying similar breakdowns in the private and the public spheres brought on by reality television and the digital public sphere, the late 1990s and 2000s witnessed the breakdown between producers and consumers through the formation of participatory cultures and transformative works. Significant changes to television technology thus occurred as "television" itself began to encompass paratextual media such as fan reaction videos, web series, video recaps, and remixes. The last of these, remixes, is the subject of the third chapter, "The Aborted Spectator: Affective Economies of Perversion in Televisual Remix." It examines Sienna D'Enema's *Jiz* (2009–2016)—a reimagining of the children's animated series *Jem and the Holograms* (syndicated, 1985–1988)—in which the colorful glam rocker is transformed into a profane, violent, and drug addicted abortionist. Using *Jiz* and other queer video remix TV series, I trace the role of nostalgia in remix culture, in which television series from the past are inserted beyond their cancellation dates into a future punctuated by digital mediation and participatory culture. If remix is, in today's digital cultural studies, used to promote cultural literacy, I argue that this is because of its capacity to pervert and corrupt. Remix may infuse creative potentiality into the wistful objects of one's past, but only through taking as its premise the risking of innocence conjured by those very objects.

If reality television and participatory culture represent two key stories describing the changes to postmillennial television, another story is the question of *story*: of increased serialization and sophistication in scripted narratives, tied to the medium's cultural legitimation. The fourth chapter, "The Spectator Plagued by White Guilt: On the Appropriative Intermediality of Quality TV," considers what has been called a new golden age of serialized drama; these current programs feature antiheroes and are heralded by critics and scholars as "literature" or as "cinema." Examining why a dislikable or morally repugnant protagonist is presumed to be a necessary component for televisual risk-taking, and why both have been branded as "art," I use discourses surrounding *The Wire* (HBO, 2002–2007) and popular police procedurals (such as *CSI: Crime Scene Investigation* and *Law & Order: Special Victims Unit*) to read intermedial appropriation—the disavowal of televisuality in favor of a more legitimated art form—against theories of cultural appropriation tied to White guilt.

Finally, the last chapter, "The Woke Spectator: Misrecognizing Discomfort in the Era of Peak TV," forms the conclusion to this book, asking what comes next, or what happens when we are fully immersed into televisual discomfort. In distinguishing between the periodization of postmillennial television here and the television of the late 2010s and into the 2020s (including how the COVID-19 pandemic disrupted television production and reception), I chart the shift from the acculturating function of discomfort present in postmillennial television to a more politicized function of discomfort seen in formations of "woke TV." Woke television is advanced by this era's characterization as "Peak TV," since more options enabled by SVOD platforms and algorithmic narrowcasting have led to more series that deal explicitly with questions of social justice and that feature the creative talents of cultural minorities. Because of this explosive rise in the number of viewing options, I examine a variety of series and their construction of wokeness as a scripted spectatorial affect that signifies a viewer's progressive politics. I then turn to two examples of racial misrecognition—blackface in the critically acclaimed comedy *30 Rock* (NBC, 2006–2013) and whiteface in the critically acclaimed comedy *Atlanta* (FX, 2016–present)—to illustrate the emergence and limitations of woke spectatorship. Audiences, I argue, are now so acclimated into discomfort that it may be acknowledged and used productively as a form of resistance, but this resistance is possible only by rewriting the very terms of the spectator's relationship to pleasure.

Taken together, these chapters make an intervention into analyses that examine television after TV, demanding that television studies synthesize work in affect and performance into its methodological repertoire. This book is intended to provoke discomfort among its readers, who must account for their own spectatorial pleasure in the popular texts of a pervasively neoliberal American culture. While such discomfort might ultimately be nothing new—American television has never claimed to be an authoritatively antagonistic force against the status quo (until perhaps, as the conclusion argues, the current moment of Peak and woke television)—my intention here is to stress how the perverse and the popular, how ideological and affective critique, and how scriptive things and spectators all circulate when we consume postmillennial TV. It has not been emotionally easy to write a book on discomfort, especially when whatever pleasure that may have originally been derived from textual perversity mutates and exhausts upon repeated viewings and critical reflection. Yet television often provides pleasure through establishing the individual viewer as part of a larger community, even if that community is imagined. To break the fourth wall for a moment (something television is known to do occasionally), I invite you, the reader, to share in this discomfort, so that together we may reroute affect through critical pathways and make sense of the television we love—and the world we inhabit—in more fruitful and politically engaging ways.

one

the irritated spectator affective representation in (post)millennial comedy

Pleasure and Its Discontents

WHY HAS postmillennial television gravitated toward discomfort, and why is this fixation on discomfort seemingly as popular as ever? Discomfort manifests as a signal not only of being external to familiarly pleasurable things but of being external to notions of normative life in general—as in vague senses of not belonging or not being able to adhere to social norms. Discomfort generally refers to inconveniences or hardships that do not threaten one's immediate health, and most dictionary definitions of the word distinguish discomfort from definitive physical pain, though the etymological roots of the word also tether it to feelings like sorrow, distress, and defeat. Meteorologists use the term "discomfort index" to account for the effects of humidity on temperature—the index itself an admission of perception's structuring effects.[1] In this sense, discomfort is meant to be perceived momentarily and thus is subject to change over time. Yet permanent states of discomfort are often normalized the more they are repeated, and these repeated performances deviate slightly as they stretch out across time, such as in Elizabeth Freeman's description of *chronicity* as a correlation "with a certain shapelessness in time . . . seem[ing] to belie narrative altogether."[2] To be made uncomfortable over time suggests an approximation of discomfort, with each iteration muddying and clarifying the boundary between comfort and pain.

Despite indicating an individually perceived state of being, our shared understanding of what constitutes discomfort is historically contingent, shaped profoundly by social and technological forces. Discomfort often accompanies new sets of knowledges or experiences, such as in the alienation felt by traveling in a foreign country without knowing the native language, or in the embarrassment felt when trying to operate a new technological object for the first time, or even in the disorientation often produced through an encounter with a theoretical argument. Yet as expressions of external sensations, notions of discomfort change when standards of comfort do as well. On a widespread scale following World War II, for example, new norms on what constituted comfort (and new ways of advertising these norms) emerged to promote consumer technologies and household goods—including, importantly, television itself—that would ease domestic labor while signifying a family's middle-class status. Watching television has always been figured as a sedentary act of comfort, the set itself a palliative technology promising to help those in pain.[3] States of discomfort appear to challenge the accepted narratives of technological progress and the quality of life associated with postwar America. The transition from a manufacturing economy to an informational economy in the mid-to-late twentieth century, with its faith in the computerization and digitization of a range of services, has shifted the primary expression of discomfort from physical registers to emotional ones, creating new vocabularies with which to describe the affective distress that proliferates across a growing number of media platforms. Indeed, a modern relationship to technology appears to be a significant force in disseminating general and often amorphous feelings of discomfort—manifesting themselves through states of anxiety, dread, and fear—via the ubiquitous accessibility of smartphones (and an overexposure to screens in general), the melodramatic rhythms of repeated twenty-four-hour news cycles, and the use and maintenance of social media.

Television is often absent from such recent panics regarding the use of technology, although advances in accessing content first through DVD releases and then through streaming platforms have altered viewing habits to include bingeing multiple episodes of a series at once. While I unpack this practice more fully in the next chapter, an episode from the second season of the satirical sketch series *Portlandia* (IFC, 2011–2018) illustrates television's capacity to move easily between registers of pleasure and discomfort. In "One Moore Episode," Doug and Claire (series cocreators Fred Armisen and Carrie Brownstein, respectively) sit down to watch the first episode of *Battlestar Galactica* (SyFy, 2003–2009) on DVD, only to find themselves hopelessly addicted: despite soft promises to watch "just one more," the couple furiously plow through episodes without interruption until finishing the series.[4] After seventy-six continuous episodes of Cylon warfare, the consequences are substantial: Claire thinks she has a bladder infection (but says she'll seek treatment "after the next episode"), she also loses her job, and both complain of salty eyes from gazing too intently at the screen, a reminder of *Battlestar*'s status as quality television requiring an attentive and immersive gaze. Yet *Portlandia*'s use of satire, here traced through the intentionally affectless tone of Armisen and Brownstein, render all these effects as merely uncomfortable: actual physical pain or economic insecurity do not inhibit the couple in any significant way, and the episode later finds them tracking down *Battlestar* creator (and Portland resident) Ronald D. Moore in an attempt to continue the story. This narrative arc, which loosely connects the various sketches across the episode, succeeds in part because as newly unemployed, Doug and Claire have nothing else to do.

Portlandia thus presents television as the vehicle by which spectators learn to embrace mild forms of discomfort as the cost of thrilling storytelling. Importantly, Doug and Claire are not the nuclear family of TV lore but are instead childless, cohabiting middle-class hipsters. As such, they easily access the rewards of postmillennial television: the leisure time to watch multiple episodes of a series at once on demand; the ability to comprehend sophisticated serialized narratives demonstrative of quality television; and the opportunity to engage more directly with showrunners as fans of a series. But as they delve deeper into *Battlestar*, they accumulate signifiers of discomfort in their bodies, which become mediated through flattened expressions in body language and verbal tone. Bladder infections, firings, unpaid bills: these symptoms of what is otherwise economic precarity are archived by Doug's and Claire's spectatorial bodies in order to be subsumed into televisual flow. As Mimi White and others have argued, variety sketch series have historically relied on intertextual references, self-promotional advertisements, and parodic modes of address in order to create television's referential imaginary, a template for audiences across which connections can be forged in the name of increased viewer pleasure.[5] *Portlandia* uses such references—the real-life Ronald D. Moore appears in the episode (though not as himself), as do *Battlestar* actors Edward James Olmos and James Callis—in the name of such intertextual pleasure, but this pleasure is also tempered by the episode's framing of embodied spectatorship. Doug and Claire spend the majority of the skit glued to the couch, their bodies aesthetically paresthetic. This acknowledgment of the body's capacity to incite action through its destruction and the destruction

29

1.1 Doug and Claire binge-watch *Battlestar Galactica*. *Portlandia*, "One Moore Episode," Season 2, Episode 2.

of leisure time illuminates the ways in which pleasure and discomfort can be thought of as conjoined categories. Doug and Claire are typical, if not ideal, spectators of twenty-first-century television: in their desire to consume, the deterioration of their bodies circulates with the particles of light transmitted from the television to compose the affective atmosphere of discomfort common to postmillennial TV.

But throughout "One Moore Episode" Doug and Claire are also supremely *irritating*: in their consensual abandonment of responsibility for aimless televisual enjoyment; in their whiny pleas to Moore to reboot *Battlestar*; and in their minimization of problems that would otherwise substantially affect a Portland resident's economic survival. Most reviews of *Portlandia* capture this vibe; in the words of *Variety*'s Brian Lowry, the series crosses the "not-so-fine line between intelligent satire and smug, irritating self-indulgence."[6] The characters invented by Armisen and Brownstein are too White, too privileged, too selfish, and too willfully ignorant to be granted any amount of sincere empathy from the audience, even if, as satire, the series never cared about such empathetic gestures in the first place. If Doug and Claire represent postmillennial television's ideal spectators who become radicalized into obsessive fans, it is because they can easily afford DVD box sets, widescreen televisions,

chapter one

on-demand food delivery, and fast-streaming internet service. From the vantage point of *Battlestar* fans, Doug and Claire are annoying, expressing their fandom by making demands of writers and actors and complaining when those writers and actors resist, rather than through productive forms of fandom such as by making video remixes or other transformative works. As Julie Levin Russo has documented, *Battlestar* fandoms "threaten the established order through their intimacy with technology and their communal proliferation."[7] Within *Portlandia*, however, Doug's and Claire's smug actions do not threaten; instead they merely alienate.

Portlandia introduces us to postmillennial television's rich entanglements of discomfort and pleasure that structure this book's arguments. This chapter advances some of these key articulations through an engagement with television's history with affect studies. My projects in this chapter are twofold. First, I situate television within the affective turn, demonstrating how television's commitment to upholding (and occasionally subverting) hegemonic social norms regarding representation require conceiving of TV's affective flows as always already embodied and thus as partially ideological. Drawing from these fields—and especially from their intersecting interlocutor, the British cultural historian Raymond Williams—I lay out a theory of affect for postmillennial television, one that coalesces around the idea that televisual affectivity is dependent on the fiction of meaningful representation. This statement and various ways of reading it led to this chapter's second project: irritation. Irritation is not supposed to be appealing, but I argue that it can be wielded as a productive reading practice through which to approach the study of representation. In considering what affective energies television scholars, critics, and fans deploy while gaining pleasure from texts containing muddled (at best) or problematic (at worst) representational content, irritation emerges as a minor but no less important form of discomfort, well suited to late capitalism's appropriation of identity politics. Through a reading of the HBO series *Girls* (2012–2017) and the polarizing reactions to the series and its creator, Lena Dunham, that emerged in print and digital journalism, I examine the convergence of irritation and the politics of representation. As an affect of inadequacy, and as itself an inadequate affect, irritation serves as a useful affective barometer for postmillennial television, which is marked by profound changes to both capitalism and the medium itself. That is to say, we might embrace irritation *as* representation in order to articulate and challenge the political stakes and viewing positions of televisual neoliberalism.

Affects and Their (Mediated) Others

The notion of a spectatorial atmosphere in which viewers watch and react to television requires attending to the interdisciplinary field of affect studies, a field of thought that has gained quite a bit of attention within the humanities over the past two decades—not coincidentally, overlapping significantly with the period of time during which this book stakes the ossification of neoliberal governmentality within the American cultural imaginary. The transition from a manufacturing to a service economy, the increasingly blurred distinctions between work and leisure, and the imperative to optimize the self fuels this episteme of affect to such an extent that making sense of popular cultural texts and media technologies from this period requires tracing their affective atmospheres and reading these structures and effects alongside embodied performances of cultural identity. As a way to assert the body's role after being largely absent from semiotic readings within structuralism (and, to a lesser extent, poststructuralism), the renewed interest in affect across the humanities and social sciences has cut a wide swath with regard to its relationship to identity (through designating specifically non-White or queer affects, for instance) and agency (through attending to nonhuman or environmental animacies). As Eugenie Brinkema cogently asserts, "We might be better off suggesting that the 'turn to affect' in the humanities is and always has been plural, a set of many turnings that are problematically lumped together in a false unity that imagines that one singular intellectual arc could describe them all."[8]

This description of affect studies parrots my point in this book's introduction about earlier categorizations of neoliberalism (and even television) as similarly and definitionally untenable; despite attempts to map out their unfixed coordinates, all these concepts appear to be stretched so wide as to defy singular delineations. Although significant differences exist within the literature on affect as to whether or not affects, emotions, and feelings are distinct from each other or as to the role the conscious interpretation of affects plays in their ontological state (differences I tender shortly), common ground suggests that affects are mobile—that they move in between and beside bodies and things—and that they prompt some sort of action, even if that action is in their very legibility. Affects disrupt and recalibrate, working together to structure psychic coherence through their adaptability. They accumulate, foster, and act as commodities in the new service economy; they are not unlike the service economy itself, which requires its labor force to be flexible, contingent, and on the move. When the cultural effects of late capitalism "trickle down" into everyday programming, the term *circulation* better describes how television structures everyday life; it is, I would speculate, a more appropriate model for demarcating contemporary televisual flow.

The turn to affect in critical theory has created space for conceiving of embodied individual experience beside the construction of knowledge; as Clare Hemmings has observed, the affective turn has thus been positioned as a privileged "way out" of the impasse between epistemology and ontology in cultural studies or between inscription and incorporation in performance studies.[9] Over the past two decades, this turn to affect has coalesced into two camps. The first draws from Gilles Deleuze and Félix Guattari, themselves drawing from thinkers such as Baruch Spinoza, William James, Henri Bergson, and Alfred North Whitehead. This coterie views affect as pure potentiality: as a presubjective response in excess of consciousness, "an enterprise of desubjectification" (according to Deleuze and Guattari), or as "irreducibly bodily and autonomic" (according to Brian Massumi).[10] This line of thought draws an important distinction between affects and emotions: affects are nonsignifying intensities or forces split from the socially signifying functions of emotion. Here, signification is the problem to which affect is the solution; as Massumi writes, "Emotion and affect—if affect is intensity—follow different logics and pertain to different orders . . . emotion is a subjective content, the sociolinguistic fixing of the quality of an experience which is from that point onward defined as personal. Emotion is qualified intensity . . . into narrativizable action-reaction circuits, into function and meaning."[11] Importantly, under this model, it is only after affects are routed through the signifying mechanisms of individual consciousness that they can then be considered personalized feelings or socially shared emotions. This distinction is, in fact, what gives affects their very power: supposedly without form or structure, affects exist with certain abstractivities that allow them to be transmitted across bodies and sensory systems.

The second camp culls from feminist, queer, and anti-racist cultural studies to position affect as also deeply corporeal but without such presubjective conditions. Here, affects and emotions are frequently read interchangeably, and most of the thinkers in this camp (Eve Sedgwick, Lauren Berlant, Sianne Ngai, Mel Chen, and José Muñoz, to name a few) insist on the importance of emotion as equally embodied, as in Sara Ahmed's elaboration: "Certainly, the experience of 'having' an emotion may be distinct from sensations and impressions, which may burn the skin before any conscious moment of recognition. But this model creates a distinction between conscious recognition and 'direct' feeling, which itself negates how that which is not consciously

33

the irritated spectator

experienced may itself be mediated by past experiences. I am suggesting here that even seemingly direct responses actually evoke past histories, and that this process bypasses consciousness, through bodily memories."[12] Ahmed's intervention here lies in viewing the body as a repository of meaningful functionality. For her, the body is not a clean system through which sensation and perception are complementary mechanisms; emotion may be qualified by "bodily memories," but the physical body carries these memories and traps affective forces as they are relayed to consciousness and recognition. Reading affects as emotions, then, enfolds sensation within the internal histories of the body; and while emotions may be figured as determined by social contexts, this does not make them purely social—as opposed to corporeal, or socially corporeal—constructs. To claim a separation between presignifying affect and signifying emotion insinuates that emotions are somehow *not* always already part of the body, ironically deprivileging the body as an archive with the capacity to redirect and shape affective forces.

Obviously, much more has been said about the aforementioned approaches to studying affect. Yet my crude scaffolding here illuminates two important points relevant to a study of postmillennial television. First, most theories of affect and affective spectatorship within media studies have historically turned to film, and not to television, as their primary expression of mediation. This suggests that while, like all moving images, television has the capacity to incite affective responses within its viewers, its historical appeal to the lowest common denominators of cultural expression (heard in the tinny laugh tracks of three-camera sitcoms and seen in the melodramatic gesticulations of a soap opera, for example) makes "the boob tube" an unreliable case study for affective inquiry. Second, the majority of scholarship within film studies has been oriented around autonomist notions of affect, an approach incompatible with the various contexts of distribution and reception common to postmillennial TV.

In his groundbreaking work *The Cinematic Body*, Steven Shaviro divides affective reactions to a film from preoccupations of signification and ideology, methodologically marking a radical departure from film theory's deployment of psychoanalysis. Instead, he redefines spectatorship around the encounter between the filmic object and its audience: "Film is inescapably literal. Images confront the viewer directly, without mediation. . . . We respond viscerally to visual forms, before having the leisure to read or interpret them as symbols."[13] Shaviro later reflects on this sentence, however, stating that it was "exactly wrong, because it simply sides with the literal against the figurative, or with presence against mediation, instead of rejecting the binary altogether."[14] In

34

clarifying that one should not abandon processes of signification entirely, Shaviro then emphasizes sequence, noting that "the cognitive—far from being opposed to the visceral or bodily—*grows out* of the visceral, and is an elaboration of it," thus indexing a temporal structure onto the act of spectatorship.[15] The alignment of presubjectively visceral affects with film spectatorship, however unintentionally formal, represents what Eugenie Brinkema calls a defensive theorization of affect "as an omission, a forgotten underside to film and media theory."[16] Yet, in the years since, this attunement has become a norm within the field, expanding affective inquiries into specific senses, proprioceptive aesthetics, and states of suspense.[17] While many of these attempts recoup form and structure in their description of filmic affectivity, with few exceptions do they complicate the ideological readings that preceded them, demonstrating the captivating pull of autonomous affect across film theory.

Television is almost entirely absent from texts like *The Cinematic Body*, for some probable reasons. If early theorizations of affect and media attempted to reorient the field away from psychoanalytic critique, film was the obvious object choice: the medium has a much richer engagement with psychoanalysis than television does.[18] Yet this is not to say that television studies has been wholly ignorant of affect—far from it—but rather that the discipline has engaged affect on different terms. Analyses of television may have resisted, by and large, the kind of affective critiques so heavily saturated within film theory because television has mostly been theorized and historicized as a cultural forum, instrumental to the dissemination of hegemonic ideologies while lacking the experimental or avant-garde techniques associated with overthrowing the status quo. Within discourses of television, affect itself, in Lynne Joyrich's words, is "most often figured as a 'feminine' trait, [thus] necessarily involv[ing] a relationship to gender," and thus necessarily involving a relationship to signification.[19] Foundational work in television studies has noted how television's affective investment has always been in service to a consumer society. In her work on classic soap opera, for example, Tania Modleski asserted that the dispersed and fragmented ways a presumed female audience would identify with the narrative mirrored the rhythms of domestic labor.[20] While scholars such as Joyrich and Massumi are not using terms like affect and emotion in commensurate registers, this body of work indicates that understanding television's context of reception—the environments in which spectatorial labor is performed—is necessary in order to locate the medium's affective potential.

What kind of labor do spectators perform while viewing? To think about this labor is to recognize the way in which the body shapes affective perception as itself a recording technology, one not so different from the many recording options available to viewers and fans alike. Writing from performance studies, Rebecca Schneider has called for a more thorough investigation into the way in which the body functions as an archive of performance and as a physical record of experience. What makes affect so seductive, she argues, is how it positions itself between bodies rather than between a body and a text. "The affective turn is extremely interesting," she writes, "in regard to the fact that it seems to resist the binary still so virile in the linguistic ties of the performative turn—that is, the binary between writing or textuality on the one hand and embodied gestic repertoires of behavior on a seeming other."[21] Returning to Shaviro's corrective to his earlier polemic, resisting the binary between the "literal" and the "figurative" shifts the focus more to concepts like *repertoire*: a collection of learned and repeated intensities that can be performed or triggered spontaneously. Just as the televised performances watched by spectators represent an aggregate of bodily tics, gestures, and expressions, so too are the intensities viscerally perceived by spectators similarly conditioned.

The Feeling of Flow, The Flow of Feeling

A "hermeneutic of discomfort" is my attempt to think through the development of television studies and affect studies as both parallel and overlapping vocabularies for describing the representation of everyday experience. This can be accomplished through a historical pairing of both fields. Television was initially conceived as both a technological and a cultural form, a "cultural technology" in the words of Raymond Williams, who seminally identified one of its distinctive qualities: flow.[22] Responding to Marshall McLuhan's technologically deterministic view of the medium, Williams based his research on his personal interactions with television, in the process highlighting his own spectatorial labor. In *Television*, he famously describes the disorienting experience of watching TV in a Miami hotel room in 1973, which due to American television's commercial network structure resulted in his mistaking of promotional ads for the episodes themselves. Developing three orders through which to read the segmentation of television, Williams articulated the concept of flow as suggestive of the medium's definitive difference from print or film; in his view, the flow between segments characterizes the viewing experience instead of the content of programming. He writes: "It is evident that what is now called 'an evening's viewing' is in some ways planned, by providers and then by viewers, *as a whole*; that it is in any event planned in discernible sequences which in this sense override particular programme units."[23] In declaring that sequence overrides specific content, Williams describes certain spectatorial choices (such as when or what one watches) that structure viewer attention as well as bodily movement, as in genres of instructional programming such as cooking or home decoration programs or in live-broadcast programs that encourage viewer participation.

When Williams provides an exhaustive breakdown of a San Francisco news broadcast, first by its general segment topics and then shot-by-shot, he directs our attention to devices such as repetition, continuity, and distancing, techniques that create the affective conditions for viewer concentration. Note, for example, how in his final "Commentary" following his shot-by-shot recounting of the news, his language is increasingly rooted in the sensory:

- "Most evident, perhaps, is a sense of the announcers spinning items along, following a rough schedule";
- "Yet the flow of hurried items establishes a sense of the world: of surprising and miscellaneous events coming in, tumbling over each other, from all sides";
- "The sense (in general, false) of instantaneous, simultaneous happening is similarly sustained . . .";
- "If an interest cannot be satisfied . . . it is nevertheless stimulated."[24]

Why is the word *sense* so apt, here, to characterize television's mirroring out onto the world (and its refracting of that world into the home, into an encounter with the viewer)? One can tell from his thick description that this *sense* is something individually perceived by the viewer, and presumably perceived by himself from his own viewing experiences. The "flow of hurried items" enacts the approximation of chaos, but this chaos both is and is not entropic: events (the release of an American prisoner of war from China, a speech by the vice president about the economy, a headache) happen at different times around the world, consumed in highly planned and structured doses of mediation. The "sense of the world" described by Williams indexes the affective processes by which viewers perceive television: as a segment shifts abruptly, it triggers an affective response within the TV viewer that helps that viewer distinguish between a news broadcast and a commercial, while simultaneously not dwelling too much on that reaction.

If Williams uses the word *sense* to approximate analogous units of time with the experience of everyday life, he does so without providing any indication as to *how* spectators are supposed to sense. Of course, Williams is well-known for also documenting the junction of experience and everyday life in an entirely different register, one in which mass media is primarily absent. I am referring here to his short essay "Structures of Feeling," in which he insists on the historical structuration of socially shared experiences. Structures of feeling generate affective epistemologies: they are "concerned with meanings and values as they are actively lived and felt" that talk about "characteristic elements of impulse, restraint, and tone; specifically affective elements of consciousness and relationships: not feeling against thought, but thought as felt and feeling as thought: practical consciousness of a present kind, in a living and inter-relating continuity."[25] Here, the idea of practical consciousness—"what is actually being lived, and not only what it is thought is being lived"—differs from "official consciousness" or "the reduction of the social to fixed forms."[26] But, as Williams makes clear, this is not the same as the unconscious (which, he says, "bourgeois culture has mythicized"). Instead, his description of the circuits of practical consciousness more closely resemble schemas of affect: "It is a kind of feeling and thinking which is indeed social and material, but each in an embryonic phase before it can become fully articulated and defined exchange."[27] For most of the short essay, Williams develops this notion as a "cultural hypothesis" before claiming that structures of feeling are most linked either to "the rise of a class" or "at other times to contradiction, fracture, or mutation within a class."[28] This soldering of the concept to that of class struggle, while not a surprise coming from Williams given his Marxist views, has been embraced by generations of minoritarian scholars who are similarly interested in describing most social identities as in process. Writing about Latinx performance, for example, José Muñoz has maintained that *feeling* functions as a critical repository of politically cogent information that resides outside the public sphere of speech and action, and thus that certain ethnic or racial subject positions can inhabit a shared structure of feeling in oppositional contrast to legibly White and national affects of America.[29] Similarly, the AIDS activist Gregg Bordowitz has identified a queer structure of feeling "as an articulation of presence forged through resistance to heterosexist society," while laying out specific criteria for inclusion in this structure (such as "if self-identified queers produce the work, if these producers identify the work as queer, if queers claim the work has significance to queers, [and/or] if the work is censored or criticized for being queer").[30] These interventions, central to the work of anti-racist, feminist, and queer studies, test Williams's cultural hypothesis through delineating and tracing the affective circulation of and between bodies.

What does it mean to read these two pieces of writing together, as part of a larger intertextual universe on the mediation of affect? To my knowledge, no substantial attempts have been made within television studies to stitch together Williams's work on television with his work on affect. Structures of feeling, like the experience of watching television, must be perceived as emergent, serving as what Lauren Berlant describes as "a residue of common historical experience sensed but not spoken in a social formation, except as the heterogeneous but common practices of a historical moment would emanate them."[31] The "present" tense intrinsic to "practical consciousness" can be found in the way television organizes the spectator's sense of time: in television's deployment of liveness as its ontology and ideology, in its insistence of technology as a-live, in its backward construction of "real time" in reality programming, and in convergence culture's revealing of television as always already intermedial.[32] Richard Dienst, however, has taken issue with Williams's notion of flow, arguing that the concept "remains the blurry images of unresolved metaphysical impulses in the theorization of television" in part because Williams gives it too much power, constructing it in a totalizing way as a byproduct from commercial systems and thus "absorb[ing] the entirety of the televisual textual process."[33] Similarly, so too might Berlant's description of structures of feeling as "sensed but not spoken" conflict with television's reliance on rhetorical address, self-referentiality, and stock character stereotypes: never turned off, and always in the service of its commercial imperative, television simply speaks *too much*. Yet as early scholarship on soap opera and female audiences within television studies has demonstrated, television's flows may replicate the status quo, but its repetitions also create spaces for change and subversion. Moreover, since television desires a stable audience, it simultaneously seeks to expand viewership while also rewarding loyal audiences; the effects of this desire—narrowcasting and rebooting old programs, to name two examples—produce affective systems that are similar to structures of feeling, just as they encompass television's many media flows.

Williams posits both watching television and structures of feeling as profoundly social experiences: television is not just a technical apparatus, for example, but an inseparably social technology (as evidenced in the subtitle to his book, "technology and cultural form"). One way that affects are socially transmitted is by sharing the same time, another is by sharing the same space. Thinking of affect as transmitted through social, and never solitary, environments insists on relational networks of community, however constructed they may be. Long perceived as a medium characterized by "flatness," television finds affective complexity in being so stretched out, creating what we might call an *affective intertextuality*. These ephemeral connections help spectators apply hermeneutic processes not just to questions within a text but also to the feelings within a text and within a spectator's relationship to that text. Consider, for example, Katie Stewart's account of how "a weirdly floating 'we' snaps into a blurry focus when one enters a mall, or when one is flipping through reality TV channels, watching scenes unfold."[34] If in his experiential misrecognition Williams found "a single irresponsible flow of images and feelings" to account for the affective methods by which spectators ultimately submit to the ideology of mass culture, Stewart shows us how flow enfolds through "watching scenes unfold" across categories of space and time: in seeing from a distance (etymologically the definition of "tele-vision"), television imprints a "blurry focus" onto its viewer.[35]

The effects of this focus now bring us back to the definitional tensions within affect studies: Where does television sit as an arbiter of ideology and as a medium of representation? Reiterating from earlier: to claim that affect is truly distinct from emotion would then suggest that affect is entirely independent from ideology and, because it is presignifying, prior to ideology altogether. As Ruth Leys has incisively pointed out in a key intervention into this debate, "The disconnect between 'ideology' and affect produces as one of its consequences a relative indifference to the role of ideas and beliefs in politics, culture, and art in favor of an 'ontological' concern with different people's corporeal-affective reactions."[36] But television is, as Jane Feuer has canonically argued, defined by its liveness *both* ontologically and ideologically, as even programs that are not recorded "live" are organized to appear exactly as a "live" broadcast. Indeed, this occupying of both positions—ontology and ideology, and thus affectivity and representation—implies that the affectivity of television is experienced as immediate, present, and vital. Furthermore, this is a necessarily *ideological* reading. Feuer frames this question differently, "at the level of aesthetic superstructure"; yet, the contradiction she identifies within television as a text also employs the neoliberal language of affect studies: "Is television a thing-in-itself (i.e., a specific signifying practice) or is it merely a means of transmission for other processes of signification (cinema, news, 'live' events)?"[37] Indeed, to think of television as "merely a means of transmission for other processes of signification"—as a vehicle for other semiotic or intertextual associations—casts the ephemeral medium in a similar light to an inscriptive body, destroyed in the process of forming the dissociated subject. Furthermore, it prefigures television's status as a central platform within convergence culture, in which the television set increasingly becomes a means of transmission for media forms divorced from live broadcast (such as streaming platforms and gaming consoles).

chapter one

Of course, postmillennial television has a different relationship to liveness, with reports of the demise of traditional network and cable broadcasting repeated ad nauseam by both trade journalists and scholarly critics. Amid this changing relationship to liveness, Karin van Es has modified Feuer's claims to argue that "*always* a construction, the live has never *not* been social" and that it is best studied "as the product of particular interactions among institutions, technologies and users/viewers."[38] Van Es helpfully emphasizes liveness through its ability to circulate across media platforms and audiences, describing "constellations of liveness" that script different mediations and audience expectations, in effect evoking the metaphor of the affective atmosphere of a particular live event. Most live broadcasts are, of course, not really *live*: it has been the custom for radio and television to delay live broadcasts by a handful of seconds in the name of censorship. Following the controversy during the 2004 Super Bowl Halftime Show known as "Nipplegate"—in which performer Janet Jackson had a "wardrobe malfunction" that partially exposed her breast on live television—the FCC mandated a five-second broadcast delay for all live events, further changing the parameters around which American audiences perceive liveness. Yet this reception reveals how affect, like the live, is "more than just a matter of technical performance" in van Es's words.[39] Televisual affectivity, then, is dependent on the fiction of meaningful representation. But what *meaning* can be extracted from the phrase "the fiction of meaningful representation," or even from the various valences of a word like *meaningful*? Below, I identify three possibilities.

Meaningful representation could refer first to the process by which a viewer makes meaning from a narrative text, a process of reading. The contours of such a process—how one approaches a text, what one looks for within its complexity—occupy a central concern of the field of literary studies, with textual strategies having been frequently analyzed as systemic (if not scientific) processes. The act of making meaning requires the adoption of the role of a critical consumer of narrative. Thus, the statement that televisual affectivity depends on the *fiction* of meaningful representation gestures toward the slippages between the perception of affect and affect itself. But if to read the affectivity of television as immediate, present, and vital is to engage in a necessarily ideological reading, we thus require the fiction of meaningful representation to inhabit TV's temporal flows, built as they are on segmentation and repetition. The affectivity of television, this reading implies, has been there all along in how we watch as organizational grammars of time and space.

Second, the fiction of meaningful representation gestures toward a claim often repeated throughout this book: that to privilege a television series or

41

genre as inherently more *meaningful* than others plays into one of the television industry's cultural logics. This has been propagated throughout contemporary television criticism, an industry itself that has grown exponentially with the medium's so-called legitimation, as well as by digital platforms that allow fans to publish their transformative works of art and their critiques of a series, challenging the traditional profile of a "television critic." This is not to say that all critics, bloggers, fans, recappers, industry correspondents, or academics buy into these hierarchies of cultural value. Rather, televisual affectivity means reorienting claims that some television programs and genres carry more meaning than others toward assessments of affective charge. The statement thus can be inferred to mean something like this: whether detached from processes of signification or not, affects do not discriminate between high art and low culture. Both are meaningful.

In ending this chapter, however, I focus its energies and its affects on a third reading of this statement. Television may traffic in this notion of representation as re-presentation, referentially, of delimited identities, but attending to affectivity expands our understanding of what "meaningful representation" itself might mean. This reading pressures the term *representation*, consorting with its definition as an action on behalf of someone else, as in the example of a political representative. As the world's predominant electronic media form for most of its history, television has always foregrounded and interrogated the category of meaningful representation through its deceptively simple portrayals of different gender, race, socioeconomic class, national, religious, and sexual identities. And as a medium that primarily entered the national imaginary through the domestic space of the suburban home, television has always emphasized intersectional questions of gender and sexuality in particular; television studies has thus uniquely contributed to the study of representation as a discipline closely tied to feminist theory and analysis.[40] Nevertheless, its responsibilities to industrial conventions, multiple audiences, and creative talent have historically produced a cautious embrace of (as well as a critical distance from) stereotypes of marginalized identity groups. Taking care not to universalize all members of a particular group, meaningful representation could be thought of narrowly as a structural impossibility, as no series will be able to satisfy the representational expectations of everyone within or outside of a particular identity group or audience demographic. Someone will feel alienated from a program's politics of representation; someone will disidentify with a protagonist who phenotypically and demographically resembles herself. Someone, in other words, will be irritated.

chapter one

Television is a medium dependent upon repetition, and Michelle Dean is not looking to repeat herself, even though she already has. In 2012, Dean was a blogger about popular culture for *The Nation* (since then, she has written a book of essays and penned the Hulu miniseries *The Act* [2019]) who wrote a post titled "The Internet's Toxic Relationship with HBO's *Girls*." The post is organized around Dean's affective reactions to news that the series had been renewed for a third season:

> I've written about Lena Dunham in this space before, and I'm not looking to repeat myself, but the gist of my take on *Girls* is: it's fine. Just that. Not the Second Coming of twentysomethings (which one shudders to contemplate anyway), nor some brave new art form. *Girls* has some good jokes embedded in unremarkable-to-sloppy plotlines and acting, but otherwise I generally prefer control and artfulness to Apatowian craft-of-no-craft. That said, I watch it faithfully for the occasional flashes of talent it contains. So there was no reason for the queasy feeling I got when I heard that the show had been renewed for a third season. I mean to say that I actually felt a pit of dread begin to open in my stomach. I interrogated this overreaction, and concluded: my objection is not so much to the show as it is to the endless amounts of think pieces—as I once saw someone put it, Very Important Essays—*Girls* inspires. There are think pieces about think pieces and now I suppose you could call this a think piece about the general phenomenon of Internet think pieces about television shows, so yes, on some level, I'm a hypocrite to point that out.[41]

Dean describes feelings of exhaustion, resignation, loyalty, pleasure, dread, and guilt before moderating this "overreaction" of spectatorial affectivity with critical thinking (as if critical thinking were itself somehow free from affect!). Yet the tone of her think piece is chiefly one of frustration: with *Girls* for not being quite good enough; with her peers for a continuous desire to think about and comment on *Girls*; with the internet for creating and popularizing the think piece as a "very important" form of writing; and ultimately with herself for hypocritically participating in an economy that commodifies criticism. In her words, *Girls* is a mediocre text, and there is something irritating about having to read too much—that is, to fashion meaning—into something that is the "craft-of-no-craft."[42]

Dean and Dunham may be a few years apart, but they share much in common: they both write across media forms, often attracting controversy

43

for their polemics about millennial culture and everyday life. Additionally, they both participate in the "craft-of-no-craft." A craft as having no craft at all describes the formal style of a think piece, a form of writing defined by the *Oxford English Dictionary* as "presenting personal opinions, analysis, or discussion, rather than bare facts."[43] This strange text, perhaps formerly called an essay or a review, has become a way to ruminate about the steady stream of popular culture—what is currently trending or has recently gone viral—through the expansion of digital publishing (an expansion that has resulted in employing fewer full-time journalists and more freelancers). Think pieces are robustly citational, horizontally deploying hyperlinks to provide evidence to their claims and to promote the think pieces written by their peers (in the process legitimizing themselves as forms of criticism). In what might be a think piece, David Haglund notes that since the 1930s the term was used derisively by journalists to incite panic about the quality of their craft; think pieces, according to *The Nation*'s Paul W. Ward in 1936, were "dispatches that in major part are the product of the reporters' communion with their own imaginative souls," prefiguring the accusations of being a "craft-of-no-craft" that would come nearly three-quarters of a century later.[44] To commune with one's own imaginative soul evokes the kind of meditative writing found in American transcendentalism, which has occupied a prestigious place in the canon of American literature, and this is both the aim of and criticism leveled at the think piece, which epistemologically epitomizes the paradoxically unique, mass individuality of digital media. Creative yet calculated, reflective yet narcissistic, the think piece has a cultural value and reach higher than the self-published personal blog but lower than seemingly objective, fact-based journalism. Opinionated, yet often inaccurate and requiring "updates" that correct facts and tone, it inhabits a temporality that continuously undermines itself, for it neither can be definitive enough nor have the last word.[45] In short, the think piece announces itself as rich in content, even though it is manufactured quickly and cheaply.

The commodification of televisual criticism—how think pieces become just another form of "content" in the digitized media industries—produces a "toxic relationship" according to Dean, who claims that the audience of such think pieces "spend way too much time reading and thinking about what they find on the Internet." Dean aligns think-piece criticisms with the act of trolling, insofar as think-piece audiences (defined by Dean as "journalists, bloggers, and, yes, comments sections") consist of people immersed in digital culture, not dissimilar to Gabriella Coleman's characterization of the function of the "troll" as "commenting on the massification of the Internet—a position that is

44

chapter one

quite contemptuous of newcomers."[46] Dean, too, sees the internet's discussion of *Girls* as exemplifying what Maura Johnston coined as "trollgazing," which works on the troll's logic of "annoyance": "doing what you know will annoy people, even if your cause is a just one."[47] The compulsion to write about HBO's *Girls,* Dean concludes, stems from the irritating nature both of the series and of the medium and form used to comment on the series.

But what to make of this toxic relationship between a millennial form of knowledge ("the internet") and a millennial TV text (*Girls*)? In Mel Chen's powerful work on queerness, toxicity, and affect, toxicity has a rhetorical valence when applied to minoritarian identities: "If the definition of *toxin* has always been the outcome of political negotiation and a threshold value on a set of selected tests," Chen writes, "its conditionality is no more true in medical discourse than in social discourse, in which one's definition of a toxic irritant coincides with habitual scapegoats of ableist, sexist, and racist systems."[48] The internet, with a never-quite-fulfilled promise of anonymity and the erasure of identity, becomes susceptible to toxic affects through debates surrounding the question of representation; such a porous structure of exposure and publicity undergirds the point of entry by which toxicity, in the form of hate speech, infects the proclamation (and contestation) of identity, both on TV and across its discourses. After all, in the knowledge economy and its attendant platforms of democratized (yet economically precarious) criticism, Dean's irritation forms the affective labor for the production of content.

Representing Imperfections through Imperfect Representations

Apart from its televisual and think-piece mediations, *Girls* is irritatingly toxic through its relationship of the identity of its main character, Hannah Horvath (played by Dunham), to its creator: a White millennial feminist. Just as the think piece metonymically stands in for the internet, and for the forms of knowledge production and networked audiences it typifies, so too does Lena Dunham represent the artistic desires and limitations of White millennial feminism, and this rhetorical linkage is perhaps what is most polarizing about Dunham, her series, and millennial culture as a whole. As one of the first television auteurs to come from the millennial generation, most profiles of Dunham, including those written by her detractors, assert this linkage; it is so ubiquitous that an exhaustive list of its appearances in recaps, think pieces, and other reportage on the series would be impossible. To select just one example: Meghan Daum's 2014 profile in the *New York Times* in anticipation of Dunham's book *Not That Kind of Girl* characterizes her "as a proxy for the collective aspirations and insecurities of her generation, or at least a certain educated, mostly white, mostly urban-dwelling microdemographic therein."[49] The linkage is perhaps not so surprising for viewers of *Girls*, for in the series' pilot Dunham's character, Hannah, while high on opium, tells her parents, "I don't want to freak you out, but I think that I may be the voice of my generation—or at least a voice of *a* generation." Here, Hannah (Dunham) alludes to media stereotypes of millennials as socially coddled and entitled to being heard (as well as being casual drug users) but also to neoliberal logics of dividuation, in which anyone with a blog or social media account can be "a voice of a generation." For Dunham, this generation is certainly one of privilege: most profiles of Dunham will also comment on her Whiteness, her Tribeca upbringing, and her wealthy artist parents. Moreover, *Girls* publicly struggled with its treatment—or lack thereof—of issues of race, as its four main leads are all White, and People of Color make scant appearances on the series (and when they do, many critics noted, they are either tokenized or stereotyped). While Dunham publicly stated in interviews that the series would rectify this lack of diversity during the second season, her solution—a two-episode arc in which Hannah dates a Black law student named Sandy (Donald Glover), who also happens to be a Republican—was roundly criticized for its inauthenticity.[50]

The episode in which Hannah and Sandy break up ("I Get Ideas") is telling for how it inscribes irritation as the series' fundamental affective relationship to race.[51] The majority of scenes documenting their short relationship are set in private spaces away from *Girls'* main settings, such as in small independent bookstores or at Sandy's apartment. The one exception to this is a brief scene in the bathroom of the apartment that Hannah shares with her gay friend Elijah (Andrew Rannells). In the scene, Elijah confronts Sandy about his political beliefs and insinuates, through a number of thinly veiled comments, that Sandy is homophobic, the effect of which is to emphasize both Sandy's ideological otherness as well as his racial otherness. Tired of being characterized in Elijah's flat stereotypes, Sandy tells Elijah: "I'm not doing *this* with you." He eventually leaves, pointing at Elijah and Hannah (shown in the screen in the bathroom mirror) and saying, "I get this. I don't approve, but I get it." This is the only scene from two episodes in which Sandy is shown with one of Hannah's friends, and his entrance into her world (and thus the world of the series) is marked by conflict (and judging by the size of the bathroom, this is a small world, indeed). Sandy's two remarks are punctuated by different uses of the word *this*: in the former, *this* signifies the tedious explanation of one's political identity, but in the latter, it flips the script of social conservatives and

1.2 Sandy exits Hannah and Elijah's bathroom. *Girls*, "I Get Ideas," Season 2, Episode 2.

becomes a sarcastic acknowledgment of the normative logics of the series, as Sandy challenges the Whiteness of Hannah's world and the gay-friendly feminism it purports to represent.

The slippage between the narrative insularity of the series and discourses about this insularity becomes fully apparent during Hannah and Sandy's breakup at Sandy's apartment. Hannah is upset that Sandy has not read her writing. But he has, he admits: "It just wasn't for me," to which she replies, "It's for everyone," in an allusion to the dogged critiques of representation within *Girls*' first season. Yet if the series is engaging in a sort of trolling of its critics, it does so by establishing Hannah's character as stubbornly defensive about the supposed universality of her creative efforts. She insists that Sandy call out the flaws of the essay but then frequently interrupts him with her sloppy rebuttals: he felt as if nothing happens in the essay; she felt as if "a girl's whole perspective on who she was and her sexuality changed." When Sandy attempts to explain himself further, Hannah complains that she has something in her ear, associating feminist critique and her own physical embodiment as challenges to his point of view. Lamely, Hannah offers one final justification for her obvious discomfort at hearing criticism of her writing: that getting such criticism is, in fact, a good thing, insofar as it constitutes a dialogue about her work that mirrors the dialogue of his political beliefs. But this, too, becomes a smokescreen for Hannah to voice her opinions on gay

47

marriage, gun control, and ultimately how "two out of three people on death row are Black." Hannah's rant tenuously yokes together Sandy's politics with his race, an explicitly verbal mirroring of Elijah's earlier discomfort. Sandy counters by noting the racial fetish of White girls new to Brooklyn, commenting how the "Black boyfriend," like the fixed-gear bike, acts as a visual signifier of hipster femininity. As the recipient of well-trodden criticisms of straight White millennial females characterized as "basic," Hannah claims to be unaware of the ways in which race is organized within her social world. She misrecognizes, this critique submits, the consumption of racial difference with the active support of Communities of Color; she will fantasize about her "jungle fever lover" (as NBA legend Kareem Abdul-Jabbar characterized Sandy in one think piece) without fully integrating him into her life.[52] In language that uncannily reflects Dunham's own excuses for the lack of cultural diversity within the series—in one NPR interview, Dunham claimed it was by "accident" that the four leads are White—Hannah deflects with a bothersome obliviousness that is notable for its Whiteness as well as for its aggravation.[53] "The joke's on you because you know what? I never thought about the fact that you were Black once," she tells him. "I don't live in a world where there are divisions like this." She requires an excess of words to communicate her cultural sensitivity and adherence to postracial ideologies, but Sandy needs only two to call out Hannah's (and Dunham's) Whiteness: "You do."

"We hate white girls because we are white girls," Hilton Als bitingly reminds us, and thus this controversy surrounding the lack of cultural diversity in *Girls* exemplifies the irritatingly White logic of the series itself and the think-piece echo chamber that calls our attention to its logic.[54] Before the series even premiered and during its initial reception, reviews praised its originality while bemoaning its racial and class homogeneity.[55] In a critique of the premiere that went viral across social media, Jenna Wortham (here writing for *The Hairpin*) ethnographically turned to Twitter to distill reactions, which inevitably centered on expectations of referential representation: "They are us but they are not us. They are me but they are not me."[56] The allure of *Girls'* verisimilitude is a profound moment of potential identification for Wortham (who identifies as Black), as she speaks of how the series "gets So. Many. Things. Right" about being in one's twenties, but in particular praises the series for being "painfully self-aware of its characters' entitlement," a trademark characteristic of many members (i.e., White, middle-class) of the millennial generation. Indeed, it is because *Girls* is "actually good" that the lack of racial representation within the first three episodes that Wortham reviewed stings that much harder.

Yet while this argument points to fissures in *Girls'* representational politics, it also reinforces an understanding of race as supremely visual and a notion of TV as a site for visual reflection: Wortham closes her think piece by stating, "I just wish I saw a little more of myself on screen, right alongside" the four friends of *Girls*. In this statement, the visual field defines Wortham's notion of representation, and her desire to suture herself into the scene appears through direct mirroring or projection. As many Black feminist scholars have argued, however, the visual field often amounts as a scene of punishment in which White people (and especially White spectators) assert a normative idea of subjectivity as defined against the racial Other, most often through the reproduction of racial stereotypes.[57] The impossibility of being sutured fully into the diegetic world anchors representation as rooted in lack, and given the way in which *Girls* reifies femininity as appearance (propped up by, among other things, Dunham's frequent nudity), Wortham's final comment contains a telling recognition of Kara Keeling's figuration of the "Black femme," a figure of difference who in making herself visible "offers us time in which we can work to perceive something different, or differently."[58]

But what is the object of this labor—what can be perceived differently—in these reflections? If the object of this labor is representation, Wortham's think piece, like much online writing about *Girls*, positions this representation as imperfect, insofar as it will not fulfill any spectator's fantasies about what legitimately constitutes the imagined "girl." For the representative icon of millennial feminism is simultaneously very much and certainly not Hannah, in many respects a flawed inheritor to Carrie Bradshaw of HBO's *Sex and the City* (1998–2004). *Girls* cannot quite get postfeminism right, for its subjects are not the comparatively mature women of Generation X claiming their place in the workforce but rather those whose access to the workforce has been restricted by the Great Recession. Yet the series also complicates its own performance of its economic precarity, with many online commentaries focusing on the socioeconomic disparity between Dunham's wealth and her character's perceived destitution: Hannah is an imperfect representation of a "real" poor person, and *Girls* is an imperfect representation of millennial economic precarity. Many scholars writing about *Girls*—particularly from the vantage points of postfeminist critique—note how its "failure, disappointment, and vulnerability" illustrate a fundamental ambivalence toward postfeminism, arguing that Dunham is clearly satirizing, to some extent, her annoyances with the circulation of postfeminist ideologies in a bad economy.[59] Throughout the series, Dunham focuses heavily on moments of self-loathing, daring audiences to hate-watch and to disidentify with her character by highlighting larger structural issues (misogyny, the Recession, poor mental health) that, despite the rhetoric of empowerment in which she was raised, prevent her from realizing her full economic and cultural potential. Here, both the object of *Girls* as well as its critique are steeped in the language of failed potential, reminiscent of Hollis Griffin's keen observation that "ideological critique often suggests a profound sense of 'failure.'"[60]

Discourses about *Girls*, and about Hannah in particular, emphasize flaws: Dunham's self-promotion of her imperfect naked body (itself a critique of "flawed" ideologies surrounding appropriate femininity and body size); the perceived entitlement of its characters; their general lack of sexual self-confidence (suggesting a millennial sexual immaturity full of anxiety); and, of course, its tone-deaf Whiteness.[61] These flaws are what give *Girls* its complexity and thus the kind of realism associated with its HBO brand. But as Taylor Nygaard has prudently observed, the controversy surrounding *Girls* is also a product of HBO's "inconsistent and conflicting branding strategies, which worked to subsume Dunham's female auteur identity within the masculine tradition of the HBO quality brand."[62] This imperfection is, I would argue, the backbone of and for an affectation of irritation that serves as both *Girls'* ontology and epistemology as well as its textuality and reception. Much of the interesting scholarly work on *Girls* has focused on its comedic affect, part of a larger genre of postmillennial comedy that invites audiences to "cringe" at the scenes on screen. Nygaard and Jorie Lagerwey claim that *Girls* inaugurated a cycle of programs about "Horrible White People," inviting affective disorientation among audiences who never know where, precisely, to direct their laughter.[63]

These programs—many of which portray millennial "girls" as mentally ill or as socially and physically awkward—deploy a variety of formal techniques to reinforce this characterological trope. In Julia Havas and Maria Sulimma's reading of the genre, "cringe aesthetics . . . depict millennial female protagonists who frequently violate social and physical taboos in embarrassing narrative situations, while failing at communication, exhibiting unawareness of expected social behaviors, and having their self-images diverge from the ways others perceive them," a description that uses the language of representation as its foundation.[64] Trapped within the discourse it cannot help but produce, *Girls* exposes the rawness of a visual representation premised on imperfect approximations. Rebecca Wanzo has thoughtfully read this condition of irritation via Julia Kristeva's concept of abjection, noting that Hannah's narcissism, her claiming of difference, and her sense of alienation from normative social life forms the basis for her agency as a millennial female subject. In documenting how much she "repels" others throughout the series (most notably in professional settings), Wanzo observes that "abjection can thus become what Hannah is and what she creates" through the act of writing and giving language to otherwise unrepresentable affects.[65]

In Sianne Ngai's apperceptive theorization of irritation, she remarks that "whether 'irritation' is defined as an emotional or physical experience, synonyms for it tend to apply equally to psychic life *and* life at the level of the body—and particularly to its surfaces or skin."[66] Her reminder of irritation's dual role as mild anger and as soreness prompts a reassessment of the epidermal in *Girls*. This metaphor appeared extensively throughout one critic's own prolific writings on the series. In 2012 (writing for *New York Magazine*), Emily Nussbaum claimed that *Girls* revealed "an aesthetic that's raw and bruised," as opposed to the "aspirational" aesthetic of *Sex and the City*.[67] In 2013 (now writing for *The New Yorker*), she likewise claimed that the series "teaches you to thicken your skin" through its privileged wit. *Girls* may be trying to teach us to thicken our skin, but in so doing it provokes discomfort by being too vulnerable or too honest about the failures of authentic representation. Its messy narratives undergird a certain porousness: how it dilutes the distinction between oneself and one's critics and how it highlights the discomfort of being "in one's own skin." Indeed, skin is precisely what *Girls* is accused of revealing too much of, with much media attention focused on Dunham's nude scenes, often figuring them as a feminist aspect of the series (or at least an aspect representative of Dunham's particular brand of millennial feminism). This may be most clear in the awkward scenes of sexual exploration in the third episode of the series ("All Adventurous Women Do"), in which Hannah is diagnosed with HPV, the sexually transmitted virus that causes skin and mucous membrane infections: transmitted, according to public health campaigns, "skin-to-skin."

The sensations that such discursive metaphors elicit are racialized as well as sexualized. As a mood that uses external sensations to elaborate internal states, irritation, Ngai points out, is always already racialized, since society's primary way of reading race is through the visual signifier of skin color. Furthermore, since this irritation can operate "only in conspicuous surplus or deficit in proportion to its occasion," *Girls* irritates both through an excess of its representative capacity (since it is too privileged, too White, too narcissistic) and through a deficiency of the same capacity (since it will never be realistic because it lacks "authentic" diversity).[68] The flattened schema of representation within *Girls* thus entraps it within a metric of appropriateness that it subsequently refuses, and the constant restaging of this affective gap is what gets under the skin of the spectator and of the porous, networked surfaces throughout online criticism.

Throwing Stones at Beach Houses, and Other Forms of Irritatingly Neoliberal Resistance

Irritation is an imperfect affect insofar as it lacks an explicit object: it simply *is*. In fact, Ngai initially ascribes to it a limited political valence: irritation "might be described as negative affect in its weakest, mildest, and most politically effete form. One is tempted to vote it the dysphoric affect least likely to play a significant role in any oppositional praxis or ideological struggle."[69] If this were true, this chapter would end on a rather depressing note. In fact, the political stakes of this book often seem particularly stymied by the forms of neoliberal citizenship made uncomfortable by TV. What political good can materialize if the viewer is too busy (or too addicted to) bingeing or live tweeting in order to process political issues, or even to recognize them, within the programs they watch? This is not to ask about the political possibilities imagined by *Girls*, which in this particular recounting (a recounting of its already existing many recountings online) amount to a politics of representation that is defined by the profound disappointment that such a well-written show can be so supremely irritating. Without a proper object, irritation as a political critique appears to be a bite with no teeth. *Girls* is irritating enough for many critics to make pointedly misogynistic proclamations about the future of (White) feminism, but it is not irritating enough to project a positive feminist utopia free from the commodification of postfeminism.

In closing, then, I want to highlight the ways that irritation attempts to be reclaimed as a form of resistance against the terms of postrecessionary precarity, at the same time that it embraces late capitalist and postfeminist logics of mass individualism. If irritation can be thought of as buttressing a politics of representation in millennial feminism and in postmillennial television, is irritation as a form of resistance elastic, like the skin metaphors common to *Girls* and its critiques? How might spectators take that form and stretch and contort it toward alternate political ends? How might a productive irritation with and of *Girls* open up a different reading of the series? A scene from the third-season episode "Beach House" uncovers what joys might be located in the act of exposing irritation for what it is, in all of its many imperfections.

"Beach House" appears at a moment during the third season when all of the characters within *Girls* are irritated with one another, to the point where Marnie (Allison Williams) scores a weekend house on the North Fork of Long

Island for the purposes of reconciliation.[70] Marnie is optimistic that healing will occur during their time together, and she has gone to great lengths to ensure that this will happen, from placing vases with hand-cut flowers next to each friend's temporary bed to planning activities such as writing down their wishes on slips of paper that are then to be burned in a bonfire in order to ensure their fulfillment. "Beach House" is thus about feelings and how the processing of feelings can help a group of friends regain their footing with one another. Marnie's efforts, however, are wholly unsuccessful: Hannah runs into Elijah and three of his gay male friends in town, and she invites them back to the house; now, with the number of people having doubled in size, a boozy pool party commences, complete with a choreographed dance number. While the partying is fun, Marnie is unhappy that it has prevented more intimate moments of friendship among the women from occurring, and after a rather dense dinner of duck originally intended for four yet now stretched eight ways, what was originally intended as a time for healing quickly becomes a disaster.

The highlight of the episode (written by Dunham, Apatow, and *Girls'* executive producer Jenni Konner) comes when Shoshanna (Zosia Mamet) hears Marnie's call for honesty among the girls and lets loose with a stinging indictment of each character, calling Hannah a narcissist ("I wanted to fall asleep in my own vomit all day listening to you talk about how you bruise more easily than other people"), Marnie a bad cook and a neurotic ("You are tortured by self-doubt and fear, and it is not pleasant to be around"), and Jessa a robot who recites the trite spiritual language of recovery ("Seriously, Jessa goes to rehab for five fucking seconds, and we have to listen to everything she comes up with?"). Shoshanna goes from sitting on the sofa in the corner, nearly a cameo in the episode's action so far, to standing up, with the camera panning around her as she delivers her verdict: Hannah and her friends are "mentally ill and miserable," a millennial generation pampered by entitlement and post-Recession ennui.

To troll, to call out, to indict, to irritate: these are the weapons that *Girls* uses (and that girls must use) to survive as millennials. These are forms of acknowledgment and recognition that are not tactful, polite, or diplomatic. Sara Ahmed has described in wonderful detail the position of the "feminist killjoy" who destroys the possibility of happiness in social situations through her embodied actions (such as Shoshanna's exaggerated eye rolls) as well as through her words. She instructively notes that the term feminism "is thus saturated with unhappiness" insofar as its very construction identifies a refusal to locate happiness in heteropatriarchal society. Indeed, her very presence may incite antagonistic feelings, altering the affective atmosphere of a room, like an

1.3 Shoshanna calls out her friends. *Girls*, "Beach House," Season 3, Episode 7.

airborne pathogen: "The feminist killjoy 'spoils' the happiness of others; she is a spoilsport because she refuses to convene, to assemble, or to meet up over happiness."[71] Ahmed notes how the position of the feminist killjoy is closely tethered to figurations of the "angry black woman," and this is suggestive of how racial difference helps amplify affective intensities: anger is coded as racially Other, in contrast to more minor and more White forms of negative affect, such as irritation. Shoshanna's outburst at the end of "Beach House" articulates a politics of acknowledgment and recognition anchored around identifying the unhappiness among her group of friends, even if, by exposing the tensions present within their friendship, she threatens the stability of the series itself. But if her rant indeed kills joy, it also opens up the possibility for that joy to emerge again, as such acknowledgment fosters viewer pleasure through breaking the fiction of politeness and assuming the porous boundary between text and audience.[72] This represents some of the paradoxes of representation and desire, irritation and pleasure: as Shoshanna occupies the narrative role of the killjoy through calling out each character's flaws, she enacts a formal irritation onto the series' relationship with its audience and with its genre. *Girls* is technically a comedy, though like much postmillennial comedy, it frequently and performatively withholds immediate laughter in response to its jokes. As Shoshanna's barbs are not particularly that witty, the series redirects the pleasure found in laughter to the act of calling out itself, a queer celebration of the failure of friendship.

chapter one

1.4 The four friends dance while sitting down at the end of a long weekend. *Girls*, "Beach House," Season 3, Episode 7.

"Beach House" presents *Girls* as a lacerated narrative, barely intact after the affective wounds of a weekend of (non)healing. Its characters askew from the images of perfect, upper-class postfeminism presented by previous HBO series, *Girls* shows a lot of skin in its version of millennial culture, but this skin, while preserved on the outside, exists to communicate the raw feeling interiorized within. The image that *Girls* presents of its characters as irritated and as irritating enables the series to reconfigure the politics of representation, trolling itself to the point of literal exhaustion. Little action happens after Shoshanna's rant, and the episode closes with the four friends sitting on a curb in town, waiting for the bus that will take them back to Brooklyn while vaguely reenacting the dance they learned the night before. In what might be read as telling of both their affective familiarity with one another as well as their exhausted state, they can only do bits of the dance while sitting down, communicating comfort through friendship but also through a lack of energy. Here, the girls remain a cohort, in sync with each other even while appearing to be distant from each other (and from the audience as well).

Imelda Whelehan has read this scene as being without "obvious catharsis," diagnosing it as a symptom of the limitations of postfeminist friendship: "Friends, like social media 'friends,' might just be a convenient, and empty, social label."[73] Yet Hannah and her friends' inability to perform the rites of friendship in upright posture lays bare the consequences of being chronically irritated or irritating, presenting those conditions as momentarily pleasurable while having debilitating long-term effects. Four seasons later, the effects of these "toxic relationships" overwhelm the series' narrative; in the penultimate episode of the series, the four again process their friendship, with Shoshanna again the agent of provocation (and here summarizing the feelings of the audience): "I have come to realize how exhausting and narcissistic and ultimately boring this whole dynamic is. And I finally feel brave enough to create some distance for myself . . . I think we should all just agree to call it."[74] Calling out has now become calling *it*, and the series ends with its friendships mostly torn apart.

Troubling the viewer's ability to forge empathetic attachments to its characters, Shoshanna's harangue foregrounds *Girls'* larger effort to address the show's critiques of White narcissism while still maintaining a complex negotiation between audience identification and disidentification. Indeed, this rupture helps to resist the demand of representation itself, as it calls into question the belief that it can have value in a predetermined, privatized entertainment industry. If televisual affectivity depends on the fiction of meaningful representation, Shoshanna teaches us that the fiction of meaningful representation, its complicit turning in on itself, does not have to produce only irritation but can also create solidarity in its exposure. In addition to giving voice to its trolls—a neoliberal yet effective way to call attention to the racialized and gendered logics at work in producing postmillennial television—*Girls* suggests that by probing sensations of discomfort we may better understand the way late capitalism shapes future generations, such that we may be ever vigilant to lash out and expose it for the irritating mechanism by which we, in turn, smile, laugh, and explode with joy.

chapter one

two

the addicted

spectator

tv junkies

in need of an

intervention

One might extend the concept
and the experience of drugs
far beyond its legal, medical
definition, and in a space at
once idiosyncratic and public,
arrange all sorts of practices,
pleasures and pains that no one
could rigorously show to be un-
related and without analogy to
drug addiction. The possibilities
are innumerable and quasi-
idiomatic. Every phantasmatic
organization, whether collective
or individual, is the invention
of a drug, or of a rhetoric of
drugs, be it aphrodisiac or not,
with production, consumption,
semi-secrecy, and a semi-
private market.
—JACQUES DERRIDA

It wasn't even like I was
watching an addict; it was
more like a person who just
really sucked at acting.
—"MEL"

DRUGS, OR THE RHETORIC OF DRUGS? An
addict, or one who cannot act, one who "just
really suck[s] at acting?" Is a poor performance
of bodily misfortune required for spectators to
gain pleasure from—or to get high off of—reality television? The addict and the spectator of
reality TV: Are these distinct subject positions,
or might they converge?

We are not watching an addict; instead, we
are watching someone who cannot perform
her addiction adequately *enough*. While these
metrics may not yet be clearly defined, it is
obvious that Linda has problems. A former
professional television extra, Linda allegedly developed the connective tissue disorder
Ehlers-Danlos syndrome (EDS), which produces fragile joints, muscles, ligaments, and
blood vessels. Some forms of EDS can cause
severe musculoskeletal pain brought on by
frequent joint dislocations. For this condition,
Linda was prescribed fentanyl, a synthetic
narcotic analgesic approximately a hundred
times more potent than morphine. Despite her
excessive use of fentanyl—she consumes seven
200 mcg lollipops daily, three more per day than
FDA recommendations—Linda claims that she
continues to suffer from chronic pain, locating
some of the pain's sources as emerging from aza-
lea bushes, the act of making left turns with her
body, and cell phone towers located in Connecticut. Her Chinese immigrant parents have come
to visit Linda in Agoura Hills, California, thou-
sands of miles away from the pain-inducing

2.1 Linda sucking on a fentanyl lollipop. *Intervention*, "Linda," Season 7, Episode 1.

cellular infrastructure of New England. This sunny suburban community is the location of Linda's intervention, a carefully staged event that occurs in a nondescript hotel conference room. During the intervention, family members read letters that meticulously chronicle how Linda's behavior has affected them: her history with fentanyl has depleted her parents' savings and retirement fund, and forced her younger brother to become her caretaker. But Linda's intervention does not go well. Running from the hotel and into the parking lot with a burst of profanity, Linda desperately attempts to convince her mother of the intensity of her pain. This, too, fails, and ultimately Linda, through the pleas of her family, agrees to go to a rehabilitation center in San Diego, where two months into her treatment she is diagnosed with a delusional disorder.[1]

While perhaps overly descriptive, the above summary delineates two bodies of knowledge as presented on a 2009 episode of A&E's wildly popular and critically acclaimed documentary reality series *Intervention* (2005–present). The first body of knowledge is clinical: communicating scientific facts about fentanyl (its recommended dosages and possible side effects) and the connective tissue disorder that prompts its consumption. Beyond these direct facts—illustrated in title cards between segments depicting Linda's fentanyl use—this body of knowledge also situates Linda's consumption of fentanyl within medical and psychological discourses of addiction. The second body of knowledge is primarily narrative, depicting a carefully choreographed intervention (and a series of events that leads up to it) that not only indexes interference in

chapter two

the subject's daily routine but is shaped by a constellation of affective relations: emotional pleas, threats to withhold money or social support, and the re-creation of the subject's past while under the influence of the addictive substance. Highlighted in this body of knowledge is the performance of addiction—in this case, how Linda manages her chronic pain through excessive use of narcotics—which is often edited to appear as a spectacle or as entertainment. Ultimately, such a performance is rendered doubly unsuccessful: Linda's family remains unconvinced that she suffers from such amplified pain, and some viewers, such as "mel," see Linda not as an addict but as "a person who just really suck[s] at acting."

Taken together, these bodies of knowledge contribute to the technologies of citizenship that promote self-sufficiency and self-discipline within reality television, which experienced an explosion of global popularity at the turn of the millennium. As numerous critiques of the genre have detailed, the confluence between reality TV and neoliberal forms of citizenship is quite extensive, from the entrepreneurialism and agonism indicative of competitive gamedocs to the cries of consumer-oriented "lifestyle" empowerment present in makeover television.[2] While these forms of citizenship often construct the "good" citizen as a competent consumer with uniquely individual tastes, this chapter focuses on the "bad" citizen who must be stigmatized for the ease with which they excessively consume generic products, as in the case of addicts consuming a drug.

This chapter annotates a model of addictive spectatorship as a useful frame with which to understand the popularity of reality television. First, I consider the representation of addiction on reality television through a subgenre I call *recovery television*, in which the behavior of compulsive or addicted individuals must be diagnosed by experts and corrected through direct confrontation. If, as Anna McCarthy has asserted, reality television is indeed a "theater of neoliberal suffering," then part of this chapter's goal is to give shape to the mise-en-scène of recovery television.[3] Next, I position the TV viewer as addict as a necessary counterpoint to the mechanisms of neoliberal citizenship inherent in reality television. Asking that scholars of television and popular culture take seriously the notion that television can function as a drug, I show how television's drug-like properties have become a critical mechanism of late capitalism's constant pathologizing of cultural affect.

These twinned assertions index the transformation of the sedentary, lethargic couch potato (formerly the iconographic figure of the television spectator par excellence) into the hyperactive, amped-up TV junkie who gets high from multiple media platforms. While notions of the TV viewer as addict have

the addicted spectator

frequently been used to disparage the medium and its viewers, I ask what happens if, instead of using this image to dismiss television (and television studies), we give it more consideration. Reality television is an apt textual metaphor for American culture's relationship to discourses of addiction and recovery in the early twenty-first century. This discourse can be traced first through the therapeutic daytime talk programs of the 1990s and then through the postmillennial subgenres of "makeover" and "recovery" television found on cable networks. Last, I situate my reading of reality television's addictive impulse within the larger scholarly terrain of analyses of media spectatorship. Using Linda's episode of *Intervention,* I demonstrate how reality television produces an addictive impulse while also providing audiences with a motive to disidentify with its subjects—a spectatorial practice of embracing discomfort—in order to disavow one's own addictions.

Bingeing on Reality?

At first glance, reality television may appear to be an unusual genre to which to ascribe addictive impulses. Indeed, most television criticism discusses practices of binge-watching in relation to new technologies of distribution and to serialized, critically acclaimed dramas, not in relation to "low" TV, like reality programming. Writing in the *Los Angeles Times* in 2012, television critic Mary McNamara gave binge-watching TV a dictionary definition, one that, in a moment of honesty, implicates practices of criticism: "Binge television: *n.* any instance in which more than three episodes of an hourlong drama or six episodes of a half-hour comedy are consumed at one sitting. *Syn.:* Marathon television and being a TV critic."[4] Though tongue-in-cheek, McNamara's definition unintentionally underscores the synthesis of addiction and TV spectatorship, offering a layperson's definition to a question with which all addicts wrestle: How much is too much? Tellingly, to binge on television is not simply to watch television aimlessly, surfing idly between channels to pass the time. Rather, the verb requires a consumable substance of a single series (a dosage?) available on a streamlined platform. According to McNamara, these changes to the distribution of programming and to technological dissemination have changed the very character of the medium itself: "Television has become something to be gorged upon, with tales designed to be told over months consumed in a matter of hours. It's television as novel rather than serialized story."

Other chapters in this book specifically address the persistence among critics' claims of "television as novel rather than serialized story." My focus here, however, is on the close association between bingeing as viewing practice and television's narrative form. In some respects, bingeing can be viewed as similar to the rhythms of substance use and abuse: both promise short-term bodily gratification through immediate consumption while deprioritizing concerns over health in the long term. In one feminist psychoanalytic account of bingeing, for example, Marlene Boskind-Lodahl implicitly stitches together the bulimarexic's bingeing on food with the high that comes from the consumption of recreational drugs, writing, "The binge brings about a union between the mind and body. One gives one's self to the food, to the moment, completely. There is a complete loss of control (ego). It is an absolute here-and-now experience, a kind of ecstasy."[5] The transposition from appetite to viewing practices similarly surfaces in Michael Newman's exegesis of bingeing, in which the act "makes one more conscious of the season as a narrative unit . . . as a meaningful narrative category."[6] Part of this, he concludes, has to do with the collectability of televisual content: whether on DVD or available via streaming, postmillennial TV can be *re*-consumed, giving shape to the figure of the TV viewer sequestered in front of a flat-screen TV, laptop computer, or mobile device, catching up on a series over the course of several hours, days, and weekends. Boskind-Lodahl's observation that to binge is to immerse oneself completely in the present can be found in Newman's own assertion that "bingeing intensifies the pleasure of [an engagement with characters] by making characters all the more present in our lives." Bingeing elicits pleasure in the subject, but this pleasure stems from being out of control, from fully succumbing to the gluttony of excess.

But I want to step back and note that the distinction between bingeing on television and what I am calling addictive spectatorship is fundamentally a matter of cultural evaluation. Furthermore, this discursive framing of these practices better illuminates the gendering of both addiction and reality television. First and foremost, it is difficult to imagine what the flipside of bingeing on media would resemble—that is, the "purging" part of the bulimarexic's ritual. Would it be, for example, to turn off the tube, to disconnect from online viewing platforms, and to refuse to consume media altogether? Dissociation from TV seems to run counter to the activity within purging, which requires an aggressive expulsion of the more sinful or impure elements of culture. According to Boskind-Lodahl, purging requires a separation of mind and body, the assertion of control via the subject's ego, a preoccupation with future perfection, and the stubborn fear that past binges will result in undesirable bodily change, none of which translate easily to the consumption of postmillennial television.[7]

Second, such media gluttony is forever enveloped in the discourses of "good" and "bad" consumption and of *quality* and *trash* television. To binge on television is not so structurally dissimilar from the practices of fandom, in which members of a subculture associated with a particular text engage in activities surrounding their shared enjoyment, which often results in obsessive watching and re-watching. The act of binge-watching quality or even cult television is implicitly to valorize them as so-called good objects worthy of consumption. These assumptions about bingeing—as a practice but also as a discourse—were corroborated by the corporation credited with introducing the term into the everyday spectator's lexicon: Netflix. In a study published in December 2013, Netflix already declared binge-watching "the new normal," enlisting the expertise of a cultural anthropologist, Grant McCracken, to explain its popularity.[8] McCracken explicitly situated the phenomenon as a result of the aesthetic and technological changes to television in the post-network era: "I found that binge watching has really taken off due to a perfect storm of better TV, our current economic climate and the digital explosion of the last few years," he writes. Although McCracken does not clarify what he means by "better TV" in the Netflix study, in a May 2013 article for *Wired* magazine, he suggests that audiences are more likely to binge-watch series out of a desire "to craft time and space, and to fashion an immersive near-world with special properties," and the series he lists as immersive are all coded as "quality."[9] This serendipitous increase of both technological innovation (more platforms and interfaces to watch) and the quality of TV series produces a more assertive viewer.

As both McNamara's definition of binge-watching and McCracken's ethnographic research reveal, bingeing is also a curiously self-aware practice, one often worn by spectators as a badge of pride—at least when it comes to quality and cult television. Reality television, by contrast, has traditionally been seen as more difficult to binge-watch, at least in the time period of interest here. Lacking the narrative complexity of serialized prime-time drama, and lacking the possibility for widespread syndication that is typical with many sitcoms, reality television has inherited the medium's own former low cultural status; in the words of critic Kelefa Sanneh, "Reality television is the television of television."[10] Prior to 2016, streaming platforms did not produce original series that could be classified as reality TV, and those platforms preferred to use the category "unscripted" as a synonym of "reality." As technology columnist Rebecca Greenfield noted in the *Atlantic* in 2013: "Reality TV—the scourge of television programming—for example, doesn't play well on Netflix. The service dropped a slew of A&E's 'unscripted fare' like *Pawn Stars* and *Ice*

Road Truckers because when given the choice of what to watch on their own time, its subscribers didn't binge on reality television."[11] Greenfield's observation is based on the long-standing economic principle of commercial television that successful series require a large viewership. Reality TV's particular spectatorship—which, under this logic, is not conducive to binge or repeat viewing—also derives from the fact that many reality television programs have a privileged relationship to the live, particularly given the popularity of competitive gamedocs in which a contestant is normally eliminated at the end of each weekly episode. Binge-watching at a later date risks the possibility that viewers could easily be spoiled by learning the outcome of the competition, making it similar to other live performative events like sports that constitute a critical part of live television's appeal.[12]

Thus there emerged a discursive paradox of cultural taste: postmillennial audiences did not want to binge on reality television and binged instead on quality programming. Here, the distinction between bingeing and addictive viewing becomes crystallized; even though the two practices might share structural features (uninterrupted viewing of multiple episodes of a series, often on multiple platforms), the affective register of each both determines and is determined by their reputation. It is this emphasis on affective difference— on why being addicted to reality television summons conflicted feelings of guilt, shame, and excessive pleasure, for example—that my theory of addictive spectatorship addresses. Bingeing on television and being addicted to television may be two sides of the same coin, but my aim is to recuperate addictive spectatorship as a meaningful way to watch television because of how it helps audiences renegotiate their own affinities to "bad," "dangerous," and "obsessive" substances, including, importantly, television itself.

Obsessed with Mass Culture's Obsessive Power

I find addiction a compelling yet underinterrogated framework for studying television spectatorship because the medium has long been understood as requiring moderation. The metaphor of addiction is nothing new to media criticism: from Harlequin romance novels to soap operas, addiction to certain media forms has always been colloquially and liberally read as a feminized, domesticated phenomenon.[13] Victor Fan, for example, has astutely proposed a "poetics of addiction" that sheds insight onto how Hollywood constructs a feminized spectatorship, finding in the *Twilight* film franchise (US, 2009– 2012) an example of an addictive substance through its negotiation of (a predominantly male) stardom replete with sexuality that is both excessive

63

and destructive. Addiction is thus both an apt descriptor for how Hollywood brands a franchise and also a way to theorize the epistemological economy that undergirds the franchise's representation of heteronormative sexuality. What this presumably feminized audience is addicted to, Fan argues, is not simply sex, but rather "the contradiction or structural incongruity in the way our society defines sexuality."[14] While I share Fan's framing of addiction as a negotiation between the producers, the texts, and the audiences, I want to consider not only how being addicted to a text or set of texts dramatizes the negotiation of the spectator's knowledge of desire but also how this negotiation is itself deemed a threat to the spectator's health. Psychologists and neuroscientists, for example, theorize addiction to television in terms of its potentially detrimental effects on viewers, situating television as a singular object that dangerously acts on a consenting subject. Most famously, Robert Kubey and Mihaly Csikszentmihalyi's 1990 tome *Television and the Quality of Life* frames "heavy viewing" as an affliction that may not fit the formal criteria of an addiction according to authoritative doxa such as the American Psychiatric Association's *Diagnostic and Statistical Manual of Mental Disorders*, but one that nonetheless has perceptual effects.[15] A subsequent *Scientific American* article by the two researchers makes several connections between television and addiction, claiming that "most of the criteria of substance dependence can apply to people who watch a lot of TV."[16]

As Jason Mittell has pointed out, the history of television has always been associated with metaphors of drugs and addiction, which frame television as a "social problem requiring political action."[17] In challenging this deployment of metaphors, Mittell provides a useful history of the antitelevision movement, which was present from the late-1970s through the early-1990s and consisted of the loosely organized advocacy group TV-Free America, parenting groups, psychologists (including Kubey and Csikszentmihalyi), and cultural pundits. Under the auspices of advocacy, TV-Free America and its supporters framed television as a crisis of public health that primarily preyed upon children while mobilizing race- and class-based anxieties.

Such an antitelevision movement is the clear inheritor of the anxieties provoked by the introduction of television into the family home. Lynn Spigel has documented how the threatening aspects of television called into question who was really in "control" of the home while stressing the dangers TV could have on children. An excess of television was seen as a potential threat to the carefully organized temporal and spatial rituals that governed postwar American family life.[18] Becoming "glued to television," in the words of one 1951 *Better Homes and Gardens* article, was the likely effect of this invasive medium, which distracted children from the learning processes of social development and encouraged spontaneous outbursts of aggression and violence. Civic advocacy promoting moderate viewing was therefore aimed at active parents—who would, in turn, control their "passive" consumer children—through social scientific and medical opinion.

Yet while television has historically been situated as an addictive substance, excessive media consumption, by and large, has not always carried the same discursive stigma. As I previously mentioned, fan studies bypasses the active-passive binary that describes the spectator's relationship to mass culture. Fandoms, however, carry with them attachments to gender stereotypes that are inherent in the discursive framing of different media forms. For example, a number of film scholars have drawn attention to the formalist and masculinist postures within a concept such as cinephilia.[19] Similarly, Suzanne Scott has posited the influence of the "fanboy auteur" in contemporary cult TV series, whereby self-identification as a fan is instrumental to managing the relationships between fans and producers.[20]

A theory of addictive spectatorship for TV, then, must insist on new connections between gender, addiction, and spectatorship. I see Linda as an important figure for deciphering what it is about reality television that makes it so profoundly addictive, like the fentanyl lollipops she ingests. Her own reception among *Intervention* fans and online commentaries as someone "who just really suck[s] at acting" emphasizes the performativity not only of addiction but also of reality television, in which real life is edited to appear as sensational as possible, in digestible segments, to maximize pleasure.

Getting High by Thinking Television Narcoanalytically

Addictive spectatorship views the discourse of addiction as a critical metaphor for understanding postmillennial television's embrace of discomfort. If reality television's pedagogical imperative is to encourage individuals to undergo regimens of self-improvement, the discourse of addiction lends critical purchase not just to understanding reality TV's structuring logic but also to understanding the affective spectatorial positions that these regimens foster. The "bad object" of reality television itself must function like a drug.

Jason Mittell, for one, decidedly advocates for denaturalizing the "metaphoric linkage between television and drugs."[21] Drugs, he argues, are inherently bad substances within the American cultural imaginary, and it would be best for television, reality or otherwise, to distance itself from any associations with such substances. Yet in making this argument, he casts the category of

65

drugs, and their signifying connotations, in expressly negative terms: perceiving drugs only as social ills that require the kind of "war on drugs" that Richard Nixon initiated and that the Reagan and first Bush administrations used as an ideological trope for managing poor and non-White populations. Following Mittell, television should "Just Say No," as Nancy Reagan's largely unsuccessful campaign cautioned, to drugs writ large.

Rather than uncritically viewing drugs as toxins meriting a crisis in public health, one might explore the variety of materials, operations, and affects involved in addiction, including addiction to and on reality TV. This is precisely the goal of *narcoanalysis*, which is defined by Dave Boothroyd as "the critical approach to culture from the perspective of its articulation with and by drugs."[22] As a conceptual rubric, narcoanalysis stretches the boundaries of drug well beyond any physical substance (as in Derrida's notion of a "rhetoric of drugs"), demonstrating how the notion of a "drug" itself is porous and elastic, encompassing categories such as the therapeutic and recreational, the legal and illegal, and the public and private.[23] Boothroyd writes, "To theorise about drugs openly and open-endedly, without prejudice and free of the pressure to produce results that either confirm or reject in one form or another the current polarised politics of drugs, involves the attempt 'to be true to drugs' as agents of differentiation. It is to aim at a conceptual and critical thinking of them *otherwise*."[24] While the term narcoanalysis historically has been used to refer to a mode of psychotherapy, I follow Boothroyd and Avital Ronell in their use of the term to signify a theory of and on drugs. Ronell, whose 1992 book *Crack Wars* was one of the first to use the term in this way, argues that "drugs resist conceptual arrest . . . act[ing] as a radically nomadic parasite let loose from the will of language."[25] Language, it seems, cannot adequately capture the affective and embodied energies that drugs enable, and thus it is all too easy to dismiss these energies as insufficient bodies of knowledge—or as insufficient reactions that prevent the body from gaining knowledge—that do not fit into accepted figurations of the public sphere. Similarly, Caetlin Benson-Allott's recent narcoanalytic formulation of a "poetics of inebriation"—a set of formal and narrative devices that presumes an audience high on marijuana and that assists sober viewers to relate to such a condition—situates the stoned spectator as prone to distraction, hyperfocus, and paranoia, qualities that prevent a subject from acting rationally or with proper control of their language.[26]

A narcoanalytic approach to studying reality television, then, resituates the genre's drug-like properties within the terms of neoliberal culture—which defines all phenomena in terms of their potential for either inhibiting or optimizing success—and thus positions the TV addict's plight as a failure of free will. Even taking into account a rising cultural acceptance in recreational drug use, a difference must be maintained between framing television as a drug that audiences can use casually and the compulsive consumption of programming to adverse effects. Yet neoliberalism has successfully recast the terms of such a difference as a question of individual property and economic freedom. Several prominent economists of neoliberal orthodoxy, for example, have previously advocated for the legalization of drugs, viewing drugs not as immoral substances but instead (and perhaps rhetorically) as property subject to consumer choice and the rules of the free market. Writing in a controversial *Newsweek* article in 1972, Milton Friedman lectured readers that with respect to the prohibition of drugs, "even if you regard present policy toward drugs as ethically justified, considerations of expediency make that policy most unwise."[27] Friedman, the leader of the University of Chicago's experiments with neoliberal policy in Latin America, then proceeds to assert that the legalization of drugs would create an incentive for their increased quality while also reducing "street crime" (a problematic denomination that he refuses to define).

Similarly, a number of scholars, most notably Ronell and Sedgwick, have pointed out how addiction itself is located at the extremes of personal freedom and responsibility. Sedgwick posits the ability to choose freely as the object of addiction, though she clarifies that "addiction, under this definition, resides only in the *structure* of a will that is always somehow insufficiently free, a choice whose voluntarity is insufficiently pure."[28] Sedgwick historicizes the emergence of a distinctive addict identity, opening her essay "Epidemics of the Will" by substituting "the homosexual" with "the addict" in Michel Foucault's famous adage from *The History of Sexuality, Volume 1*: "The [opium-eater] had been a temporary aberration; the [addict] was now a species."[29] In her view, the transition from opium-eater to addict had stretched to its very limit at the time of the essay's original publication in 1991, so that one cannot even conceive of individual voluntarity without the impure qualification of addiction. An emphasis on impurity is important here, because it allows the rhythmic, habitual cycles of voluntarity and excess present in casual consumption to be diagnosed as disease, albeit one that can be cured with postindustrial consumer capitalism—including reality television.[30]

Ronell and Sedgwick wrote their narcoanalyses in the early 1990s; since then, neoliberal attitudes toward drug use have only grown, as reflected in the widespread growth in the use of psychiatric medication for managing emotional pain such as depression (and subsequent constructions of a "Prozac nation") and the legalization of marijuana, first medicinally and then recreationally. This highlights the trope of addiction as a disease of the will, a notion of contaminated voluntarity present in early theorizations of the addict identity—the moment, Sedgwick says, when the addict becomes a species—and that became particularly rampant in the late twentieth century, with medical science and psychology prioritizing the identification of root causes of addiction (in addition to diagnosing and treating it). This narcoanalytic detour exposes the importance of approximate language in describing, and thus categorizing and regulating, addiction-as-disease. Just as, for Ronell, drugs enable a reckless detour from the subjective constraints of language, Sedgwick finds that "the locus of addictiveness cannot be the substance itself and can scarcely even be the body itself, but must be some overarching abstraction that governs the narrative relations between them."[31] Following this, America's addiction to reality television demands an interrogation of the governing cues that provoke and shape spectatorial response, a decoding of the narratives on reality TV so that we might better understand our addictive impulse. Television studies should not insist on the elimination of drug metaphors for theorizing television spectatorship. Rather, television studies should attend to the resonances between drug culture and media culture in order to theorize television's critical engagements with desire and affect and, tellingly, with the structural logics that shape each.

Amped-Up Programming: Locating Addiction in Reality TV

While the paradigm of addiction-as-disease and the models of recovery that developed to cure this disease emerged midway through the twentieth century, it was through the popularization of daytime talk programs in the late 1980s and 1990s that discourses of therapy and self-help reached a mass public with narratives of addiction and recovery. Addiction was no longer something that was repressed, and the recovering addict came to share a narrative temporality similar to survivors of sexual abuse and exploited children who came to define that historic moment in terms of popular psychology, feminist identity, and national sentimentality.[32] In this temporality, an individual comes to understand his or her belonging to a class of people who can reconcile past traumatic events through a regimen of therapeutic self-discipline. Daytime TV talk shows—important genealogical antecedents to the documentary reality fare of the 2000s—often framed questions of addiction both as spectacle and as public therapy. While often reveling in the spectacle of drug economies themselves (for instance, Geraldo Rivera famously broadcasted a botched drug bust on a 1986 syndicated special), the programs also included drug users and addicts in various stages of recovery as on-air guests as well as among the hosts themselves (such as Oprah Winfrey, the queen of self-confessional talk, who admitted in 1995 to having used crack cocaine with a former lover).[33] Confessional regimes—acts of disclosure in which personal secrets are revealed—help structure these programs both in terms of narrative (providing a moment of revelation followed by interpersonal discussion about it) and in terms of content (because such secrets are often about societal taboos like aberrant sexual behavior or drug use).

Scholarly work on these programs has demonstrated how television transforms confession in the very gesture of its production, another indication of its influence on recovery television, in which confessionals with addicts, family and friends, and experts move the narrative forward.[34] Like in other "low" genres, confessional regimes are deployed throughout daytime talk shows as a discursive strategy. As Mimi White argues, "Confession and therapy are engaged toward finding one's 'proper place' as an individual and a social subject, even as they are mediated through the apparatus of television. This proper place is overdetermined by family/gender relations and models of consumption."[35] On the one hand, this scholarship demonstrates that such confessional regimes are premised upon an affective charge linked to the discursive magnification of aberrance or criminality. But on the other hand, these programs also allow for the increased visibility of minoritarian subjects, destabilizing any hegemonic notion of the public and private and gesturing toward the possibility of the formation of alternative counterpublics.

While the confessional mode of address characteristic of daytime talk programs facilitates the first step toward recovery, it predates the emergence and explosion of the kind of reality television that works in tandem with neoliberal governmentality to reform compulsive behavior or substance abuse while also providing audiences with an addictive spectacle. Reality television's command over network and cable programming since the turn of the millennium is indisputable. But the generic category of "reality" is, as many scholars have noted, an inherently problematic category. Laurie Ouellette and Susan Murray, in one formative scholarly anthology, define reality TV "as an unabashedly commercial genre united less by aesthetic rules or certainties than by the fusion of popular entertainment with a self-conscious claim to the discourse of the real."[36] Invoking the "discourse of the real," however, summons a tenuously constructed category at best. While reality television frequently comes under attack for how scripted such "discourses of the real" appear to be, it is precisely the way that reality TV plays with the distinction between the scripted and the improvised, the unusual and the ordinary, and the exaggerated and the authentic that is the genre's strength, making it so easy to consume.

The proliferation of reality television brings us to a 2003 *Business Week* article pronouncing "America's Reality-TV Addiction." Written by industry correspondent Michelle Conlin, the article makes repeated reference to reality TV, then in the midst of its ascendancy, as "network crack" and as "crack TV" that affects both producers hooked on a business model of quick and cheap production and consumers oversaturated with endless variations on the same premise.[37] The article's use of "crack" here serves many functions: as a metonym for reality TV's perceived audience of lower-income Americans and People of Color; as an index of the low cultural status of this freebased form of programming that can be mindlessly inhaled; and as symbolic of addiction par excellence. As Ronell notes, "As synecdoche of all drugs, crack illuminates an internal dimension of *polemos*—opening up the apocalyptic horizon of the politics of drugs."[38] Just as crack moved the polemics surrounding drugs toward the racially coded rhetoric of apocalypse, so too did reality television inaugurate similar fears among cultural elites convinced that these series were "weapons of mass distraction."

More Than Just a Makeover: Viewing Recovery Television Ironically

While not young in the history of television, reality television has grown to encompass a number of different subgenres within its elastic boundaries, including, among others, competitive gamedocs, docusoaps, celebrity profiles, legal programs, and makeover programs. I use the term *recovery television* to add another category to this incomplete list: a group of series that focus on subjects with some sort of practiced *behaviors*—rather than, as with makeover programs, physical appearances—that fall outside the norms of acceptability and that must then be tempered through professional expertise. These programs focus on habitual actions or patterns manifested through repetition and an endangerment of the subject's health, from the exorbitant consumption of *Hoarders* (A&E, 2009–2013) and *Hoarding: Buried Alive* (TLC, 2010–2014) to its inverse, the needless improvidence of *Extreme Cheapskates* (TLC, 2012–2014) and *Extreme Couponing* (TLC, 2010–2012). Additionally, the subgenre has concerned itself with habits of eating and not eating, as in the E! documentary series *What's Eating You?* (2011), and misguided sexual energy, as in *Bad Sex* (Logo, 2011–2014). There are also programs that profile people with aberrant and outlandish obsessions, such as an unnatural fixation with a particular object or practice, as in *My Crazy Obsession* (TLC, 2012–2014),

My Strange Addiction (TLC, 2010–2015), and *Collection Intervention* (SyFy, 2012). There are programs that highlight an individual's management of anxiety, as in *Obsessed* (A&E, 2009–2010) and *The OCD Project* (VH1, 2010). And there are programs that explicitly center on an individual's dependency on illegal drugs or otherwise unhealthy substances, such as in *Intervention*, *Addicted* (TLC, 2010), *Relapse* (A&E, 2011), and *Celebrity Rehab with Dr. Drew* (VH1, 2008–2012).

My aim in cataloging these programs is not only to document the emergence of this subgenre in the late 2000s and early 2010s but also to think about the differences between these programs and the large number of reality programs that deal with self-improvement. Many of the aforementioned series, for example, have been categorized as "makeover" programs because of their emphasis on a personal transformation between an abject "before" subject and an expert-educated "after" subject.[39] In her comprehensive study of the subgenre, Brenda Weber describes three "common themes" that unite seemingly disparate series under the header of "makeover television": a narrative of progress through personal transformation; the use of shame to interpellate an imperfect subject into this teleological narrative; and a "big reveal" moment that celebrates the work of experts who located and reconstructed the subject's sense of self.[40] For Weber, the narratological structure of the makeover must correlate to definitive improvement, even if that improvement is incomplete or never actually achieved. "Even when the makeover offers 'where are they now' updates," she writes, "the imagined zone of reality TV does not allow for the messiness of real lives."[41]

Recovery television, however, tests the boundaries of this "imagined zone" in its distinct narratological guarantee: the televised circuits of addiction, recovery, and relapse within these programs indicate a cyclical rather than linear relationship to progress. Just as in makeover television, experts such as trained interventionists or clutter psychologists offer institutional pathways to self-improvement. But a crucial difference exists: rather than emphasizing the necessity to the narrative of a successful transformation, recovery television revels in the spectacle of the inappropriate behavior, offering only vague commitments to change—a desire to declutter, a stint in rehab—as narrative linchpins. The indulgent descriptions of the subject's loss of control are highly gendered as well, feminizing the subjects through staged humiliations set to melodramatic music.[42] The big reveal of recovery television, then, is typically the result of a struggle between the experts and the subject, in which the subject must accept a diagnosis or admit to an obsession. Such a reveal may amount to a reconstruction of the subject's sense of self (following Weber), but one without any necessary material effects; subjects could fail to complete rehabilitation and relapse, for example, or they could return to old habits of hoarding.

The "big reveal" constitutes the first step in recovery discourse: the well-known performative utterance of "Hello, my name is _____, and I am an addict" (or an alcoholic, or a hoarder, or someone with a crazy obsession). This statement grants the addict a politics of visibility and identification, one in which group solidarity can be formed. This identification, however, cannot be divorced from the pathologization of addiction as a disease, through which the addict can pursue or be coerced into "self-help." Such a neoliberal co-opting of identity politics requires that the freedom to identify as an addict be put to the services of the contemporary service economy. Thus, an entire industry has emerged and developed to accommodate addicts: twelve-step programs; residential treatment facilities; sober housing; psychologists, counselors, and therapists; and pharmacotherapies such as methadone.[43]

Prior to the subject's indoctrination into this industry of rehabilitation via the "big reveal" moment of the acceptance of diagnosis, of course, viewers are treated to crafted narratives that illustrate in visceral detail the consequences that these detrimental behaviors have on its subjects. In *Hoarders*, for example, rotten food is graphically displayed to demonstrate the obscured functionality of a house. These sequences are often the most memorable part of such programs, provoking affective reactions of disgust, pity, and occasional laughter from viewers. Yet even beyond eliciting viewer affect, these moments also have immense value in the larger arena of popular culture, including ongoing narrative value and general reinforcement value for neoliberal discourses. One of *Intervention*'s most well-known subjects, Allison, went viral in many digital outlets following her hallucinatory disclosure in 2008 that she was "walking on sunshine" after huffing aerosol spray cans of dust cleaner.[44] Her popularity among both frequent and infrequent viewers partially stemmed from the shocking revelations of her personal trauma; in addition to her addiction, she confessed to being anorexic, a survivor of parental abandonment and child molestation (an incident to which she later testified at trial), and someone who engages in self-mutilation. These events serve as a narrative justification for her addiction; she is an addict who is, as Ronell described Emma Bovary, "apparently a grand self-medicator."[45]

Clips from the episode in which Allison describes the euphoria that comes from huffing Dust-Off have millions of views on YouTube. In addition to posting excerpts from the episode, a number of fans uploaded remix videos that parodied Allison's declaration, often set to the 1983 Katrina & the Waves song

"Walking on Sunshine." In accordance with convergence culture, in which reality television easily lends itself to digital memes and repeatable GIFs, Allison's "fame" within the larger population of reality TV subjects is notable for the ways in which the segment distorts paradigms of visual identification. In figure 2.2, we see Allison under the influence of drugs, and her intoxication can be read via her face, in her splotchy skin and intense, twitching eyes. Her body is not an index for the practices of abstinence and rehabilitation that denote a narrative of individual progress; rather, it is the subjective shorthand for the extraordinary exhibition of her abject state. Taken out of context from the episode's interventionism, the segment invites viewers to laugh at Allison, not to root for her recovery. Framed by a mutated confessional mode of address that is both therapeutic and ironic, Allison represents reality television's unique relationship to addiction: she reveals suburban domesticity gone awry as her body literally ingests the consumer cleaning products marketed by broadcast television. If, for Weber, makeover television resists the "messiness of real lives," recovery television requires the explicit spectacle of such messiness, the visual signifier of the deleterious consequences of compulsive behavior. The complex mix of empathetic identification and parodic disidentification that Allison incites in viewers is the central mechanism for inducing spectatorial pleasure while serving as a distraction from the success or failure of any expert-induced involvement.

As another example both of the genre and its own diagnosis, consider a May 2008 *Good Morning America* profile of Candi Kalp of Easton, Massachusetts, a self-proclaimed reality TV addict who claims to watch an average of twenty reality shows each week.[46] Kalp's insatiable desire for reality TV encompasses not just an excess of programming but an excess of the technology necessary to record and rewatch programs multiple times: the segment highlights Kalp's two DVRs and several television sets, including one in her bathroom. Like many users, Kalp is addicted to reality television because it boosts her confidence. "The reason I watch reality TV is because it makes me feel better about myself," she reveals. "You're looking at all these other people, and they're really a bunch of losers. So, it sort of validates yourself, like, 'Oh, I'm not that bad.'" Kalp describes an atmosphere of reality television spectatorship, bringing the subjects of reality television (Kalp, the audience member) and the subjects on reality television (the "bunch of losers") together in moral relation. Her statement is thus suggestive of what Susan Douglas specifies as "ironic viewing," the reception effect produced when "reality TV shows use idiotic, arrogant, or self-destructive behaviors which we are urged to judge and which are designed to make us feel much better about ourselves:

2.2 Allison under the influence of drugs. *Intervention*, Season 4, Episode 18.

however dumb or selfish we were today, at least we weren't like *that*."[47] This definition of ironic viewing resonates with Ien Ang's 1992 description of ironic viewing as dependent on a thorough knowledge of a program's textual tricks and codes. In Ang's writing about *Dallas* (CBS, 1978–1991), this comes about because "ironizing, i.e., creating a distance between oneself and *Dallas* as 'bad object,' *is* the way in which one likes *Dallas*."[48] Kalp, for example, is allowed to indulge in the spectacle of reality TV's partying twenty-somethings, teen moms, and junkies in need of an intervention only through a wink and a nod to the industrial, aesthetic, and promotional discourses that surround the genre of reality TV. As long as she knows that what she is watching is coded as a bad object, she can disavow her pleasure in such trash by self-identifying as an ironic viewer.

Kalp's segment on *ABC News* aired three months prior to Allison's episode of *Intervention*; whether Kalp watched Allison, or Linda, or any of the other subjects of recovery television, is, of course, impossible to confirm. Had this situation occurred, however, Kalp would no doubt have watched Allison huff one of the eight to ten cans of Dust-Off she inhales daily, and given Kalp's own comments on her viewing pleasure, she would have done so within the parameters of a morally ironic spectatorship. Following Douglas, such a spectatorship would have given Kalp a reassurance as to her own gender or class performance; but this same reassurance obscures the addictive dimensions of such ironic viewing. The identity of an addict, whether self-acknowledged (Allison eventually acknowledges her own addiction over the course of the

chapter two

episode) or acknowledged behind the addict's back by family and friends (in Kalp's case, it is her two friends, the GMA segment explains, who are "somewhere between concerned and appalled" at Kalp's addiction), fits uneasily within claims of ironic viewing, as the addict could be said to latch onto any justification for her viewing compulsion. Thus, we must attend to the narrative of recovery to better understand the seductiveness of ironic viewing as a dismissal of addiction.

Demystifying and Documenting Narratives of Addiction and Recovery

Addicts may suffer from a disease that causes them to forge inappropriate relationships to freedom and the free market, but they can find a redemptive path to recovery through rigid acquiescence to the practice of self-discipline and the mantras of personal responsibility, that is, through the changing of their own subjective narrative. As a concept, addiction structurally resembles the narrative logic of many common reality programs. Robin Room, a sociologist who has written prolifically on drug and alcohol dependency, characterizes addiction as "what is perceived and defined as a mystery: the mystery of the drinker or drug user continuing to use despite what is seen as the harm—such as causalities, damage to health, and failures of work and family roles—resulting from use."[49] Room's ontological framing of addiction as a "mystery" involves the construction of a narrative text in which a reader identifies the hidden factors undergirding the subject's unhealthy lifestyle. Reality series that profile compulsive behavior and the interventions that steer the subjects toward professional expertise and self-improvement use such mystery narratives to justify the subject's participation in the program, with episodes punctuated by references to turbulent upbringings and traumatic experiences.

In this way, reality television incorporates the discursive tropes of addiction. According to psychologist Gene Heyman, the stories shared by addicts regarding their addiction "establish a larger narrative—a natural history of drug use, constructed from the contributions of individual drug users," much like how recovery television has become a way to trace the topography of drug culture under American late capitalism.[50] Similarly, sociologist Craig Reinarman has conceptualized addiction as a disease containing two processes that shape the individual subject's identification as an addict and her trajectory through recovery. First, Reinarman identifies a pedagogical process marked by the acquisition of a specific terminology of disease and recovery from the multitude of licensed actors: social workers and counselors, therapists, judges, lawyers, correctional staff within the prison industrial complex, nonprofit workers and case managers, and, importantly, other addicts. This process prompts addicts to "retrospectively reinterpret their lives and behavior in terms of addiction-as-disease," a paradigm revolving around the aforementioned narratology of mystery. Second, Reinarman describes a performative process in which "addicts tell and retell their newly reconstituted life stories according to the grammatical and syntactical rules of disease discourse that they have come to learn."[51] This is the discursive utility, for example, of the meetings of Alcoholics Anonymous (AA), a semi-anonymous gathering of individuals who ritually confess their narratives to the group as part of a regimen of sobriety. The twofold process described by Reinarman is, to some extent, naturally episodic. At each meeting, subjects recount narratives to influence or support other addicts but also to reinforce their decision to get sober; these testimonials are bookended by specific rituals such as the Serenity Prayer. Moreover, each meeting begins and ends with rituals that guide the confessionals that occur during the middle of the meeting. When televised, this narrative exploits the "anonymous" aspect of the therapeutic aesthetics of the reality genre's public sphere while clearly acting in the service of commoditized entertainment. In the words of A&E executive Rob Sharenow, "Interventions are quite dramatic. They come with a built-in climax, which makes for powerful TV."[52]

The aesthetics of reality television have often been negatively compared to those of cinema verité documentary. As Susan Murray has compellingly noted, the unstable line between "reality television" and "documentary" situates audiences so that they may take into consideration the logics of commercialism and cultural taste, applying each label as they see fit.[53] The dramatic narratives of recovery television invert the formal conventions of documentary by injecting the sensational into the serious and by enabling the option of ironic viewing. Bill Nichols, in his textbook study of documentary cinema, attaches the "discourse of sobriety" to the genre, claiming that "sober" documentaries speak to social and historical realities within rational topics and disciplines. For these "social issue" documentaries, the discourse of sobriety dictates that "style is secondary to content; content is what counts—the real world as it exists or existed."[54] Nichols contrasts the social issue documentary with the "personal portrait documentary," centered around a poetic of subjective discourse, in which form and style take at least equal, if not greater, precedence over content. In personal portrait documentaries—which are most like reality docuseries—the emphasis on subjective narrative repudiates sober aesthetics and must be read instead as a kind of narcoanalytic text, a text that alters the affective atmosphere of the narrative.[55] The bodily sensations that are prompted by both the narrative and the form of recovery television can never be distinguished from their documentarian context, in which the desire to view "real" people and events allows for identification to occur, but only in the abstracted space between the structure of the genre (a rhythm of addiction and recovery) and the personalized subject (the ordinary individual with a specific, contextual narrative of compulsion).[56] Addiction, here, is not merely the narrative subject of recovery television but also its primary affective category, replete with somatic investment.

Hallucinating Authenticity: Affective *Intervention*s

Ironic viewing may provide certain audiences with a justification for excessive consumption, but sometimes that justification is not convincing to friends and family members. The authenticity of the addict is always suspect, because often the addictions are so extreme that they cannot possibly seem real *enough*. Remember how, as "mel" wrote on an *Intervention* bulletin board, when watching Linda "it wasn't even like I was watching an addict; it was more like a person who just really sucked at acting." What is Linda's specific narrative of addiction and recovery, and why was "mel" unpersuaded by her (failed) performance of failed management?

"Linda" was the season premiere of *Intervention*'s seventh season, immediately following its win for Outstanding Reality Series at the 2009 Emmy Awards. Yet *Intervention* operates by disavowing—at least to its on-air subjects—its status as reality television. Each episode follows one or two participants who believe that they are being filmed for a documentary about addiction, and the participants are supposedly unaware that they will be the subjects of an actual intervention by their close family members and friends (although some figure it out immediately prior to the actual intervention). This sleight-of-hand inscribes a certain degree of authenticity into the participant's narrative, since the program proclaims from its opening credits that it is a documentary of sorts (or, more accurately, that it aspires to the cultural status of documentary). The majority of addictions covered on the series are drug- and alcohol-related, though the series also covers addictions to gambling, shopping, video games, sex, plastic surgery, and exercise. Episodes tend to follow a particular form: first, the program introduces the subject and documents the addiction; next, it portrays the addiction's impact on the individual's family and friends; and then there is the actual intervention, in which family and friends read aloud letters to the individual that specifically outline the consequences if treatment is refused (such as divorce or being cut off from one's family and/or children). At the end of each intervention, the individual chooses either to go immediately into rehabilitation or to continue the addiction and accept the specified consequences. Each episode closes with an update on the individual's condition—whether the subject has beaten addiction or not—and the program occasionally checks back in with former subjects in subsequent episodes and paratextual webisodes. Shortly after receiving its Emmy Award, for example, *Intervention* producers claimed that 130 out of 161 interventions conducted since the series premiere in March 2005 ultimately resulted in sobriety (although in 2015, this statistic was revised to 151 sober individuals out of 270 attempted interventions).[57]

"Linda" is organized around Linda's addiction to fentanyl, but it is also narratively broader, as it documents her unusual management of pain and questions whether the pain stemming from Ehlers-Danlos syndrome necessitates such intense use of fentanyl. The episode restages this generic problematic, making the moment of revelation a confrontation between Linda's Chinese immigrant mother, who desperately wants to believe that her daughter is not merely acting, and the rest of her family, who do not believe that Linda is in pain and instead view her EDS as an excuse for her addiction. Linda's family backstory narrates a familiar immigrant tale: her parents leaving China following the Chinese Revolution of 1949, and then opening up a laundromat and managing rental property in order to gain entrance into the American middle class. Linda's mother is depicted as a very frugal woman, and Linda expresses resentment toward her mother at multiple points throughout the episode, claiming that she was denied a "normal" childhood because she had to spend her childhood working in the laundromat: "I did wish I was more like my American friends and their families," Linda says, "it didn't seem as if they had as many expectations." In this way, Linda marks the source of her problems as based on national and racial difference rather than on medical grounds.

The racialized language that Linda uses to construct the narrative that will later serve as the basis for her eventual addiction is of note here. Linda's father explains that "in China, children help parents. It's as a matter of fact. It's nothing unusual about it." His broken English and the required subtitles serve to reinforce the dichotomous value systems of two different nations and ideologies of parenting. The episode thus references a larger archive of cultural texts that frame Chinese parenting as overly disciplinarian in nature.[58] After Linda's parents arrive in Agoura Hills for the intervention, they call Linda to tell her they are nearby, and Linda freaks out, yelling at an off-screen producer that, rather than helping, the presumed documentary about pain management is "risking [her] life" by bringing her parents so close. Within the segment, shots alternate between Linda's parents in their hotel room (with subtitles to translate both language and cultural difference) and Linda, who interrupts her father with bursts of sound indicating pain. This continues until the episode cuts to commercial following a scene filmed with a handheld camera moving frantically around Linda's bedroom as she yells, "Get out!" underneath a nondiegetic cacophony of shrill xylophone tones.

When the episode resumes, Linda confronts her parents at their hotel, explaining to them that they carry radiation and electricity from Connecticut that trigger her joint pain. As her mother sits in front of a blue screen for an interview, Linda forcefully pounds on the door, interrupting the shoot and causing the producers to attempt to calm her down. Throughout this scene, the camera cannot decide on what, exactly, to focus its lens: some shots are of the arranged mise-en-scène of the presumed documentary, with corresponding props within the frame that allude to this metatextual set, and some tracking shots are of Linda's erratic movements outside of the hotel conference room (at least, until she proclaims, "We're done," and places her hand over the camera's lens). Most shots, however, include some kind of obstacle to a clear, uninterrupted view of any of these characters (as in figure 2.3), with walls and angular corners serving to block our access (even while, paradoxically, announcing access). These impediments serve to guarantee the episode's narrative as spontaneous and unexpected and, therefore, authentic. The affective excesses present within the narrative and mediated through aesthetic choices preclude the possibility of rational, direct address, and thus appear symptomatic of the poetic discourse present in personal documentary—or in what Benson-Allott calls a "poetics of intoxication": whether one believes her addiction or not, Linda is certainly not "sober." In this way, the unpredictable camera movements evoke the cinema verité documentary aesthetic that is so important to reality television while also mimicking Linda's own inability to control her body, with the camera's quick motions analogous to her own motions under the influence of fentanyl. This excess—of both the camera and Linda's character—is instructive for the audiences of reality TV. Misha Kavka links such uncontrollable expressions of televised subjects to the affective climate engendered by reality television, in which spectators rely upon affective cues to determine the authenticity of the performance that they are watching: "The reality of the camera-performer relation in reality TV is thus twofold: it inheres on the one hand in the affective syntax of performative gestures, those 'tics and gestures and wrinkles,' at the same time it registers

79

2.3 Linda confronts her parents. *Intervention*, "Linda," Season 7, Episode 1.

the everyday negotiations of *being watched* by an unowned gaze, which structures subjectivity itself."[59] Linda's capacity to disrupt the narrative—and to exceed the racialized and gendered strategies of containment—sticks to the episode's framing of addiction through overlapping (and, at times, competing) dynamics of citizenship, the family, and medicine. These dynamics yield affective excesses, which primarily produce spectatorial disgust in two ways. First, Linda is figured as an addict requiring moral judgment, an object to be viewed ironically. As TV critic Melanie McFarland writes of *Intervention*, "The viewer is not left to contemplate the subject's healing process as deeply as how messed up that person is. We get 25 percent recovery, 75 percent chaos."[60]

Second, disgust is registered through Linda's inability to perform her addiction competently. In Linda's case, the affective signifier *addict* (implying her own exacerbation of her symptoms by her own drug use) becomes an impediment to viewers' taking her embodied pain seriously; it impedes even the extent to which she is read as an addict—and an addict of some knowable substance—by fans of the series. The episode conjures up a spiraling of (bad) performance and addiction: on the one hand, if Linda's pain is faked, it "really" proves her addiction to fentanyl; on the other hand, if her drug addiction is faked, it "really" proves that she is addicted to attention from spectators, including that of her family, doctors, and viewers. Television, in this case, is the cause of her pain (as she tries to evade the cameras that she claims are harming her) but also the obstacle to her believability. The episode informs the audience, via a title card following a montage of still photographs of Linda

chapter two

with various television celebrities from the late 1990s, that Linda experienced her first instance of joint dislocation while working as an extra on set (thus leading to her fentanyl prescriptions). Linda's reputation as a failed actress who appears only on television's periphery is a position overdetermined by her race and gender. Indeed, Linda's televisual identity is doubly "extra," both in terms of her profession and in terms of the affect she displays, and this extra remainder comes to define the habitual rhythms of compulsion and voluntarity present in recovery television.

Tactile Glances, Addictive Gazes

As spectators consume this remaindered narrative, they become dependent upon a rationale of synesthetic affect that functions as the guarantor of the operations of neoliberal governmentality prevalent within reality television. This affect coordinates the processes of distantiation (such as ironic viewing) that allow the ideological imperatives of the text to go unnoticed by the spectator. Addictive spectatorship is, for example, partially explained by Bernadette Wegenstein and Nora Ruck's formulation of the physiognomic "cosmetic gaze," a gaze "through which the act of looking at our bodies and those of others is already informed by the techniques, expectations, and strategies of bodily modification; it is also and perhaps most importantly a moralizing gaze, a way of looking at bodies as awaiting an improvement, physical and spiritual, that is already present in the body's structure."[61] Wegenstein and Ruck utilize the term "gaze" transhistorically, constructing a media archaeology of cosmetic surgery and body modification through a physiognomic reading of the body.[62]

Their formulation of the cosmetic gaze is helpful for framing the larger narrative action of the makeover (a process of making over) in a somewhat analogous way to that of the addict. As a process of making over, the cosmetic gaze reveals the physical, mental, and affective labor necessary to achieve the makeover's goal of self-transformation. Wegenstein and Ruck write, "The beautiful body in makeover culture thus reveals that it is anything but lazy; rather, it is the new site of inscribing a late capitalist culture's ideals of self-realization: besides the 'beautiful' outcomes of the renewed bodies, what we are supposed to see is hard work."[63] The same logic is clearly at work here when transposed to the register of recovery, with experts reminding everyone that getting clean entails hard work. But this kind of labor is not given significant screen time on recovery television, which instead demonstrates the labor the addicted body must enact *to perform its addiction* proficiently:

81

the set of affects required to convince friends and family that such a trans-formation is needed. When one sees an addict on television, the "techniques, expectations, and strategies" of recovery are always already present, along with the end-goal of recovery, or sobriety, acting both as transformative goal (what the addict aspires toward) and as the true nature of the self (what the addict always was, until the addictive substance came along). "What we are supposed to see" in these mediated narratives of addicts is the affective labor required to maintain an addiction and to move toward recovery, which mir-rors our own affective labor required to manage our own consumption of television. This recognition thus renders the subject positions of on-screen addict and off-screen spectator unstable; the addicted spectator's dodging glances (between the screen and another point, perhaps another device) allow the look to be projected onto a screen exemplary of society.

In this schema, the subjects of reality television function as the screen. Kaja Silverman offers one definition of the screen that is recognizable to addicted spectators: the screen is "the site at which the gaze is defined for a particular society, and is consequently responsible both for the way in which the inhabitants of that society experience the gaze's effects, and for much of the seeming particularity of that society's visual regime."[64] Silverman's definition harmonizes with theorizations of reality television that comment on how eas-ily the genre lends itself to moralizing spectatorial positions, as in the case of ironic viewing. Spectators see this in how the subjects of reality television are introduced: in Linda's case, for example, there is the juxtaposition of her background narrative as an extra in Hollywood and her current state of de-pendency on fentanyl. The contrast between past and present locates addiction very clearly as a form of moral disorder indicative of imperiled selfhood, as title cards providing medical facts about the drug also reveal the dirty secrets of Linda's ability to sustain her addiction (that she obtains her prescriptions, for example, by having visited over fifty physicians in the last eight years). No matter their condition, the spectators of these kinds of programs exercise a certain moral superiority necessary to shore up the affective definition of an addict: they may also be recreational drug users or social drinkers, but they are positioned as confident that they do not inhabit the "rock bottom," as do those they view. Subjects are presented on these programs as always already more excessive than the presumed spectator precisely through the program's scripted cues: their stories can only be told through a trajectory from rock bottom to rehab via the intervention.

The structural formula of reality TV intervenes to amplify this screen as well, since the genre devotes a significant amount of camera time to behind-the-scenes, rather than on the product or outcome. Writing in a different context (that of dance studies), Kate Elswit argues that the behind-the-scenes process in reality television enables a set of possibilities for personal engagement beyond the experience of the staged event, such as in her example of a dance performed on a gamedoc like *So You Think You Can Dance* (Fox, 2005–present).[65] This same kind of process occurs in *Intervention*. Linda participates in a staged event, an "intervention" deliberately constructed and scripted by the producers and by the expert, a trained interventionist. The event is staged to the point where a "pre-intervention" occurs, allowing for the interventionist to brief family members and close friends on the precise process of how the intervention will unfold, to recap information from the first part of the episode, and to detail what threats need to be made by the group in order to entice the subject to enter rehab. In this sense, the pre-intervention functions as a sort of dress rehearsal, an opportunity for the family to work out any inner conflicts and to emerge prepared for the intervention as a unified unit dedicated to individual self-discipline. Importantly, this event behaves as a dress rehearsal not only for the addict's support system but also for the audience, who must prepare themselves for the "big reveal."

But Linda's intervention improvises from the script. As Linda rushes out from the hotel conference suite, we see several shots of the behind-the-scenes machinations: a camera operator, the blurred-out face of a producer, and the accidental inclusion of a hotel housekeeper who is almost knocked over during Linda's sprint down the hall. The affective excesses, too, still linger, the stickiness of addiction a testament to its persistence in the act of recovery (and, in Linda's case, to recovery as an embodied performance). The scene is characterized by chaos, with Linda yelling over the voices of family members, experts, and producers who are attempting to begin her journey toward recovery through the performative acknowledgment of her addiction and through her addiction to performance. Space becomes crucial, here, as the affective energies that characterize Linda's breakdown cannot be confined to the nondescript hotel; thus, the narrative action moves to a strip of lawn in the parking lot, where Linda, stretched out on the grass, finally hears her family's pleas for help. Notably, Linda's mother is absent from the final moments of the intervention, as she is sent away by Linda's other family members on the suspicion that she would "believe" her daughter's claims of pain caused by EDS. On the grass, her body wildly contorted, Linda unleashes a flood of excessive gestures, only to acquiesce, finally, to her family's demands to enter rehab. The intervention may have technically been successful, but the sense of Linda's intervention having failed, to some extent, persists, as the spectator

83

2.4–2.6 Linda leaving her intervention, running down the hall, and confronting her family outside. *Intervention*, "Linda," Season 7, Episode 1.

works through evaluating her authenticity prior to deploying ironic judgment or compassionate association. In refusing the script, Linda's is a failed performance, which, paradoxically, makes her seem like *more* of an addict to TV performance itself, if not to drugs.

Linda's intervention is indicative of what Anna McCarthy terms the "affective-civic relationship" in reality television, in which trauma and suffering are instructive public affects that simultaneously secure and expose the limits of neoliberal rationality.[66] Linda's resistance to being incorporated into a coherent narrative of addiction is instructive insofar as it demonstrates the power of that narrative as public feeling. For McCarthy, the onslaught of suffering—the telling and retelling of traumatic pasts, the exhibition of physical pain, the transformation of flesh into various extremes—represent the production of critical knowledges of self-organization that reality television exemplifies. But makeover television's affective influence on the narrative lays bare how these texts perform "an extended meditation on the nature of making-over—encompassing governmentality's imperative to make oneself over and the 'making over' through which traumatic memory returns, *again and again*, to constitute its subject afresh, in the rawness of the past moment, frozen in relation to others and to history."[67]

I locate a model of addictive spectatorship within this form of mediation: as audiences watch and rewatch reality TV, they find themselves constituted as addicts "again and again," fixated on the economies of addiction and recovery but never within a linear history of true recovery. In watching the breakdowns and carefully staged interventions, the addicted spectator receives the spectacular payoff of reality documentary: the moment when the televised subject acts so unpredictably that, paradoxically, she seems scripted. This moment underscores the double narrative at play: the narrative of Linda's breakdown, with its truth being stranger than fiction, and the narrative of the program, with its ideological instruction of self-transformation. The addicted spectator must maintain and manage both narratives simultaneously, and in so doing, I believe, the viewer herself becomes an addict who must find out Linda's fate, and the fate of the subject of the next episode, and the next, and so on. Each episode of *Intervention*, after all, lasts forty-three minutes, and each is so formulaic (structured through the introduction of the subject, the pre-intervention, and finally the intervention), yet also so capricious (accentuated with affective irruptions that undergird moral abjection), that it is not until the final ninety seconds that the addicted viewer receives the kind of narrative resolution or spectatorial fix she has been craving all along. Did the subject successfully make it through rehab or not? Did the subject relapse?

Have they been sober since the intervention? These questions are secondary to the dramatic highs of recovery television, for as soon as they are answered, another episode begins, with another addict on whom to fixate.

Coming Down, Again and Again: Recovery Television's Mise-en-Abyme

I have demonstrated how a commitment to understanding addictive spectatorship and to a critical narcoanalysis of reality television requires stretching the surface of television to reveal its drug-like potential. By way of attempting some closure to my theorization of addictive spectatorship—however impossible that may ultimately be—I offer a satirical web video of *Intervention* that debuted on the popular website Funny or Die in August of 2009, a few months before "Linda" aired.[68] Directed by Amy Heckerling, the segment opens with a direct invocation of *Intervention*'s title text, the familiar disclaimer that "this program contains subject matter and language that may be disturbing to some viewers." Viewers then see Fred Armisen in a car and in his house, his face grotesquely exaggerated in the act of spectatorial fixation as he watches the screens that are always nearby. (Between this and the example of *Portlandia* discussed in the previous chapter, one cannot help but wonder how Fred Armisen actually watches television off-screen.) "Fred," the segment explains, is addicted "to *Intervention*," and as the segment progresses, viewers see Fred arguing, pleading, and empathizing with the real addicts from the series through his television set and laptop. To the consternation of his then-fiancé, actress Elisabeth Moss, Fred watches *Intervention* in bed, and the voice of Allison "walking on sunshine" emerges from the laptop computer underneath the sheets. Moss then reveals what is most disturbing to her about Fred's addiction: "He doesn't just watch, he gets all involved with the people. It's like they're more 'real' to him than people he knows."

What should we make of this "real" comedian and his "real" fiancé participating in a parody of *Intervention*—one that uses "real" footage from the series as well as its fonts, music, and aesthetic design? And what to make of Moss's statement that Fred is incapable of "just" watching, that recovery television requires an investment in its subjects in order to authenticate their "real" nature? As parody, the Funny or Die clip accurately—perhaps too accurately—mimics the narrative logic of the recovery genre, condensing the action of a full-length episode into less than five minutes. And while the segment is constructed around the kind of inside jokes that require a knowledge of *Intervention* (Fred expressing disappointment that his favorite interventionist,

Candy Finnegan, isn't leading his own intervention, for instance) the message of the clip is clear: lest viewers think that they operate at a safe and perhaps even a critical distance from recovery television, the programming is simply too obsessive. Disengaging fully from the repeated narratives of addicts, the skit proclaims, requires an intervention of one's own.

The Funny or Die video, appropriately titled in repetitious fashion *Intervention Intervention*, illuminates the necessity of theorizing addictive spectatorship, of taking seriously the proposition and possibility of television as drug. If makeover television is, as some scholars have pointed out, late capitalism's version of a fairy tale—in which the self becomes improved only with the help of a benevolent private sector—then the abstract space between fable and real is precisely the space in which *Intervention Intervention* intervenes.[69] Indeed, this space resonates as the justification, as Sedgwick explains, for "[taking] seriously the self-help proposition that, understood logically, the circumference of addiction attribution is nowhere to be drawn."[70] But for me as a scholar of reality television and as someone who desperately wants to make sense of its affective excess, such an annular video hit nightmarishly close to home, prompting a reassessment of my own viewing practices. Do I binge? Do I consume addictively? Do I justify watching television in its various temporal and technological forms as the labor necessary to unpack the medium? Does the collapse between addict and spectator obscure my own epistemological desires, my own obsession with reading a text again and again?

Curiously, as the development of this book progressed (at times quite slowly), I began to notice how much television I consumed, often in order to procrastinate from writing. I was always able to defend such voracious consumption as research, but now I am not so sure such an apologia sticks. Academics, at some fundamental level, resemble the addicted subjects of recovery television: their personal libraries of unread books and their stacks of paper accumulate to *Hoarders*-like levels; they become intoxicated with the frustrations and satisfactions that come from solving some sort of conceptual problem. "We imagine that the drug addict-writer," Derrida notes, "seeks to discover a sort of gracious and graceful inspiration, a passivity that welcomes what repression or suppression would otherwise inhibit." Thus the specular rhetoric of drugs could be supplementarily extended to the compulsions of theory and research.[71] In this way, too, Linda's story is not just Fred's, or Allison's, or Candi Kalp's, but also our own as scholars and cultural critics; our viewing is a way to skim the televisual surface and to enter the narratives of recovery, again and again.

It is not that recovery television traps us within a ceaseless circumscription of suffering and self-improvement, of empathetic identification and ironic disidentification. Nor is it that the addicted spectator stands as a failed citizen, with her lack of control a reminder of the evils of mass culture. Rather, the figures of recovery television invite us to own our addictions and to come to terms with them through the narratives on-screen, so that we can better understand our own relationships to television itself. Addiction may signal the crisis of free will caused by the overexposure to economic and consumer freedom, the free market taken to a habitual extreme. But this nonpareil structuration of our relationship to freedom, the way it conditions us to absorb, devour, and exhaust cultural texts, is contrasted against an amplified pleasure that comes from fully interrogating the elastic potential of those very texts, instructively intimating to addict, viewer, and scholar alike how freedom, like other conceptual and representational substances, should be taken in moderation and enjoyed responsibly. The moments when that intimation fails, however, serve to punctuate addiction's excess, which remains unable to be underestimated, no matter how often one attempts to disavow its ideological and affective power, again and again.

chapter two

three

the aborted

spectator

affective

economies

of perversion

in televisual

remix

THE CHANGES TO postmillennial television are perhaps easiest to grasp through the normalization of fan cultures enabled by the speed and connectivity of digital culture. This narrative is incredibly familiar: technological changes that increase the availability and accessibility of programs have disrupted long-established spectatorial rhythms and identifications, with viewers forming new modes of engagement and hermeneutic practices. The well-mythologized ritual of Saturday morning cartoons—children sitting down in front of a living room TV with bowls of cereal packed with extra sugar—is perhaps one such casualty. The toyetic series of the 1980s were largely targeted to different genders of children, creating endless marketing opportunities through the tropistic figures of what Heather Hendershot has described as muscled superheroes, mechanized transformers, and nurturing caretakers.[1] The synergy between toy companies and television production is most clearly reflected in a number of franchises developed in partnership with Hasbro: *G.I. Joe: A Real American Hero*, *The Transformers*, *My Little Pony*, and *Jem and the Holograms*. In the case of *Jem and the Holograms* (1985–1988), for example, young girls could be equally as transfixed by the adventures of Jem, the colorful glam rock alter ego of music producer Jerrica Benton, as by the many ways Jem's identity could be accessed: through the cartoon itself, the collectible doll series, or the accompanying playsets (such as the Rockin' Roadster or the Star Stage).

Jem's ideological message of independent girls achieving success in the music industry through the largely male-dominated genre of rock and roll resonated deeply with these young audiences, provided that their families had the means to empower these viewers with the Hasbro line of *Jem* toys.

Then, more than two decades later, a video appears on YouTube sporting a familiar face, but paired with a deepened, throaty voice, erratic pacing, and a contemporary pop soundtrack. A wholesome Saturday morning this is not: here, in this uploaded remix video, Jem is renamed Jiz, a profane, drug-addicted, sexually ambiguous drag queen who, instead of running an orphanage like her predecessor, houses an abortion clinic for her animated young fans. In more than twenty graphic remixes ranging from short public service announcements to ten-minute-long self-contained episodes, the animated adventures of Jem and the Holograms (her bandmates Kimber, Aja, and Shana) are replaced by Jiz and the Mammograms, accompanied by irreverent story lines about sexual violence, cunnilingus, abortion, and "shitty panties." The episodes carry titles such as "A Very Special Drug Episode" and "Kimber Is a Dirty Lezzie," playfully nodding to stock forms of episodic children's animated television while functioning as an assault on nostalgia in all its sentimentalized registers.

Created by a video artist from Los Angeles who assumes the pseudonym Sienna D'Enema, *Jiz* (2009–2016) represents a radical departure from its 1980s antecedent *Jem*, both in terms of its technological mode of address and in terms of its content. These departures, however, gesture toward oppositional affective structures. The remix form of *Jiz* situates the series as a fan-produced transformative artwork disseminated online, a cultural object that has benefited from (and that in turn benefits) older circuits of production and consumption. In this way, transformation functions positively for the television industry and its neoliberal logics, reinforcing codes of cultural value premised upon expanded spectatorial agency and new networks of fan communities that simultaneously consume and produce for TV. Yet in another way, the crude content of *Jiz* renders this transformation alienating, with the ideological messages of a popular children's animated series (popular, at least, among those of a certain generation) corrupted, its capacity for empowerment defiled by Jiz's toilet humor, a juvenile comedic style popular among prime-time animated satirical sitcoms.

It is impossible to think about postmillennial television, post-network and convergent, without acknowledging the impact of digital culture as manifested in fan communities that frequently take "old" media texts and remix them as "new" transformative works. Yet the ambivalence with which this

chapter three

transformation operates within *Jiz* and in other remixed television series raises questions about the structural logics of televisual remix, which itself straddles positions of "television" and "digital media," as well as of "old" and "new." The movement between these forms—and indeed, the apparent impossibility of making categorical cleavages within remix culture—resonates on an affective dimension: to remix an old text into something new is to risk mutation on the levels of audience, representation, and modes of address in unexpected ways; a remixed text may be delivered to viewers not only on a different technological platform but on a different affective platform as well, potentially offending, alienating, and disgusting them. This chapter argues that there is something *queer* about televisual remix, and also that this queerness operates on multiple planes. Not only does it describe the transformation of an identity (the ambiguous drag queen replacing the female rocker, for example), but it also describes the act of transformation itself; to queer a text, following some minor *Oxford English Dictionary* definitions of the word, is "to put out of order; to spoil" or "to disconcert, perturb, unsettle."[2] Both *queer* and *remix* therefore share a certain theoretical resonance: each of these terms attempts to scramble existing categories of sexuality and narrative in order to subvert, pervert, and revolt against normative codes. Each of these terms is also anthimeric, sliding between noun and verb forms and between objects and actions. This chapter uncovers the side effects that occur as a result of the processes of *remixing* and *queering* as they play out in convergent television, an expanded configuration of the medium that includes short-form web series as well as paratextual media such as fan reaction videos, video recaps, and remixes. *Jiz* affords its audiences a look into the affective landscape of remix culture through its insistent replication of an aesthetics of vulgarity and taboo subject matter. Importantly, I claim that the technological changes to television spectatorship that have occurred in the convergent era overdetermine this affective landscape, with television series from the past stretching beyond their cancellation dates into a future punctuated by participatory culture.

Specifically, I track how nostalgia is transformed and reshaped through this new experience of televisual remix, theorizing an affective economy of perversion and its subsequent impact on the idealized confidence present in participatory culture's ability to eliminate the barriers between media consumers and producers. Drawing primarily from *Jiz,* I examine televisual remix from the perspective of abortion, both because it is explicitly referenced in *Jiz's* vulgarization of its source text and because it is a reference that undermines a sentimental attitude toward both childhood and reproductive processes, including the reproductive processes of media forms themselves. As the boundaries of "television" become more diffuse, encompassing streaming and user-generated video platforms such as YouTube, the ways in which remixed web series cannibalize, appropriate, and ultimately abort their source material allow for a disorienting reconceptualization of the normally optimistic stance toward participatory culture. The temporal structure of abortion, in which something is given life only to be subsequently evacuated, unhinges the debate surrounding participatory culture's claims to cultural literacy since, as Barbara Johnson has reflected, debates surrounding abortion "should refuse to settle into a single voice."[3] The gravelly, queer voices of *Jiz* dictate strange and uncomfortable ways of (re)animating and aborting the familiar scenes of Saturday morning to the multiple screens of convergent television, risking the wistful innocence of one's childhood in the name of participatory culture.

Convergent Sensibilities, Consumer Choices

Understandings of televisual remix occur in part through the rhetorics of viewer agency and consumer choice ubiquitous within convergent television. One aspect of the spectatorial conditions that distinguish *Jem* from *Jiz*—that separate 1985 and 2009—is that the idealized audience is no longer a family sitting together in front of a television but instead an isolated individual navigating a matrix of programming offerings on multiple screens and platforms. These changes to the medium have shifted the boundaries of the family room from a singular space anchored around the family unit (the living room) to multiple rooms, each with their own personal screen, airing an increasing number of channels that utilize narrowcasting strategies and algorithmic formulas to attract and maintain viewership. "Watching television" is no longer something necessarily done in a domestic space, or even in a public space that facilitates group viewing (as in a doctor's office, a bar, or an airport terminal), but occurs instead in dispersed environments that move in and out of each other and that are mediated by industrial structures of individuation. Lisa Parks notes that "industry leaders have identified the age of post-broadcasting as the era of 'personal television,'" observing how the strategies deployed by networks, cable companies, and other providers "produce the effect of enhanced viewer choice in the form of a stream of programming carefully tailored to the viewer's preferences, tastes, and desires."[4] While this kind of direct marketing may yield a more narrow definition of content, this content is flexible across multiple devices (which, not coincidentally, share data with one another in order to create a robust profile of a user's viewing habits). Here, the direct migration of a text from one apparatus to another does not correlate to a shift in cultural value, as in the next chapter's discussion of intermedial television, because the text is claimed not as being that of another medium (as in so-called novelistic television) but simply as being that of another means of transmission.

These migrations have been famously dubbed by Henry Jenkins as "convergence culture," collisions between "old" and "new" media both in terms of production and consumption.[5] Convergence culture, according to Jenkins, has transformed television's viewing communities: active audiences have more control over what content comes onto their various devices and can follow aspects of a media text as it traverses different forms, industries, and platforms. As a text migrates from one platform to another, the configuration of the audience similarly changes. Jenkins gives the example of a family watching a broadcast of the popular reality series *American Idol* (Fox, 2002–2016; ABC, 2018–present) together as a cohesive viewing unit, but individually voting for a contestant on a smartphone or tablet or interacting with other individuals in a social media fan community. Importantly, for this chapter's purposes, then, the key shift with the arrival of convergent television is not with respect to its interactivity, but instead with respect to the discursive consolidation around a single user or fan; fans may communicate with each other frequently through digital platforms, but this does not necessarily translate into shared viewing experiences. The existence of a fan culture cements participation—as opposed to interactivity—as the governing concept behind the consumption of corporate media, with the tension between how the industry and its consumers variously define participation serving as the force behind many of television's technological changes.[6] The general difference between interactivity and participation, as I see it, is one of structure and stress: interactivity is a planned choice of technological or media system in which the design of the system (a video game, a website, or a gamedoc such as *Idol*) demands an interaction on the part of a viewer/user, whereas participation is directly incited by the user. While Jenkins is clear that participatory culture, rather than spectatorial culture, is a defining characteristic of fandom, it is important to note that part of fandom entails the transformation of "personal reaction into social interaction," which I would emphasize approximates a structure of feeling: individual affective reactions to a text are considered part of a participatory culture only if they are mobilized through the communicative pathways of a fan network or community.[7] Individual fans may therefore view a media text individually, but this viewing carries with it a participatory rem(a)inder to engage with the text in a social setting, even if such a setting is entirely digitally mediated.

Most famously, such engagements entail the production of transformative works for distribution among members of a fan community. According to the nonprofit Organization for Transformative Works (OTW), which advocates on behalf of fans and fandoms, a transformative work "takes something extant and turns it into something with a new purpose, sensibility, or mode of expression," and comprises categories including "fanfiction, real person fiction, fan vids, and fan art."[8] This is a similar definition to that offered by the Supreme Court in the 1994 copyright law case *Campbell v. Acuff-Rose Music, Inc.*, in which the transformative work was construed as one that "adds something new, with a further purpose or different character, altering the first [work] with new expression, meaning, or message."[9] While a transformative work's "purpose" and "message" could, in theory, be determined by a court of law, some of the other terms within both the OTW's definition and juridical literature are subject to broad interpretation, especially *sensibility* and *expression*, two terms that evoke a text's affective characteristics, often through nonspecific and embodied language. In early texts on fan cultures, *sensibility* described the relationship between cultural forms and their audiences, highlighting the residual effects of context alongside those of text; sensibility thus inscribes certain cultural codes that shape viewer experiences with texts. In Camille Bacon-Smith's work on *Star Trek* fan communities, to name one example, she locates a feminine or "women's sensibility" in the reconstructed characters of fan fiction that realign the heroism of the all-male science fiction series' protagonists into an array of cultural values important to female fans, while at the same time often dooming such transformative works to dismissal by cultural gatekeepers.[10] The multiple and coexisting sensibilities unique to a specific text and its reception in a specific place and time, then, produce a set of relations between the audience and the cultural world; sensibility crystallizes *how* audience members digest texts in order to make sense of the world around them.

In this capacity, Lawrence Grossberg has distinguished between a "consumerist sensibility," structured around individual pleasure, and a "fan sensibility," structured around socially constructed affect. Grossberg's constructivist attempt to wield affect many years before its twenty-first-century revival (he was writing in 1992, during the inaugural moment of "fan studies") is a sharp reminder that for many scholars of popular culture, affect has always been a category of prime importance to cultural analysis, read within the labor of the audience and along lines of difference. Importantly, Grossberg maintains a distinction between affect and emotion, prefiguring later ontological work in the field. He views affect as difficult to define precisely because it is "what we often describe as the feeling of life."[11] Yet such distinctions and viewpoints should not be read as being in total agreement with a vitalist or virtualized affect. Grossberg identifies two aspects of affect, the first of which quantitatively describes an amount of energy or volition invested into an event, and the second of which reroutes that energy through pathways of inflection prior to meaning or signification. This second aspect, qualitative in nature, emphasizes "the way in which the specific event is made to matter to us."[12] As a habitual sensibility that establishes the conditions under which we make meaning from affects, this second imperfective facilitates the organization of investment, the set of mechanisms Grossberg calls "mattering maps." The affective is, for Grossberg, but one dimension that can determine the ideological, as it is the terrain of inflected investment through which difference is structured: affect's "power to invest difference" functions as a sort of filter over the spectatorial process, gesturing toward the already hybrid and multiple schematic atmospheres that structure televisual affect.

The affective sensibilities of fan culture establish the conditions for spectatorial identification around the binary opposition of fans and nonfans, or "Us" and "Them": fans "get it," nonfans do not. Transformative works require these sensibilities because of the importance of context in the creative process of transformation; remixes of a series by people who have no prior affective relationship to the source text tend to be taken less seriously (and receive less circulation) than remixes reflecting the affective sensibility shared by fans of the source text, for example. This is especially true of works that transform original texts with already complex diegetic universes, such as the science fiction and fantasy series that comprise a substantial number of TV fan cultures. The sedimentation of convergence culture around the figure of the fan who both affectively invests in a series and participates in communities yielding transformative works in the current and expansive age of digital television owes a debt, to be sure, to the work of cultural studies. As Grossberg states, "For cultural studies[,] context is everything and everything is contextual."[13] The attempt to understand the affective economies of perversion that undergird a remix series like *Jiz* authorizes the consideration of the affective sensibilities of both *Jem* and *Jiz*, which in turn involves investigating the texts themselves, the political and cultural contexts of the mid-1980s as well as those of the late 2000s, and the industrial and technological structures that allow each text to attract fans. In essence, it entails affectively mapping the intertextual engagements of a text in its moments of production and reception. Yet perhaps this age of convergence demands a remixing of context itself, one in the same vein as what Rita Felski, herself remixing Bruno Latour, expansively

95

outlines as the nonhuman assemblage that "includes not only individual novels or films, but also characters, plot devices, cinematography, literary styles, and other formal devices that travel beyond the boundaries of their home texts to attract allies, generate attachments, trigger translations, and inspire copies, spin-offs, and clones."[14] Thinking about the affective sensibility of *Jiz*, then, as akin to intertextual processes of association must begin with delineating the formal qualities of televisual remix as a unique subculture of the participatory impulse endemic in convergent television.

Remix Culture and the Value of Cultural Literacy

My interest in sketching out the affective dimensions of televisual remix stems from the figuration of participatory culture as creatively liberated from traditional circuits of production and consumption. Those who participate in these digital art practices—remixers, DJs, vidders, hackers, slash writers, meme authors, and the like—are now frequently valorized by both cultural critics and scholars as the driving force behind pop culture trends in today's buzzworthy mediaverse, creating new forms of digital reading and writing that comprise a convergent cultural literacy. (Notably, this figuration stands in clear opposition to the stereotyped Trekkies that William Shatner told to "get a life" in an infamous 1986 *Saturday Night Live* sketch.) Remix speaks with a teleological force, however coded or implicit; scholars of digital cultural studies are fond of observing, for example, that remix is *not* a strictly "new" phenomenon, precisely because most culture always already appropriates the texts and rituals from the past and transforms them into objects of the present (though such a position can often end up perpetuating unequal power relations). In the introduction to a 2009 special issue on fan/remix video in the online journal *Transformative Works and Culture*, for example, Julie Levin Russo and Francesca Coppa mischievously note that "the buzzword has gathered such momentum in cultural discourse that it begins to seem retrospectively that everything is a remix . . . remix as a trope converges with our idea of creative production itself."[15]

Eduardo Navas, a foundational scholar on this topic, makes a distinction between remix culture, a movement anchored around the free exchange of ideas and the products resulting from their association, and Remix, a discursive cultural variable espousing principles of rip, sample, cut, copy, and paste (among others). Whereas Remix is a practice, a largely parasitical way of reading and writing texts that is, in theory, without form (although form assumes a certain wiliness throughout Navas's theory of Remix), remix culture

chapter three

is the institutionalization of said praxis often overdetermined by questions of legality.[16] Remix thus appears in dimensions not traditionally bracketed into remix culture, ranging from RSS feeds (in which different stories are curated based on a time stamp), to smartphone operating systems that allow for simultaneous activities (such as screening streaming video while text messaging), to special effects that use CGI to insert an actor into a scene of a film or television program. While any discussion of television as medium is absent from Navas's extensive writings on remix—an omission, I suspect, based on its perceived low cultural status—television seems a natural fit for theorizing both remix culture and Remix. Remixes such as *Jiz* correspond to the organizational systems of remix culture as they involve sampling, cutting, and pasting ripped broadcast material owned by the media industries. Examples of this, such as the practice of vidding (a specific type of remixing in which cut footage from television series or films are remixed and set to music), often elude charges of copyright infringement and fall under the legal definition of a transformative work because of their creative reconstruction of fair-use material.[17]

More broadly, television as a medium shares several formal characteristics with Remix and remix culture, making televisual remix a particularly evocative media object. All remixes depend on the practice of sampling, even and especially on the level of structure: common online activities require copying and deleting information (in the shape of data packets) from one point or another, making the identification and handling of fragments important to Remix. This is not dissimilar from television's own formal organization, of course, often thought of through Raymond Williams's notion of flow as well as through Jane Feuer's notion of "segmentation without closure."[18] Further, television routinely remixes its own content for narrative and paratextual purposes and pleasures: both regressively (e.g., through flashbacks to earlier episodes within a diegetic narrative) and regeneratively (e.g., through the automatic updates to the chyrons common to most news and sports programming). Whereas historians of remix make a convincing case that remix culture was developed and refined by American DJs in the 1960s and 1970s, it would appear that to some extent television has always exhibited some key characteristics of remix in the concept and design of its narrative form, though for most of television history the viewer could not exert any control over the order and length of the presented segments.

As every new cultural text remixes the past through some sort of digital remediation, it also habituates new users into the semiotics of digital culture. In his 2009 indictment of current copyright law, *Remix: Making Art and Commerce Thrive in the Hybrid Economy,* Lawrence Lessig claims that

97

remix culture assists in the creation and promotion of cultural literacy as it introduces younger generations (millennials and now Gen Z) to the logics of reading and writing, cut and paste, and collage that are ubiquitous to digital culture.[19] Lessig argues that current copyright restrictions automatically criminalize a whole generation of youth who have been raised "in a world in which technology begs all of us to create and spread creative work differently from how it was created and spread before," and that a solution to such criminal activity—copyright reform—is needed in order to ensure that free culture is prioritized as a liberal democratic value.[20] In framing remixing as a variation both on citation practices and on creative expression, and thus as a more expansive and elastic form of "writing," Lessig and other proponents of Remix perpetuate an equivalence between remix culture and cultural literacy in the digital age, all too readily subsuming institutions of literacy within the social good. "We should encourage the spread of literacy here," Lessig writes, "at least so long as it doesn't stifle other forms of creativity."[21]

These accents of "cultural literacy" (in Lessig) and "creative," "efficient," and "meta" (in Navas) are not neutral terms. For one, Lessig has been critiqued for establishing a logic in which practices of copying and pirating become circumscribed within racialized dichotomies of empire.[22] Therefore, while the recoding of criminality remains considerably uninterrogated among proponents of copyright reform, remix culture, like most work within fan studies, participatory culture, and convergence culture, tends to be lauded as enabling democratic norms and institutions and thus insulated from colonialist critique; one could reach quite easily to the work of Edward Said to explain literacy as a democratic technology that constructs citizens as consumers.[23] My point in underscoring this nonneutral contour of remix is neither to discount the immense labor that remixers give their creations nor to slight the discourse of fan studies that has brought these transformative works to the attention of the often-stuffy academy. Rather, I want to pressure the logic of accumulation that accompanies remix rhetorics in which "transformation" indicates the addition of an affect that inscribes the remixed object into discourses of creativity, efficiency, and metagenre. Even in work done on nondigital remix, such as that of cinematic "found footage," terms such as "recycled images" invigorate the footage with the rhetorical weight of ecologically friendly practices evocative of a "green" economy distinct from the corporate conglomerates that populate Hollywood. These discourses surrounding Remix (as a practice) construct the transformative work as *in excess of* its source material. For those who argue that remix is a recognizable form of writing unique to participatory culture that must be legally protected in order to preserve cultural literacy, remix "adds something" to its previous iterations. I contend that this excessive remainder is overdetermined by its cultural value, necessitating an affective reading of the incremental yet significant changes between the original and the remixed.

The Tactics of Queer Remix

While Lessig's documentation of generational media literacy focuses on the need for copyright reform, Lev Manovich's assertion that "it is a truism today that we live in a 'remix culture,'" and McKenzie Wark's observation that the "cut and mix practice is now the daily life of a generation," both highlight remix as already ingrained in the mediated rhythms of society.[24] In particular, they invoke Michel de Certeau's foundational work on the routine ways of being in the world. As fragmented parts reassembled and rewritten, remix carries the potential to disrupt the temporal flows of routinization established by corporate, state, and educational institutions that structure work and leisure time (while also still easily assimilating into those institutions). De Certeau provides a rich framework with which to reconsider remix, opening *The Practice of Everyday Life* by declaring his project's goal to be the pursuit of "the ways in which users—commonly assumed to be passive and guided by established rules—operate."[25] For de Certeau, *users* (as opposed to consumers, subjects, or even persons) are epistemologically foregrounded as actors, and his introduction to his study on these operations sounds familiar to remix practitioners: "The purpose of this work is to make explicit the systems of operational combination (*les combinatoires d'opérations*) which also compose a 'culture,' and to bring to light the models of action characteristic of users whose status as the dominated element of society (a status that does not mean that they are either active or docile) is concealed by the euphemistic term 'consumers.' Everyday life invents itself by *poaching* in countless ways on the property of others."[26] Of note here are two things. First, de Certeau highlights the user as an active agent. Second, his use of the word *poach* resonates strongly with fan vernacular (as in Jenkins's 1992 book, *Textual Poachers*, which itself heavily remixes *The Practice of Everyday Life*). In everyday life, users do not blindly consume the entertainment offerings of those in power (such as corporate Hollywood) but instead appropriate them to their own ends in a constant cycle of reinvention. Remix builds on this activity of poaching through its use of the actual "property of others" as the capital from which new works of art are invented, making a direct substitution of "remix culture" for "everyday life" in de Certeau's aforementioned passage not so farfetched.

99

Paul Booth has written how remixing, and especially remixing that changes the genre of a text, is a "practical application of the de Certeauan notion of tactical reading, where alternate readings become externalized."[27] Although his comparison stops there without further explanation, the association is helpful, for it reorients the framework of media culture toward a circuit of media interactivity, a more dynamic and unstable variation of the model of production/consumption historically present within cultural studies. For de Certeau, tactics are the tools of those without power, as they represent an adaptation to the surrounding environment, often for the sake of survival; he distinguishes them from strategies, which presume levels of control and order. Tactics require constant adaptation to unfolding circumstances, thus instantiating them as an important component of practice. Televisual remix can be powerful in pointing out how broadcast television routinely tells stories from the perspectives of those in power, envisioning a world in which those from minoritarian subject positions subvert existing televisual narrative conventions.

In the *Queer Carrie Project* (2009–2010), Eliza Kreisinger creates a queer-positive re-narration of HBO's *Sex and the City* (SATC, 1998–2004), critiquing the presumed heteronormativity of postfeminism (although, in Kreisinger's words, the "issue of white, owning-class women remains").[28] Seamlessly keeping sound and visuals intact, *Queer Carrie* uses existing characters from SATC to perform the series' general premise—how the modern professional woman can find love in Manhattan—differently. The final installment, for example, describes a failed queer romance between Carrie and Natasha, a character who, in the original text, is Carrie's romantic competitor.[29] In contrast to the original series, *Queer Carrie* reverses the gendered and sexualized norms that all too often govern televisual representation: Natasha and Carrie meet awkwardly in a boutique dressing room as queer exes, and flashbacks are used to depict a tumultuous and sexually charged relationship between the two women using footage from episodes in which Carrie is having sex with Big during the affair, is meeting with Natasha post-breakup, and gets dumped by fifth- and sixth-season romantic interest Berger. Bringing a refreshing reading of the industrial practices that often bring such remixes to the digital table, Aymar Jean Christian has documented how similar variations of SATC (such as Carmen Elena Mitchell's web series *The Real Girl's Guide to Everything Else* [2010]) advance more radical perspectives on identity and representation and pitch them "not only to a community of like-minded fans but also to the industry of Hollywood, (potential) advertisers, and the media as a product created by a group of marginalized workers leveraging convergence culture for their purposes."[30] Televisual remix thus can produce a disidentificatory politics of representation that plays with both stereotype (explosively dramatic lesbian relationships) and TV form and genre (serial melodrama) while metatextually commenting on relationships between the media industries and fan communities. *Queer Carrie* intervenes through its formal commitment to its original source material, since Kreisinger merely reedits SATC to create her queer reinterpretation of metropolitan love without voice-over dubbing or adding additional sound or visual effects. Such tactics reveal the queer readings present in SATC, emphasizing the importance of subtext: the comedic elements of the original postfeminist series are entirely absent in Kreisinger's remix, with a darker, more dramatic tone used to illuminate the bad blood between the ex-lovers. Queering the iconic character of Carrie Bradshaw serves not only to remix her sexual desire but also to strip her of her joy, illuminating the impossibility of queer love within the comfortable confines of postfeminist consumption.

Jiz, too, flips the sexual script of *Jem and the Holograms*, queering nearly all the children's animated series' characters (and demonstrating the slippages between queer as a noun and queer as a verb). Most notably, *Jiz* queers keyboardist Kimber, who clashes with Jiz and the other members of the Mammograms in several episodes about her sexual identity that satirically skewer lesbian music culture while also making rote jokes about lesbian sexual practices. But it also flips the narrative of homonormative queerness, critiquing structures of queer community that are in turn invested in liberal democratic values and identity politics. In one episode, Jiz has a special message for queer youth who are being bullied about their sexual identities by their peers. Jiz's special message, as inferred by the episode title, "It Gets Worse," reverses that of the It Gets Better Project, launched by advice columnist and gay activist Dan Savage and his husband and featuring testimonials from ordinary individuals as well as celebrities who offer uplifting words of advice for victims of bullying.[31] In a medium-shot frame focusing on Jiz's head and neck and using looped footage with a dissonant voice-over, the beginning of the PSA finds Jiz passing her wisdom on to the next generation before breaking out into a sexually explicit rendition of Whitney Houston's "The Greatest Love of All":

> [JIZ]: You're gonna grow up and get a job, and it's gonna suck. And you're gonna get a relationship, and it's gonna suck. And you're gonna get old and fat and wrinkled, and it's gonna suck. But you know what doesn't suck? Gay sex. Gay sex is fucking awesome. I mean, you're gonna grow old, and life's gonna be pitiful and stupid, but at least you can look back

the aborted spectator

and remember the gay orgy that you had, there are still gonna be those memories to beat off to. So I mean, if you're gonna kill yourself, do it because life is fucking retarded. Not because you're a fucking queer.[32]

In many ways, Jiz's message to the victims of bullying comments on the temporal universality fostered by processes of socialization and aging; despite having a horizontal relationship to time, here both straight and queer youth must endure the suffering of entering the workforce, formalizing romance, and accepting bodily decay. But "gay sex" is valued not for its radical ability to thwart the repressive heteropatriarchy, or even for its ability to stage a publicity that leads to "the production of nonheteronormative bodily contexts," in the words of Lauren Berlant and Michael Warner.[33] Rather, gay sex becomes a masturbatory memory of pleasures past, an approximation of the larger, more liberating projects of queer world-making envisioned by Berlant and Warner (it is, indeed, "fucking awesome") that can be used to combat the dreary minutiae of adulthood.

Moreover, the episode of *Jem and the Holograms* from which "It Gets Worse" sources its visuals is a curious choice for Jiz's critique of the discourse of liberal rights. The *Jem* episode "Adventures in China" shows the Holograms as they perform a concert in China, with the narrative action revolving around the pair of magical star earrings that Jerrica uses to transform into Jem.[34] When the earrings are stolen by the rival girl group the Misfits, Jerrica enlists the help of a young Chinese girl, Lin, in order to retrieve them. Here, the global fan is used as the narrative device to resolve the episodic crisis, with the rescue involving a certain degree of Orientalism when Lin must defend herself using martial arts against a boy trying to steal her earrings (among many other examples). The song at the end, "Love Unites Us," sees the band wearing East Asian–inspired fashions (and matching flowers in their blown-out manes), with one shot consisting of the floating heads of Jem and Lin transparent against a background of neon stars.

"It Gets Worse" almost wholly evades the racialization of sexuality, despite remixing an episode that features many ethnically Chinese animated extras. The remix form—recycling of the visuals from "Adventures in China"—produces the unintentional alignment of the racial Other with the bullied queer and the overexuberant fan, with all three identities linked to the memory of past sexual excesses that serve as an emotional crutch for the victims of global capitalism, many of whom must "grow up and get a job" while still in adolescence. Jiz remixes the language of bullying in her PSA while erasing the (presumed queer) youth of color from the neoliberal discourses of

3.1 Jem and Lin during the song "Love Unites Us." *Jem and the Holograms*, "Adventures in China," Season 1, Episode 10 (also used in *Jiz*, "It Gets Worse").

coming out and upward mobility present in the It Gets Better Project: in the shot in figure 3.1, Jiz asks, "Whoa, wait, hold up . . . Why is my head like this? And what's that Asian girl doing there; I don't get this part." Here, remix traffics in the recycling of images, but the shifting affects and identities "It Gets Worse" produces leave, in effect, unsalvageable heads floating on the screen, an ethnically illegible message to the (presumed White) bullied queer youth. If televisual remix can demonstrate the mastery of technical editing, as *Queer Carrie* does, or the mastery of ideological critique, as in "It Gets Worse," it exercises a dexterity that is as potentially irresponsible as it is tactical. Remixing feminist television to queer ends, it would seem, risks an engagement with a slippery and tricky darkness (and, occasionally, literal darkness) to manipulate both heterosexual and queer suffering.

The Circulation of Perversion, the Perversion of Circulation

In contrast to the logic of accumulation championed by nascent remix theory, I propose an *affective economy of perversion* as a useful lens through which to view queer remix. I sample the term "affective economics" partly from Henry

Jenkins, who introduces it in *Convergence Culture* as the system produced by digital culture that can "understand the emotional underpinnings of consumer decision-making as a driving force behind viewing and purchasing decisions."[35] Whereas the affective dynamics of fan communities have been of interest to both cultural studies scholars and feminist vidders going back to the 1970s, affective economics transposes the desires, dislikes, and frustrations placed onto a text into a system that facilitates purchasing decisions and consumer citizenship. As television increasingly rewards loyal viewers or fans (the distinction often an act of self-identification), affective economics rewards the affective investment that these loyals/fans have in a series often by acknowledging the presence of fan communities through narrative and aesthetic choices: these include Easter eggs (messages or jokes embedded within a media text), nods to online shipping cultures (when fans project romantic attachments onto characters in a text), and corporate-authored platforms for interactive discussion. The emotional investment loyals/fans have in a series can be harnessed to extreme ends, as such investment is an unlimited resource as opposed to a viewer's annual income or technological sophistication.[36]

In a different register, however, I also sample from Sara Ahmed's work on "affective economies." Working from a psychoanalytic viewpoint—important for Ahmed, as it allows her to theorize subjectivity as outside the present—she posits an account of emotion *as* economy.[37] Indeed, she highlights the sociality of emotions "as a form of capital: affect does not reside positively in the sign or the commodity, but is produced as an effect of its circulation." She thus invests in the metaphor of circulation as an index of the perceived affective value of a sign. Importantly, the circulation of affect is *not* spatially limited to a movement to and from the subject; rather, it moves across a number of "nodal points," perhaps in reference to actor-network theory. In Ahmed's example of language drawn from white supremacist websites, the circulation of a publicly shared emotion works to substantiate the embodiment of racialized individuals within the nation-state as it mobilizes social, material, and psychic affective economies of hate.

But if, as I argued earlier, figurations of remix culture are effused with positive valences of accumulation, is it possible to theorize an affective economy independent from these cultural values? I would answer yes: for Ahmed, accumulation functions as a given over time rather than as a singularly psychic drive; thus, the more objects and signs engage with and across one another, the more affective they become. Yet the accumulation of affect present in all affective economies is separate from the desire to accumulate affect to maximize its value (even if it may have that effect later on). In fact, the discursive

chapter three

fashioning of remix in Western digital culture may rely upon a categorical drive to accumulate affect as a marker of cultural value that subsequently disavows its position within the capitalist market economy. As Rachel O'Dwyer convincingly argues: "Like much of the ideology of free culture, however, the emancipatory potential of remix is arguably contested and, at best, overstated. Following on a series of transformations to the relations of production, the technical composition of labor and the property regimes under which labor produces, we can no longer think of remix as operating in fundamental opposition to the market or indeed as fundamentally anti-capitalist."[38] As a practice, remix is first and foremost a process that adds messages, often to extreme degrees. Take, for instance, the way in which digital sampling culture in electronic music regularly combines a large number of songs in order to create new mashups, such as in musician Girl Talk's (Gregg Gillis) 2006 album *Night Ripper*, which sampled 164 songs across sixteen tracks, or DJ Earworm's (Jordan Roseman) annual "United States of Pop" mashup, which combines the top twenty-five songs of the year as determined by Billboard's Hot 100 singles chart. If the addition of messages resulting in a "new purpose, sensibility, or mode of expression" is a key criterion for determining the scope of a transformative work, then remixes, by definition, require the accumulation of *both* messages and affects.

Affective economies, to parrot Ahmed, suggest "that emotions do not positively inhabit *anybody* or *anything*."[39] The logic of accumulation present within remix culture is centered on messages that migrate between networked communication technologies and affects that, according to Ahmed, are themselves produced from the entangled migration between users, objects, and commodities. It is thus possible to formulate an affective economy that complicates the pure accumulation of commodifiable affect, one that risks destroying as many messages and affects as it produces throughout the course of its transformation. Even if the migration of affect implies a degree of accumulation in meaning (and in affect itself), this accumulation does not have to be situated as positive or as "adding" anything to the text. This chapter's own appropriations fixate on the rhetorical valence of queer as a force of both corruption and degradation. That is to say, when we talk about *queering* art objects—such as turning Carrie into Queer Carrie, or Jem into Jiz—we cannot escape the connotations of perversion that are enabled in such performative gestures. Like the body that archives emotional responses and that processes its surrounding material conditions as part of reading sensations within its affective pathways, to queer something shifts its paradigm of sexual identity while also imbuing that something with the historical force of abuse and insult. A (queer) theory of (queer) Remix, then, requires attending to which affects are lost, vulgarized, and elided through derivative transformation.[40] An affective economy of perversion emphasizes how, in a sense, such loss, vulgarity, and elision are naturally concomitant with transformation. Video remixes are rife with perversity, for example, in the forbidden sexual tension between characters unearthed by shippers, or in Francesca Coppa's assertion that vidders are fetishists who "*cut*, slicing visual texts into pieces before putting them together again, fetishizing not only body parts and visual tropes, but the frame, the filmic moment, that they pull out of otherwise coherent wholes."[41] Indeed, there is something queer about this figure of the geeky vidder who meticulously, though not always precisely, sees a different narrative underneath the conventional one, a private narrative that correlates to the open-secret structure central to Eve Sedgwick's axiomatic claims about same-sex desire. "In dealing with an open-secret structure," Sedgwick writes, "it's only by being shameless about risking the obvious that we happen into the vicinity of the transformative."[42] We might ask if the same logic applies to transformative works, like those that set up derivative jokes that all-too-often write themselves, or the incessant repetition of a meme that itself plays off a play on words.

But if remix culture is derivatively queer, its queerness operates through the suspension of the temporal structures that govern its open secret. This is especially true in televisual remix, in which "old" television series are given "new" texture through voice-overs and editing, often with satirical intent. Applying interventions into queer temporality demonstrates how the nostalgia for a television series connected to one's own past can function as a queer affect that can be temporally extended into the present—or into a future projection of the present. The collection of work on queer temporality, while heterogeneous, is replete with emblems of resistance to teleological experiences of time. In her remixing of Judith Butler's theory of gender performativity—mashed up with Pierre Bourdieu's notion of the habitus—Elizabeth Freeman notes how "delay and surprise" lay bare the conditions for gendered performance; her location of "temporal drag" allows for a robust sense of performance that encompasses reception as well as address, and "might capture the gestural, sensory call-and-response by which gender is built or dismantled within a given space or across time."[43] Temporal drag also appears to describe, fittingly, an affective change to our engagement with television under convergence culture in which television can be dismantled from the apparatus itself, rebuilt across multiple platforms and devices, and retransformed by new communities of disparate individuals under conditions of delay, binge, surprise, and spoiler.

chapter three

Televisual remix is uniquely perverse in how it stretches the temporal surface of programs and drags segments along to new dialogue and music. Because of such temporal play, remixing thus feels as if it is a call-and-response, an engagement between vidder and spectator. This is a counterfeit (and thus queer) feeling, since the vast majority of televisual remixes limit interactivity to commenting on YouTube or to the direct creation of other transformative works (such as reaction videos). For the spectator attempting to follow along with such dissonant perspectives of sound and image, then, the simulated feeling of a call-and-response becomes an aurally voyeuristic exercise in the logics of improvisation that govern Remix. In *Got 2B Real* (2011–2015), created by Patti LaHelle, throaty banter dubs over visual footage from interview segments from entertainment, news, and daytime talk programs (such as *Entertainment Tonight* and *The View*) with prominent Black divas of contemporary popular music.[44] The "diva variety show," as the remix series' opening credits proclaim, is meticulously edited, replacing the talking points of Patti LaBelle, Aretha Franklin, Dionne Warwick, Mariah Carey, Whitney Houston (often a disembodied voice on an answering machine), Janet Jackson, Chaka Khan, Beyoncé, Rihanna, and others with throwing shade: recurring barbs include Franklin's choice of wigs, Warwick's rampant chain-smoking, and the interchangeability of Jackson and her siblings.

Got 2B Real is exemplary of a Black digital expressive culture in which sass and shade serve as performative acts existing "in an ambiguous liminal space between the gestural and the spoken as well as the written word," as Brandy Monk-Payton (sampling E. Patrick Johnson) has keenly noted.[45] Yet the remix series also works within such liminal spaces, attaching new dialogue to the rigid gestural parameters of each diva's moving mouth, right down to embodied actions such as guttural laughter and clapping. Both larger narrative arcs as well as specific dialogue follow this structure of call-and-response; the two-part episode, made up of "Crispy Business" and "Long Time, No Seat," for example, debates Mary J. Blige's participation in an allegedly racist Burger King commercial in which she extolled the virtues of fried chicken, with every panelist "responding" to the controversy through barbed comments that speculate on what they would have done differently. Yet the commitment to televisual form—the pure segmentation of comedic affect—distorts any linear reading of sketch remix. Aymar Christian, for example, recommends that the uninitiated viewer start with *Got 2B Real*'s final episode, an insistence on an episodic temporality on a structural platform that naturally encourages a distorted seriality, since YouTube organizes a channel's video files into playlists by upload date set as a default to reverse chronological order.[46]

Call-and-response is thus structured by both technological interactivity and the affect incited by our perception of historic cultural objects as they emerge in the present day, or in other words, by the nostalgic weight these objects conjure as they enter the digital age. Yet the centrality of nostalgia to televisual remix culture should not be interpreted as it has been by scholars of the postmodern, such as in Fredric Jameson's account in which nostalgia represents a blockage to historicity resonant with cultural amnesia. Curiously, these renditions of nostalgia as ubiquitously referential in a simulated world, or as images of pastiche spread across society in order to invoke a collective past, function as affective economies (ironic, to be sure, as Jameson connects the "insensible colonization" of the postmodern by nostalgia with the waning of affect).[47] What is striking about nostalgia in televisual remix is how the programs important to one's childhood past become animated in the present, albeit becoming perverted in the process. A consideration of this, however, involves returning to *Jem* and the living rooms of the 1980s, to a time before remix culture and the use of the internet in everyday life: a time before *Jiz*.

Consuming the Contradictory Feminine

Jem premiered in October 1985, targeting an audience comprising the younger members of Generation X. Several fans and critics of the series have noted how the series lends itself to feminist readings, given how, in its narrative world, women run the music business and thus are powerful within the media industries. Although she inherits Starlight Music from her deceased father, lead character Jerrica is a music producer, and as Lizzie Ehrenhalt has observed, "The Holograms are not treated as an oddity because they are women, and the episodes focusing on African American drummer Shana and Chinese American guitarist Aja promote a more complex vision of sisterhood than, say, *Strawberry Shortcake*" (who starred in six television specials in the early and mid-1980s).[48] And yet, such a reading becomes invariably complicated by the range of female roles presented in the series. All girls may be rock stars, *Jem* preaches, but the possibility for musical prowess is highly contoured by the type of band young girls wish to emulate: either the Holograms or their rivals, the Misfits and the Stingers. "Jem really has a social conscience," Hasbro marketing executive Stephen A. Schwartz said in a 1986 *Los Angeles Times* interview. "Her world is not about shopping and dating. She is a working girl, a woman of the '80s. She's an executive. She makes decisions. She has lots of pressure."[49] In contrast to this executive humanitarianism are the Holograms' antagonists throughout the series. the Misfits. Whereas the Holograms sing about romance, friendship, and other normatively appropriate themes for young girls in songs such as "People Who Care," "We Can Make a Difference," and "I Believe in Happy Endings," the Misfits rebel against conventional norms of femininity, displaying a rather masculinist lyrical posture in songs such as "Winning Is Everything," "Takin' It All," and "Gimme Gimme Gimme."[50] Viewers are thus faced with a binary opposition between the Holograms, who run an orphanage on the side, and the Misfits, who once kidnapped a young girl and locked her in a trunk. With such a limited number of options for female roles and such a narrow vision of appropriate feminine behavior came a clear directive. Series creator Christy Marx broke down the framing of the Holograms in commentary on a *Jem* DVD release, granting, "This show was essentially about being good role models for the girls."

Although *Jem* made good on Marx's prescription, steadfastly incorporating messages about multiethnic friendship, cooperation, and generosity into its plots, it is imperative to recall that the series is toyetic, produced in part for the purpose of marketing tie-in merchandise. Hasbro created *Jem* with the explicit intent of rivaling Mattel's Barbie line of dolls, broadcasting the series four months before the first wave of merchandise was released at the New York Toy Fair in February 1986.[51] These toyetic motives lend themselves to the model of affective economies of perversion that I outlined earlier. As an example, consider a commercial for Jem dolls that aired during broadcasts of Hasbro-sponsored cartoons.[52] Advertising the inclusion of an audiocassette with each doll purchase, the commercial adopts the form of popular compilation album commercials of the time, with the names of popular Holograms songs ("Jealousy," "Universal Appeal," and "Who Is He Kissing?") scrolling up the screen while excerpts from those songs play in the background. The commercial alternates between black-and-white stock footage of crazed *Jem* fans in a stadium arena, neon close-ups of the dolls and their accessorized instruments, and human interaction with the toys: a young girl's hand places a cassette vertically into a player, and the words "FREE WITH PURCHASE" pop right back up, explicitly stressing the commercial appeal of "rock 'n' roll." Girls decked out in headbands and denim rush to grab packaged dolls off the shelf, as a female voice-over tells audiences, "You get a free *Jem* poster, too!" Following this, the happy girls proudly hold up their audiocassettes in their bedrooms (with the free *Jem* poster prominently displayed on their walls), cheerily exclaiming, "I got mine!"

The phrase "I got mine!" eerily echoes the consumerist mantra of 1980s proto-neoliberalism, in which hard-working individual entrepreneurs claimed

109

3.2 Commercial for *Jem* doll advertising a free audiocassette.

their well-deserved consumer goods. Middle- and upper-class girls growing up in the 1980s had far fewer opportunities to use entertainment technology on a daily basis than they do in the twenty-first century; the audiocassette—along with television, of course—thus represented a prime opportunity for girls to demonstrate control over domestic technology. The *Jem* dolls commercial frames the ownership of the cassette as essential for musical celebrity, and the girls in the segment practice good citizenship via smart consumer purchasing (buying a toy with a free gift included) in an overidentification with the image. These girls may not yet be successful glam rock stars like Jem, or even successful music executives like Jerrica, but through eager and diligent consumption, they can, in the future, lay claim to the entertainment industry. That the commercial is not just a commercial but one intimately tethered to other toyetic programs is also of critical importance; the convergence of cartoon, commercial, and music video forms within the *Jem* universe all belie the industrial effort to train girls as prodigious consumers—though the Children's Television Act of 1990 would end the practice of directly advertising tie-ins of toy lines and food products for a program. Lynne Joyrich's excellent analysis of 1980s television through the lens of gender and consumer culture rings especially true here: "In both their consumer appeal and their address to an audience of youths, a viewer who is not yet considered a man, music videos are in many ways exemplary... [demonstrating] the gender contradictions that may arise in a medium that is considered 'feminine' by many critics but is itself committed to appealing to the public at large."[53] While Joyrich is referring to the presumed male spectator of the music video as it aired on networks such as MTV in the 1980s, we might flip the script of her remark to expose the totality of gendered consumption as it occurs within *Jem*. Here, gender contradictions emerge not through a gendered audience (though *Jem*'s audience certainly did not entirely consist of girls), but rather through the contradictions the commercial engenders in defining appropriate feminine behavior: Jem and her friends may have a social conscience and preach sororal cooperation, but her fans must gleefully embrace private property in order to access *Jem*'s model of empowered success.

Whereas the "I got mine!" commercial reveals the perversion of feminist aspirations for girls through its contradictory address and possibilities for identification—in which the only tenable position for the young girl is that of consumer—it is not the only example I wish to discuss; for Jiz, too, has merchandise that she wants you to buy. "The *Jiz* Commercial" opens with the profane humor one can come to expect from *Jiz* ("and now a motherfucking word from our motherfucking sponsors") as Jiz invites the "ugly girl from the '80s" to shop at the Jiz Emporium.[54] The commercial mashes up a number of *Jem* merchandise commercials, replacing the glamour of the music industry with scenes of sexual violence through its alteration of sound and image. First, Jiz tells a girl in front of a marquee, "This is where you're going to have an abortion"; then "I'm going to rape you . . . and I have friends to help!" is voiced over footage of the plastic faces and neon hair of various Holograms and Misfits dolls. Furthermore, Jiz's cassette does not grant access to the sphere of feminine consumption but instead is tethered to the most morbid 1980s cultural signifier: the AIDS epidemic. The footage of the girls rushing to grab dolls off store shelves has been remixed to Jiz's voice promising, "The first thirty victims who come get an AIDS test where I read you the results," as we see Jiz's verdicts (presumably also free with purchase) emerge out of the pink cassette player:

> [VOICE-OVER]: Hey Hannah, it's Jiz . . . so I have something to tell you: you got it. I'm sorry. No easy way to say it. You are as positive as the nubby clit side of a battery. You have more AIDS than an '80s gay bathhouse. So . . . sucks for you.

> [VOICE-OVER]: Hey Lindsey, it's Jiz . . . looks like you're negative, but don't let that make you think that you're not a slut, because you know what, even whores can get lucky, all right, because we all know it's only a matter a time . . . it's only a matter of time, Lindsey. You disgust me.

In the Jiz Emporium, the girls proudly display their cassettes, which now serve as their test results: "I got mine!" is remixed to "I got AIDS!," shifting the

3.3 The audiocassette from the "80's Jem Toy Commercial + Cassette Offer" becomes remixed as a positive HIV test result in "The *Jiz* Commercial."

3.4 A negative HIV test result. *Jiz*, "The *Jiz* Commercial."

subject position of empowered consumer to diseased pariah. If, as Monica Swindle argues, "girl power is often a slogan and a marketing technique, girl an image sold to girls and women as coming from the consumption of products and other intangible commodities in new global affective economies," then what sort of image is being "sold" through this discursively immunocompromised remix?[55] What affective economies are present within this transposition of AIDS? Nostalgia functions powerfully in the Jiz Emporium, insofar as the ideological attitudes espoused by test counselor Jiz mirror the condensed temporalities and reorganization of subjectivity of People With AIDS (PWAS) during the height of the epidemic, a temporal overlap with the syndicated broadcast of *Jem*. Prior to the development of antiretroviral medications, AIDS was represented in the popular press and other media as a death sentence with little recourse; a diagnosis in 1985 would have, in fact, engendered feelings of helplessness and pity, whereas a negative test result would have been framed as having dodged the bullet—a delay in what might have been perceived as the inevitable threat of seroconversion. And although children were used in media representations of AIDS to signify innocence and the utter capriciousness of the disease throughout the 1980s and early 1990s (as Paula Treichler argues, in a strategy to "normalize their 'otherness'" and to shift attention away from gay men), girls were very rarely the victims of AIDS.[56] Apparently, the Misfits are not the baddest girls in town; in the Jiz Emporium, the body of the girl extends beyond the boundaries of legitimate consumption and into the dangerous territory of reckless abuse and misogyny, as girls are presented with a third option for identification: that of happy victim or of masochist.

Remix is crucial to the reorganization of consumer and victim identification in this affective economy of perversion. Both *Jiz* and the original commercial footage (which was also made available as part of the extras for *Jem*'s DVD release) are "consumed" on YouTube, often to sentimentalized effect. As Richard Grusin has noted, YouTube "serves as an archive of affective moments or formations, much as television has done for decades," and among the comments on one page containing the original "I got mine!" commercial are those from predominantly female commenters who proudly say they still have their cassettes or who long for their old dolls.[57] While the commercial, to some extent, suffers from the decay common to recorded video footage that has been digitized and compressed for uploading to YouTube, viewers still access their pasts through the merchandise they consumed in their youths. The commodity circulates as object, text, and nostalgic affect, although it is still anchored in its original material form. In contrast, the YouTube comments on "The *Jiz* Commercial" make little reference to material objects but rather repeat some of the more graphic (and choice) lines from the parody, effacing the nostalgic weight of the commercial (though some users also express a desire for Jiz to read out loud their future HIV test results). The textual repetition of the voice-over in the comments reaffirms the circuits of transformation to consumer culture; what ultimately is to be consumed, "The *Jiz* Commercial" suggests, is more *Jiz*, a masterful demonstration of the intertextuality present in televisual remix.

113

"Don't Give It a Name / Flush It Down the Drain": Remix's Reproductive Politics

Abortion functions as a notable trope in the *Jiz*-verse. As a character, Jiz is "pro-choice . . . really pro-choice," according to the caption to "The Abortion Episode" that I analyze here, and many remixed episodes are spent documenting her attempts to coax abortions out of all young girls who appear in the diegetic narrative.[58] Yet I propose that on-demand abortion is not only a controversially definitive trope within the remix series—even more so than the imagined seroconversion of *Jem* fans—but also, in a sense, a structural condition of televisual remix itself.

As a family-friendly medium for much of its history, television has always figured the family in its direct address, yoking together, as Joyrich has keenly pointed out, the reproductive capacities of television as a medium premised on weekly repetition and the reproductive capacities of the family that give television its audience.[59] As a number of feminist television scholars (and scholars of feminism more broadly) have pointed out, the 1980s saw television begin to incorporate more explicit and experimental topics taken up by the socially conservative campaigns in the name of "family values," specifically those surrounding reproductive rights and debates centered on the moment when life begins.[60] Abortion on prime-time narrative television, however, remained relatively taboo throughout the 1980s, even as the aftermath from *Roe* calcified within the American cultural imaginary. Following Maude Findlay's decision to undergo the procedure in 1972 in the eponymous sitcom *Maude*, only a few series tackled the issue, and the majority of these representations examined the political debate itself rather than having a female character making the decision to abort her pregnancy voluntarily.[61] These debates continue to be unresolved, yet abortion is now a more common practice, although it often remains equally sensationalized. When a teenage character from the family drama *Friday Night Lights* (NBC, 2006–2012) decided to have an abortion, for example, one television critic noted how surprised he was by how the episode was "devoid of political posturing or grandstanding. It didn't insult its viewers. It was classic 'show-not-tell' at its best."[62] The realism hinted at in his review may be read as part of a larger strategy by NBCUniversal to frame the episode as amorphously apolitical and appealing to a homogenous audience in which the boundaries between pro-life and pro-choice are not recognized as demographically pertinent, despite the character's ultimate decision to abort her pregnancy.

But Jiz does not belong to prime time, and she is most certainly not beholden to network censorship or corporate control. "The Abortion Episode" of *Jiz* is one of the remix series' most watched, attracting over 700,000 views on YouTube. In the episode, Deirdre, one of the girls from Starlight House (in *Jem,* the orphanage run by the Holograms), faces a familiar dilemma and opts to keep her baby rather than have the expected abortion induced by Jiz. Abortion (or a "self-induced miscarriage," as Jiz prefers) is figured in unequivocally positive terms. For instance, a conversation between Jiz and her boyfriend, Rio, at the beginning of the episode reveals that Jiz refuses to have babies of her own because she loves abortions too much; this conversation exists in opposition to one that acknowledges the diegetic world of *Jem,* in which the orphanage function of Starlight House serves as an outlet for the maternal. "Only live things go in my pussy, and only dead things come out," Jiz reminds Rio, establishing her own body as the space of a promiscuous sexual politics in addition to the very zone in which life and death can be established. Jiz projects the site of reproduction—and thus of her own reproductive politics—not as her womb but as her "pussy," an exceptionally insistent sexualization of abortion. Indeed, perhaps unwittingly, Jiz stumbles upon the fraught relationship between the act of sexual copulation (and its attendant affective labors, from negotiating sexual autonomy to the overcompensation for material power differences to the literal manufacture of gesture during the act itself) and the (failed) act of childbirth (as well as its attendant affective labors, from the performance of the celebration of an always racialized femininity to the regimented coordination of preparing both to give birth and to socialize a newborn). It is not only that Jiz employs the binary of penetration and expulsion as the framing device for life or death, but that she sequences it as well, first the (orgasm inducing, one assumes) act of life, then the (violent, one also assumes) eviction of that life that methodically contaminates the categories of recreative and procreative sex.[63] The mechanization that Jiz thus uses to describe "self-induced miscarriages" (in a rather "businesslike" manner, perhaps as a nod to Jem's "executive" sensibilities) presents the structure of remixed abortion as necessarily and simultaneously pleasurable, violent, intentional, and vulgar.

Abortion represents one of the most meaningfully commanding "choices" in the lives of women, yet the fact that reproductive politics has borrowed consistently, although tenuously, from the language of neoliberalism should also come as no surprise. The way in which reproductive debates within the news media and within political discourses have been cast as an issue of "choice" or of "reproductive freedom" represent an intentional strategy by pro-choice groups to maximize associations to individual liberty, self-autonomy, and private property. As Lauren Berlant has cogently documented, the figure of the fetus emerged within pro-life or antiabortion social movements and was thus introduced into the national political discourse as a living organism-citizen entitled to rights—a rather sneaky appropriation of the liberal discourse of freedom. Identifying political propaganda and popular media of the 1980s as complicit in this appropriation, Berlant stitches together vitalism with natalism and thus with nationalism: "The purpose here is to exhaust the banality of violence to the originary (read white 'American') body, to make violation once again a scandalous violence, and to reprivatize that body (within the patriarchally identified family); to recontain scandalous corporeality within mass culture and the minority populations of the nation; and to revitalize the national fantasy of abstract intimacy, but this time in a body that, visually available in its pure origin, receives protection from the juridical and immoral betrayals of national capitalism let loose by feminism and *Roe v. Wade*."[64] Berlant underscores the way in which late capitalism thrives on tactics of appropriation, showing that what is ultimately produced within the abortion debate is a strange discomfort within neoliberal ideology that, to remix Eve Sedgwick, can best be summarized as "kinda subversive, kinda hegemonic." Just as neoliberalism has co-opted choice within feminist theories of reproduction, so too has it recalibrated its economic spheres of influence to reinscribe gender stereotypes to preserve the heteropatriarchal order. The rhetorical framing of choice and rights on the one hand and life on the other hand constructs a well-known logic of false equivalence: the opposite of "pro-life" or "anti-abortion" is simply "pro-choice," an elegant investment in neoliberal terminology, and not "pro-death" or "pro-abortion."

And yet for Jiz, these are precisely the ideological positions that must be scurrilously espoused; the rhetoric of choice is entirely absent from all *Jiz*'s conceptions of abortion. By perverting the object of the debate, *Jiz* succeeds in resisting the neutralization of liberal rights discourse, although this resistance should not be uncritically valorized. Indeed, Jiz is simply against choice writ large: she demands abortions on her terms and views the act of copulation as integral to fulfilling the second and more important act of her mandate. The compulsion to abort with fascist precision simply does not compute with the rationales of the free market. But just as choice is always limited, so too does Deirdre become trapped by her pregnancy in "The Abortion Episode." Having decided to keep her baby, thereby defying Jiz's orders, she finds that this carries risks of its own. After unsuccessfully attempting to gain support from her brother, a gay prostitute, and unwilling to perform extreme sex acts in order to earn the income necessary to raise a child, Deirdre eventually decides that she wants an abortion after all, and she returns to Starlight House for the procedure. Jiz, in the meantime, has been busted by the authorities for administering abortions without a medical license and for performing them—license or not—after the eighth month (a charge to which Jiz replies, "But that's when you pull 'em out, when they're ripe!"). As Jiz and Deirdre reunite, the younger protégé confesses, "I finally realized that having babies is for retards. I realized that I don't want to fucking have a goddamn baby on my goddamn back." Her rock star mentor could not be more proud, and Kimber then rallies the group with a spritely jump: "Let's get a motherfucking abortion." The Mammograms take the stage in front of a global audience to sing their new hit, "Abortion." Kimber's line, and its ensuing repetition in later episodes, position abortion not as an individual act at all, but as one experienced collectively, a socialist/consumerist, feminist/misogynist, queer/normative celebration of abortion that represents a rite of passage for young girls. "The Abortion Episode" animates, quite literally, the potential for the rhetoric of abortion (or antiabortion) to be dramatized and pushed to its logical extreme, and Jem has been remixed into a different kind of female pioneer: the crusader who demands that every girl get an abortion to hilarious, if reprobate, effect.

It may be tempting to read these puerile abortion jokes as simply there for shock value, a way of capitalizing on the legacy of television programs such as *South Park* and *Family Guy* while transposing the valence of obscene, animated adolescents to a different aesthetic and sexual demographic. Rather than assuming a coherent political ideology, as many scholars have noted, these animated programs espouse a politics much like their comedic style and assumed audience: juvenile and fragmented, "a mode of political engagement," according to Ted Gournelos, "that is about politics and about discourse [and that mobilizes] social tropes in a consistently self-reflective and discursively active way."[65] Nick Marx has similarly read such programs as courting a demographic audience of "lost boys" who sprint quickly through the intertextual references, with the aesthetic techniques of "click culture" constructing a "false sense of comedic pluralism that elides the power differentials among comedic targets and audiences," thus undoing the program's (or the genre's?) larger claim as effective satire.[66] But perhaps abortion is doing other work here as well, representing more than an effort to shock or scandalize its viewers. In Barbara Johnson's consummate excursus on abortion and poetry, "Apostrophe, Animation, and Abortion," she articulates an inquiry into the rhetorical shape of abortion with a deceptively simple question: "Can the very essence of a political issue—an issue like, say, abortion—hinge on the structure of a figure?"[67] As she takes a keen eye to poems by Adrienne Rich, Anne Sexton, Lucille

Clifton, and Gwendolyn Brooks that give voice to women, fetuses, and readers who both act and do not act as witnesses to the event (the essay is a tour de force of close reading), Johnson advances the rhetorical figure of apostrophe—the address of an inanimate being—as the structure around which the arguments for and against abortion coalesce. Abortion is activated only as a polarizing debate, she argues, because it is *animated*, given life through a situation that is never not violent: "The choice is not between violence and nonviolence, but between simple violence to a fetus and complex, less determinate violence to an involuntary mother and/or an unwanted child."[68] The speakers of the poems she analyzes have written themselves into poems they "cannot get out of without violence," due to the formal structures of poetry, the device that was originally assigned to give life.[69] Because it must be animated, the "choice" is never without violence.

What kind of violence is present within *Jiz*'s own animation of abortion? And what, specifically, is being animated? Does language—in this case a new addressee, a literal voice-over—give life, or does it end it? I have advanced the notion in this chapter that the offensive rendering of what are undoubtedly sensitive and resonant issues for women is a kind of violence that is conjoined to the development and value of remix culture. As a tactic of remix that poaches on the territory of familiar identifications and affects, abortion emerges as a form of creative resistance, a figure of speech that stitches together a foundational violence with its capacity for revival and regeneration. *Jiz* is full of profane language that often borders on hate speech, and while many queer voices have argued against the policing of speech as a marker of a distasteful respectability politics, I am not convinced that *Jiz* and her creator, Sienna D'Enema, can be acquitted (if they ever cared about such things in the first place) by a line of defense that states, "The right to offend people is a cornerstone of the LGBT movement ... and every movement and community needs jesters," to quote trans activist Andrea James.[70] To write off *Jiz* as an equal opportunity offender, or as pure parody, would do injustice to the effects of that very violence, after all. Instead, I see in *Jiz* the abortion of nostalgia for its "parent" series. But this perversion of nostalgia has political effects. Nostalgia is not wielded in the *Jiz* episodes to gloss over the political battles over family values successfully used by conservatives in the culture wars. Rather, when a remixed Jiz encourages abortion among her girl groupies, I see the vulgarization of nostalgia, but only in such a way that requires the initial resuscitation of said nostalgic feelings. In other words, what makes *Jiz* so dangerously offensive is less its provocative slurs and more the violence enacted on nostalgia: how *Jiz* reanimates the sacred objects of one's childhood in order

chapter three

to defile them with acerbic humor. I read in *Jiz* an act of vidding apostrophe, in which the practice of Remix gives life to an older series and in doing so becomes interpellated into structures of violence. Such a reading must resist the temptation to call remix culture pure creation or an unimpeachable form of writing. Rather, we must take Johnson's import to heart: "It is as though male writing were by nature procreative, while female writing is somehow by nature infanticidal."[71] While D'Enema identifies as male, they prefer to lurk in online pseudonymity with a female name, and the queer sensibility present within their work invokes Beth Freeman's identification of queerness "as the site of all the change element that capital inadvertently produces, as well as the site of capital's potential capture and incorporation of chance."[72] This linguistic drag, in which the male writer is both procreative and infanticidal, produces a queer infanticide of the nostalgic object.

Anecdotally, when I met with D'Enema, they told me that one of the most frequent responses to their work is the comment "You killed my childhood!" To take such a flippant comment seriously, we might then stipulate that while the remix might "kill" a childhood, it can do so only because it first reanimates the feelings of nostalgia connected to one's childhood. Indeed, this repetitive cycle of apostrophic abortive nostalgia lays bare the terrain of an affective economy of perversion. *Jiz* is a perverted text that in turn perverts the memories of *Jem* fans. Its presence online functions as a rejoinder that Remix as action and remix culture as industry infuse creative potentiality into the wistful objects of a viewer's past—but only through taking as their premise the risking of innocence conjured by those objects. If remix is, in today's digital cultural studies, indeed a repertoire of techniques used to promote cultural literacy, it often has such instructive power because of its capacity to pervert. As past becomes remixed into the present, queer remixers must insist on tracing what is risked when they scramble, even to innocuous or humorous effects, for the reanimation and subsequent murder of childhood innocence; as *Jiz* demonstrates, they might embody perhaps one of the most extreme metageneric principles at stake in postmillennial remix culture.

Affective economies of perversion, I maintain, operate in subtle ways, despite the level of explicitness present within their address. Hearing *Jiz*'s voice-over is fundamentally different from reading the transcribed language on the page—as you, the reader, have done here—so much so that, during the course of writing this, it caused me no small degree of consternation. It is why I insist on the vulgarity (however unprofessional and risky in a neoliberal university system rife with "trigger warnings") as essential to animating the many uncomfortable affects present within *Jiz*'s televisual remix of abortion.

Assuredly, my task in demystifying perversely queer televisual remix has been to expose the violence and discomfort present in remix culture, no matter how much such critique would seem to run counter to the object under investigation. If, for Johnson, the uneasy terrain over which rhetorical, psychoanalytic, and political structures crawl in and out of each other emerges "in the attempt to achieve a full elaboration of any discursive position other than that of child," then I believe that *Jiz* affords us access into understanding how the formal grammar of remix culture discharges a correspondingly muddled elaboration of non-child discursive positions.[73] The problem with remix culture's teleological bent, one I have attempted to slow down and limn carefully, is that perhaps even the child has been sophomorically corrupted, and once we accept that as the case today, we risk indulging in the viewing position of the child without the knowledge of the fraught reproductive politics that enabled this juvenile remix to transpire online in the first place.

chapter three

four

the spectator plagued by white guilt on the appropriative intermediality of quality tv

What the televisual names
then is the end of the medium,
in a context, and the arrival of
television as the context.
—TONY FRY

A NUMBER OF POSTMILLENNIAL American
television series have been cited as examples of
a new golden age (sometimes called a "platinum
age") in television. As a general rule, these series
tend to be shown on cable networks, premium
cable networks, or streaming services, and they
are often heralded for their attention to visual
detail and narrative structure, attributes that
often result from generous production budgets.
The metaphoric deployment of the metallurgic
terms of classical antiquity serves to index cultural value, but this deployment is not limited to
the twenty-first century; since the first commercial television broadcast in 1941, American television has had a number of golden ages: at least
two, and probably three. That more than one
golden age exists is indicative of the fluctuation
in the perception of cultural value among different art forms and historical periods. Television
may finally have "become art" in the 2000s, in
the words of TV critic Emily Nussbaum, but
how television expresses its *artness*—what is
specific to television that renders it legible as art
in the eyes of critics, historians, scholars, and
the general public—is a product of the social
climate surrounding the emergence of the discourse of cultural value.

The possibility of locating multiple golden
ages in the history of American television
squarely critiques the position of television as a
"bad" object in the American popular imaginary.
To qualify as a golden age, a period of history
relating to a national, artistic, or technological

culture must be comparatively at its peak, a relational definition of excellence. In the case of television, this peak is always the terrain of drama: the first golden age of television, for example, was not associated with formative sitcoms such as *I Love Lucy* but instead with the hour-long anthology series that often directly adapted works of Western theater, opera, ballet, and classical music for live broadcast (dramatic in artistic weight, if not explicitly in genre).[1] The second golden age of television—though one not universally agreed upon by critics or scholars—encompassed the "serious, literary, writer-based drama[s]" (in Robert Thompson's account) of 1980s prime-time programming. While these series were often not the most popular on prime time, critics praised their incorporation of elements of serial narrative while taking pains to distinguish these series from the prime-time soap operas that dominated the Nielsen ratings.[2]

This chapter examines the discourses surrounding the cultural value of postmillennial drama, which television critics primarily refer to as a third golden age. To be talked about in such auriferous terms, according to critics, a series must showcase its construction of narrative and the talents of its writing staff and have one singular figure, the showrunner, in charge of the narrative. Showrunners shore up the anxiety of critics who wish to ascribe an authorial voice to a series, complicating the ways in which television has traditionally been perceived as an ensemble medium.[3] Seriality is emphasized within the narrative structure of the new golden age drama, but with a bounded introduction (a series premiere) and conclusion (a series finale). These programs are characterized not only by their narrative specificity but also by the specificity (even if disavowed) of their lead characters: this reemergence of *quality* has also been centered on White male protagonists who grapple with moral or ethical decisions. Dubbed antiheroes by some, these men stand in for the tragic pathos of late capitalism; they are figures who perform national angst in the late 1990s and 2000s. In many respects, the antiheroes of the current golden age stand in for the series themselves, eclipsing other cast members, as approximations of the *ur*-White male of a so-called postracial and postgender America. Thus the series that constitute this golden age—most notably *The Sopranos* (HBO, 1999–2007), *Six Feet Under* (HBO, 2001–2005), *The Wire* (HBO, 2002–2007), *Deadwood* (HBO, 2004–2006), *Mad Men* (AMC, 2006–2015), and *Breaking Bad* (AMC, 2008–2013)—are defined by their conflicted protagonists (Tony Soprano, Nate Fisher, Jimmy Mc-Nulty, Seth Bullock and Al Swearingen, Don Draper, and Walter White, respectively). As journalist Brett Martin writes in his hagiographic study of the third golden age, appropriately titled *Difficult Men*, "Not only were the most important shows of the era run by men, they were also largely *about* manhood—in particular the contours of male power and the infinite varieties of male combat."[4]

The "contours of male power" (and, although unmentioned by Martin, white supremacy as well) dramatized in these series correspond to claims made about their mediality. Critically, intermediality has emerged as the metric by which some series are perceived as quality both by journalists—plainly seen, for example, in a *New York Times Sunday Book Review* article, "Are the New 'Golden Age' TV Shows the New Novels?"—and by scholars of literature—as in literary scholar Jennifer Fleissner's contention that literary scholars should turn to studying quality TV texts under the rubric of the "novelistic" in order to study the "face-off between a 'charismatic' structure of authority (the mob, the gang) and a modern one (the legalistic bureaucracy, the school)."[5] Such a contention seemingly stands in contrast to television studies scholar John Caldwell's notion of televisuality, or the aesthetic sensibility of television that in turn produces a visually stimulated viewer who participates in an aesthetic economy associated with postmodern subjectivity and who is obsessed with programs that require immense postproduction processing. Rather than emphasizing the refined *image* (a given in the current golden age, in which many of these cable series are presented in HD), the language of the novelistic favors crafted *narrative*.

The televisual and the novelistic produce varying spectatorial stimulations that might appear to resemble the oppositional categories of form and content. Indeed, as Susan Sontag warned of such categories, "It is hard to think oneself out of a distinction so habitual and apparently self-evident."[6] Yet neither divisions of aesthetics/narrative nor of form/content can explain the terms by which quality TV becomes discursively divided from regular TV. Rather, *quality* seems to mark a kind of intersection and interaction, even as this becomes reframed as a singular distinction. Thus the challenge of this chapter is to rethink contemporary quality television in terms of its intermediality, examining the appeal of the intermedial as a marker of cultural value. This chapter takes up the thrust of critical assumptions about television of the golden age through one of its most cited examples and through some of its pivotal theorists of literature and film: HBO's *The Wire*, one of the most critically acclaimed television series of the twenty-first century (and a frequent contender for the pop culture title of the "best TV series" of recent times).

I then compare this reception with that of so-called middlebrow television, best exemplified by network police procedurals of the early twenty-first century such as CSI: *Crime Scene Investigation* (CBS, 2000–2015) and *Law & Order: Special Victims Unit* (NBC, 1999–present). Following the legitimation of certain forms of television—forms that achieve such legitimation through their very disavowal of the medium—I analyze what I term the *appropriative intermediality* of quality television, a form of intermediality by which one media form appropriates others through the work of cultural legitimation. According to scholars such as Fredric Jameson, Slavoj Žižek, and Linda Williams, series such as *The Wire* epitomize a sort of literary neoliberalism (or a neoliberal literariness?).[7] But rather than fetishize this program for its realism or for the ways in which it challenged conventional TV aesthetics and politics of the time, I am interested in how brief moments within the series contradict the feelings of comfort that generally come from audiences (figured within these discourses as White) who rhapsodically view *The Wire* as something greater than normal television. Despite being a series that regularly portrays poverty, homicide, and drug use as endemic to urban life, *The Wire* relies on racialized empathetic identifications to its characters to establish itself as a quality text that defies televisuality. Yet moments of abjection persist, a reminder of the ways in which race marks the reception of the series. If, as this chapter's epigraph by Tony Fry signals, the televisual shifts attention from a defined medium to an aesthetic context, I critique the discourse of *The Wire* for making audiences *too comfortable* with institutional Whiteness, shrouded by the veneer of golden, novelistic antiheroism.

We should not watch *The Wire* through a symbolically characterological gaze, ripe for the extraction of meaning in the name of optimizing cultural value and prestige—as the champions who insist that postmillennial television is art would have it. Rather, viewing quality television on the surface—a critical interrogation of its intermediality—reveals why a dislikable protagonist is a necessary component for narrative risk-taking and thus for artistic legitimation. In other words, series heralded and marketed as quality valorize the individual estranged from his or her family as both protagonist and ideal spectator. Appropriative intermediality, quality, estrangement from the American nuclear family: this is the topography of the third golden age. It is one in which disassociated individuals both willingly flee and are forced from the once-stable defenses of the family; such a description applies both to individuals on the screen and to those outside it, suggesting that late capitalist constructions have shifted the very ground of television's operations.

chapter four

To hear critics tell the story of television's third golden age is also to hear a sigh of relief that the medium has become something other than itself. Brett Martin, for example, begins his own history in *Difficult Men* by stating the obvious: television has held a low cultural position throughout most of its history, tethered to its mass appeal and popularity. Citing instances ranging from FCC chairman Newton Minow's infamous "vast wasteland" speech in 1961 to HBO's longest-running network slogan, introduced in 1996 (the same year the premium cable network premiered its first original dramatic series, *Oz*), "It's Not TV. It's HBO," Martin parrots the usual talking points of "this maligned medium." Television was stunted technologically in its early days, with "clunky, immovable cameras and limited recording capability."[8] Echoing the historical critiques of the medium that I covered in previous chapters, television was deemed a threat to the American family (and especially to children) at the same time as it was heralded as a technological apparatus that would keep all family members home and together. Furthermore, other cultural agents—authors such as Ray Bradbury and E. B. White and filmmakers such as Orson Welles—constructed television as necessarily trashy, apocalyptic, and technically alien.

Martin's framing of television unintentionally reveals the work of the critic in assessing cultural value; while professional critics (including Martin himself) can make careers out of appraising cultural products, such labor circulates omnipresently in and out of the culture industries. His consideration of the comments from Bradbury, White, and Welles as evidence of television's low cultural status testifies to the impossibility, as well as the inevitability, of the task of criticism itself. This is highly suggestive of what Barbara Herrnstein Smith outlines as a denial of the objectivity of value. Writing about literature, Smith states: "The value of a literary work is continuously produced and re-produced by the very acts of implicit and explicit evaluation that are frequently invoked as 'reflecting' its value and therefore as being evidence of it. In other words, what are commonly taken to be *signs* of literary value are, in effect, its *springs*."[9] Smith points to the way in which criticism that attempts to establish value constructs arbitrary criteria that affirm the position of the critic. She notes how the "test of time"—the persistence of certain texts throughout history that becomes a mechanism for canonization—serves the social, economic, and political interests of the institutions *of* criticism, creating an echo chamber of sorts.

Smith's claims help illuminate a beloved staple of media criticism: the "best-of" list, a strong example of her notion of the "contingencies of value" described in her eponymous work. The mere presence of a text on such a list guarantees its potential for future citation, a projection of its future endurance. The best-of list is authored by a single critic or controlled group of critics, differentiating it from awards given by democratic guilds or industrial organizations (such as in television's Emmy Awards).[10]

While the list form predominates, especially at the end of a calendar year or at the end of a decade, some print and media outlets have used unconventional means of ranking texts according to their own criteria. In March of 2012, for example, the pop culture website *Vulture* ran a bracket competition of its own concurrently with the NCAA college basketball tournament, asking the question, "What's the Best TV Drama of the Last 25 Years?"[11] While a quarter-century may seem an appropriate length of time to periodize contemporary pop culture (and, it should be noted, such a periodization somewhat overlaps with my own characterization of postmillennial TV), such a time length was not arbitrary. *Vulture* declared the premiere of the critically acclaimed network drama *Twin Peaks* (ABC, 1990–1991) as the beginning of television's "new Golden Age." Yet this moment of historical abstraction already carried signs of what, exactly, would qualify a series as a contender for the "best": it would not need to be legible as television as-such. In introducing the bracket, Brian Raferty situated *Twin Peaks* as "a TV show that didn't seem to *know* it was a TV show, and its mere existence conveyed a strangely empowering message to TV viewers everywhere, people who'd long been content with neuron-dimming procedurals and plod-heavy soaps: *You're smarter than this.*"[12] The best TV is smart TV, if it is TV at all. Vying for the "Best TV" title of this Drama Derby were sixteen series, all of which involved "neatly tangled story lines, grimly hilarious dialogue, and characters who inspire loyalty, love, and the occasional fan-fic dispatch" (though Raferty here contradicts himself, as these criteria obviously also extend to the two genres of "not smart" TV he cites earlier: the procedural and the soap opera). Notably, the series selected by *Vulture* were predominantly male—only two featured female protagonists (*My So-Called Life* and *Buffy the Vampire Slayer*)—and while the sixteen were split between broadcast and cable/premium cable networks, the "final four" all came from cable, with the "championship round" featuring two HBO series, *The Sopranos* and *The Wire* (see figure 4.1).

In arbitrating this final match between these two programs, television critic Matt Zoller Seitz offered six criteria for the *best*: influence and transformation; philosophical sophistication; characterization; formal daring; influence

DRAMA DERBY: WHAT'S THE BEST TV DRAMA OF THE PAST 25 YEARS?

A different all-star writer judged each round. Click the winning shows to read their deliberations!

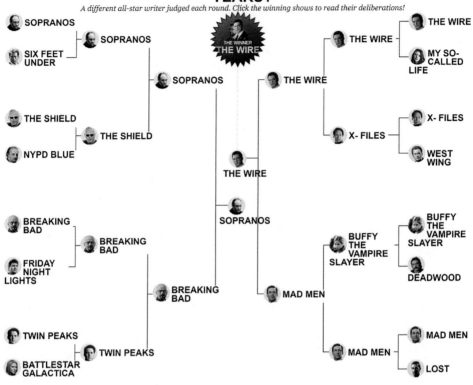

4.1 The final results of *Vulture*'s 2012 "Drama Derby."

on the medium; and consistency.[13] What is apparent from Seitz's explanation of the criteria is that what makes a television series the best is relative not to attributes unique to television—that is, whether or not such a series embodies an essentialized notion of *television*—but instead to attributes recognized as best in other forms of art—that is, a series' ability to be misrecognized as something other than television. *The Wire*, Seitz concludes, is "one of the most intelligent, moving, and politically astute dramas ever aired on American TV, and a rare series that truly deserves the adjective *novelistic*," while *The Sopranos* "is novelistic, but it's also short-story-like, and poetic, and at times has qualities of stage drama, opera, and even Renaissance painting and great twentieth-century pop music." *The Wire* edges out *The Sopranos*, Seitz decides, because he had "to strain less when arguing the greatness of *The Wire*," an interesting commentary on the critic's labor in and of itself.

127

the spectator plagued by white guilt

This kind of intermedial comparison has graced the newsprint pages of television criticism since at least 1995, when Charles McGrath published a lengthy article in the *New York Times Magazine* declaring the "triumph of the prime time novel."[14] Like clockwork—or perhaps more appropriately, in a rather serial fashion—the past two decades have been punctuated with headlines that spur such comparisons; thus, to claim that quality television programs are the "new novels" is not, in fact, all that new of a claim.[15] Digital media studies, itself a significant influence on the convergence of postmillennial television, has emphasized the role of the "new" as one indexing repetition: "new media" can emerge only against its opposite, "old media." In this vein of archaeological criticism, television is rendered as old, trapped within its pedantic laugh tracks and annoying commercials, while TV-as-literature, with its complexity and ability to be consumed in large blocks of time, has revitalized an even older form of narrative: the novel or even, as Sean O'-Sullivan has claimed, "oral performances" such as poetry, "narratives governed by metrical organization, iteration, and variation."[16]

Elsewhere, Michael Newman and Elana Levine have advanced cinematization (as opposed to novelization) as the most prominent strategy in the larger project of legitimating certain kinds of television, arguing that a number of factors activate a move to the cinematic. Among these are the emergence of high-definition television that shifted the aspect ratio for broadcast programming, the collectability of programs via the DVD box set and its attendant "bonus" disc of special features, and practices of spectatorship that shift the screened temporality of a series (as in bingeing—though their analysis comes right before streaming services such as Netflix appropriated the term). Such factors, Newman and Levine contend, mean that "certain kinds of television and certain modes of *experiencing* television content are aligned with movies and the *experience* of movies."[17] Newman and Levine's astute analysis offers many correctives to the teleological narrative that television has somehow "gotten better" throughout its history, but they omit any recognition of the fact that claims of legitimation require attention to affect. Their use of the word *experience* in the above passage, for example, suggests that there can be an identifiable set of affects that certain television texts and certain films share. While they do not view such parallel experiences as affective, I wish to emphasize the role that experience plays in cinematization, extending it to all processes of intermedial criticism.[18] What does it mean for a program to *feel* like cinema, or to *feel* like literature? And more importantly, stitching together this affective form with its corresponding content: Why are feelings of intermediality tethered to such unlikeable protagonists, the antiheroes with mired ethics and unsavory behaviors?

"Neuron-Dimming" for Everyone:
Popular Perversity and the Procedural

Before turning to *The Wire*'s extensive use of intermediality, I find it important to offer a generic counterpoint to the intertextual, quality drama of postmillennial TV. Of the sixteen series included in *Vulture*'s Drama Derby, only two—*NYPD Blue* (ABC, 1993–2005) and *The X-Files* (Fox, 1993–2002; revived 2016–2018)—really fall within the generic boundaries of the procedural, the middlebrow television much maligned by Raferty as "neuron-dimming."[19] While procedurals may not be fully recognized as quality under the markers of the critics of the new golden age, they historically have attained some recognition through traditional metrics (for example, in composing the majority of the Emmy nominations for Outstanding Drama Series throughout the 1970s, 1980s, and 1990s), as well as through their incorporation into previous golden ages (for example, *Hill Street Blues* is considered a seminal text of the second golden age of the 1980s). Throughout the most recent golden age, however, procedurals retained their popularity among wider audiences, with *ER* (NBC, 1994–2009) and various instantiations of the *CSI* and *Law & Order* franchises routinely included among Nielsen's Top Ten. Such popularity appears to exclude procedurals from the rubric of quality television, however, since their longer seasons (22–25 episode seasons, as opposed to 10–13) and aspirations toward syndication (in which episodes can be marathoned without respect to order) represent the conventional narrative frameworks of television's past.[20] Yet, in the example of "TV gone too far" found in this book's introduction, critic James Poniewozik uses the example of *CSI* (#1 in the Nielsen ratings from 2002 to 2005) as demonstrative of the harmony between popularity and perversity, reading the two together as indicative of television's free-market logic ("When the greatest plurality of viewers choose to watch a show they know to be graphic, can that show be beyond the pale?").[21]

The *CSI* episode Poniewozik refers to in his article is "King Baby," a season 5 episode that was the Nielsen most-watched show over the week, beating out ratings juggernaut *American Idol* by over three million viewers. A closer analysis of the episode reveals the affective logics at play in this middlebrow procedural.[22] In the episode, the investigation into the murder of a prominent Las Vegas casino magnate reveals an obsession with infantilism: the victim

129

wore enormous cloth diapers, defecated recklessly across the carpet, built a secret nursery decked out with giant baby furniture (including a toy chest with a hidden compartment containing information about the magnate's enemies), drank human breast milk from oversized bottles, and received anal douching from an aspiring lounge singer dressed up as his babysitter and caretaker (who laced the magnate's last bottle of breast milk with LSD, which ultimately led to his death from a fall off the mansion's balcony). Excessive perversity dominates the episode's general mise-en-scène; following the discovery of the crawlspace that leads to the nursery, for example, the analeptic sequences that represent the detectives' speculative re-enactment of the crime depict the sexual scene gone awry, with exaggerated gestures of bottle nursing and enema preparation.

For many, including Derek Kompare and Steven Cohan, such flashbacks can be indicative of the series' overall use of visual signifiers invested in the ultimate veracity of scientific evidence. For Kompare, CSI "[inhabits] a kind of extra-realism ... whereby the conventional codes of narrative realism apply, but are first worked through an expressive and eclectic palette of audiovisual styles." Yet the series' tableaux of the evidence of criminal perversity does not alienate the viewer, who rather "share[s] in its principal characters' insatiable pursuit of 'evidence.' In these ways, CSI is unapologetically comfort food television: heavy on spectacle and drama, but still easy to digest."[23] These critical assessments of the series align its commitment to excessive aesthetic representation with its diegetic setting—Las Vegas, Nevada, whose alter ego "Sin City" promises an "anything goes" attitude regarding sexual desire and consumer capitalism. Full of freaks, the Las Vegas setting allows for the series to showcase its gruesome murders and fetishes while more-or-less adhering to conventional dialogue and episodic form, and thus CSI is subversive only in training its mass audiences to accept technological supremacy uncritically through visual display or what a number of scholars call the "CSI effect."[24]

This televisuality, however, does not mean that spoken language is insignificant to the procedural's production of affect. As opposed to the seamless intertwining of multiple story lines found in the serialized quality drama, middlebrow television such as procedurals feature "special effects" on the level of character that sterilize and temper sexual fetish to make it appeal to a broader audience as "unapologetically comfort food television," as described by Kompare. Throughout "King Baby," the detectives adapt two distinct postures toward sexual infantilism. It revolts Crime Scene Unit assistant supervisor Catherine Willows (Marg Helgenberger), who describes its fetishists as "freaks" in an emphatic tone and who appears to be affected

chapter four

4.2 Grissom finds the LSD-laced enemas in the secret nursery. *CSI*, "King Baby," Season 5, Episode 15.

by the kind of labor required of the investigation, sarcastically remarking that whoever gets to analyze the blood, urine, and fecal samples found at the crime scene is a "lucky girl."[25] By contrast, supervisor Gil Grissom (William Petersen) is measured and matter-of-fact toward the fetish, approaching it with a nondescript affect reserved for the scientific process. Grissom offers multiple amateur psychoanalytic theories about how and why someone might derive sexual pleasure from infantilism: an adult-sized pacifier is a "transitional object" that "helps [children] with anxiety," and he namedrops Freud while speculating with a matronly employee of an adult-baby fetish store that the poles of maternal love—its excess or its absence—form the root of such perverse play.

The series also offers moments of direct education through the explanation of random scientific and medical facts. In "King Baby," Grissom explains to Willows that the LSD found in the enema bottle would not have shown up in the toxicological blood screens because the drug "is in and out of your system in twenty minutes." His short lecture is juxtaposed with flashback sequences of the casino magnate having a bad trip in the nursery that zoom in on and show flashing nerve synapses in his brain. The combination of these aesthetically excessive flashbacks with Grissom's voice-over positions viewers as in an educational film, deploying, in David Pierson's terms, "forensic and abject gazes."[26] As a function of character, these opposing tones conform to expected gender stereotypes; with respect to the investigative hierarchy and

the spectator plagued by white guilt

the mastery over forensic bodies of knowledge, Grissom must contain Willows's occasional betrayals of intuition in order for the crime to be solved. And as a product of neoliberal regimes of emotional management, Grissom's performance requires a lack of affect to enact this instructive grammar, which constructs the ideal spectator as a true believer in the scientific method (or, in Martha Gever's keen phrasing, a "a self rendered so transparent that it vanishes or remains perceptible only as the sum of inscriptions").[27]

csi thus represents the neoliberal impulse to correct one's intuitive reactions to the spectacularized display of gruesome bodies and sexual perversity with scientific and medical bodies of knowledge that serve as affective and textual *pharmakon*. By contrast, the episode of *Law & Order: Special Victims Unit* (svu) that aired the same week as "King Baby" is also symptomatic of that series' construction of procedural affect, but it does so without a depersonalized investment in scientific knowledge.[28] Like most svu episodes, "Hooked" occurs at the intersection of sexual desire and criminality, with detectives Elliot Stabler (Christopher Meloni) and Olivia Benson (Mariska Hargitay) investigating the murder of a fifteen-year-old girl that ultimately exposes a child pornography and prostitution ring in which many of the teenage girls test positive for HIV. As in csi, sexual desire is granted a certain kind of autonomous empowerment—teenagers who quite literally wear their promiscuity on their wrists, with the colors of each rubber bracelet corresponding to different sexual activities—in line with the general epistemological preoccupation with sex acts inaugurated by the late-1990s investigation into and subsequent impeachment of President Bill Clinton. Excessive videographic signifiers abound within the episode's lurid representation of illicit sexual desire: the body of the victim is framed circularly by a telescope belonging to a local Boy Scout troop; medical examiner Melinda Warner (Tamara Tunie) uses a computer model "used by the CDC to calculate the spread of HIV in urban areas" in order to geo-locate the victim's sexual partners; surveillance cameras find the victim's friend Angela (Hayden Panettiere) performing oral sex on a retail employee; and the prostitution ring itself is exposed through a pornographic film of a three-way between the victim, Angela, and Dr. Derek Tanner (Alex Crammer), the doctor who prescribed HIV medications to the teenage prostitutes and the victim's lover (and who is found dead midway through the episode). As in csi, these signifiers not only demonstrate the necessity of visual evidence for solving crimes but also allow for narrative moralizing (condemning casual sex between teenagers, for example) through making visible the sexual exploitation of women.

chapter four

Yet the character dimensions in "Hooked" reveal a more emotional language than in *CSI*, a grammar that uses feminine nurturing affect as the basis for both possible criminality and successful detective work. Notably, "Hooked" allows for a glimpse into the domestic lives of its protagonists when it is revealed that one of the victim's sexual partners is a classmate of Stabler's daughter, Kathleen (Allison Siko). Fearful that Kathleen may have been exposed to HIV, Stabler rushes to his daughter's school, asking her if she had sex with the potentially infected classmate. She responds negatively, and he protectively embraces her. The motif of Stabler as a tender protector is reinforced at the end of the episode, when Stabler elicits a confession from Angela that she killed Dr. Tanner; Angela hugs Stabler and tearfully exclaims, "I'm so sorry . . . I just wanted my life back." Lisa M. Cuklanz and Sujata Moorti have described the character of Stabler as a "proto-feminist family man" who, throughout the series (and with the prodding of his female colleagues), "realizes a key feminist insight that sexual crimes often defy rationality"; thus, *svu* promotes "a key feminist idea that separating the public and private arenas is an untenable ideological device."[29] These "key feminist ideas" (that allow the series to be claimed as a feminist text more so than *CSI*) emerge through the emotional performances of the male protagonist across several episodes and ultimately function as a palliative device of care for those exposed to criminal sexual perversity. *svu*, with its sensationalized plot twists, its representation of police and prosecutorial misconduct, and its latitude in dramatizing actual crimes, can be read as symptomatic of what Sarah Projansky has identified as the complexity and pervasiveness of rape culture within postfeminist discourses.[30] Following this logic, part of what makes the sexual assaults portrayed on *svu* so popular are the unsettling responses generated by the program, responses that shift the audience's conceptions of justice away from legal culpability and instead toward extenuating circumstances. That all of this occurs on a major broadcast network within a procedural format in which individual episodes follow a similar narrative framework challenges the assumption of Janet McCabe and Kim Akass that serialized programming on exclusive premium channels is the preeminent site for provocatively reprobate content. It might, however, demonstrate the effects of original premium programming on its network counterparts; *svu*, it can be argued, had to "evolve" through a narrative and aesthetic excess that complicated any straightforward moral message about sexual assault in order to keep up with its more serialized competitors. Detective Olivia Benson, for example, finds herself kidnapped by serial rapist and murderer William

Lewis (Pablo Schreiber) at the end of season 14; the kidnapping, her escape, and Lewis's trial become a more serialized story line across five episodes in the following season, allowing for Benson's backstory (she was a victim of sexual assault numerous times throughout her life) to support her dedication to capturing perpetrators of sexual assault. SVU therefore distinguishes itself from previous police procedurals in its empathetic address and character development while reinforcing television's larger therapeutic imperatives.

Both SVU and CSI have been noted for their narrative ability to present stories "ripped from the headlines," transforming the realism found in *Hill Street Blues* and NYPD *Blue* into distinctly more perverse and explicit territory. Their individual episodic plotlines graphically depict sexual fetishes, sexual assault, and child abuse as proximate to criminal behaviors, using established character stereotypes and backstories in the service of criminal investigation. Yet despite the abundance of sexual perversity present in each, neither series invests significantly in viewer alienation, using instead televisually forensic and therapeutic representational strategies to scaffold their moralizing of deviant criminal behavior. These series inoculate audiences to perverse content over the course of many seasons, but they are neither intermedial nor antiheroic in and of themselves.

Appropriative Intermediality as Legitimation: *The Wire*

The distinction between quality and middlebrow representations of the crime genre extends into university classrooms: certain programs may be perceived as novelistic or literary, for example, because they are taught as such in literature departments. This fact in and of itself is not really that noteworthy; as Newman and Levine explain, one sign of the legitimation of television can be found "in the spread of attention to television beyond radio-TV-film and communication studies curricula"; they single out courses on *The Wire* in other disciplines to note that "it is significant that these kinds of television courses are oriented around specific or individual series and that the series so chosen are among the most lauded of contemporary TV."[31] One such lecture course, called "Storytelling in *The Wire*," offered in a comparative literature department, opens its syllabus with a quote from Mark Twain's *The Gilded Age* before proceeding to encapsulate the course's goals: "*The Wire* has received attention from fields like sociology and urban studies, which tend to read the work as a fictionalization of their observations about cities. It has not received as much attention from departments of literature, although it should. In our course, traditional categories of literary study will be wedded to the investigation of contemporary problems that emerge from the work."[32] The syllabus covers a wide range of texts, genres, and mediums: Greek tragedy (Sophocles's *Antigone*), Marxist economic history (David Harvey's *The Condition of Postmodernity*), urban social policy (William Julius Wilson's *When Work Disappears* and Michelle Alexander's *The New Jim Crow*), and cinematic Westerns (Sam Peckinpah's 1969 film *The Wild Bunch*). Fredric Jameson's gloss on the series is included ("Realism and Utopia in *The Wire*," an article that I subsequently address), but the syllabus does not include readings on the televisuality of the text or on the question of representing "contemporary problems" on television. Such absences emphasize how the study of technological media and its possibilities for formal analysis fall outside "traditional categories of literary study" (and thus obscure print media's own mediality).

The syllabus encapsulates what this chapter terms *appropriative intermediality*: when one media form or discipline appropriates an art object belonging to a different media form through an active disavowal of that art object's medial specificity. It is more often than not used as a tactic for cultural legitimation, in which "high art" forms such as literature and visual art cannibalize select texts or genres from mass culture in order to claim them as their own. In George Lipsitz's account of cultural appropriation in popular music, these tactics are always already grounded in the racialization of the audience, as in the case of White audiences actively consuming genres of popular music stemming from Black musicking traditions like jazz or the blues. Such an act of consumption, Lipsitz contends, is dependent "on the ways it erases its cultural origins and suppresses its original social intentions."[33] Similar work of erasure and suppression are present in appropriative intermediality, in which a legacy of low cultural status prevents certain mass media forms from being recognized as art, at least until they are recognized as such through a renunciation of their medial specificity.

Although Lipsitz foregrounds this racialized appropriation through a desire to forget the material conditions of production—the labor of the Black bodies that wrote, sung, and performed the blues, for example—he extends his claim to thinking about categories of popular culture more broadly: "Audiences and critics want to 'own' the pleasures and powers of popular music without embracing the commercial and industrial matrices in which they are embedded; they want to imagine that art that they have discovered through commercial culture is somehow better than commercial culture itself, that their investment in the music grants them an immunity from the embarrassing manipulation, pandering, and trivialization of culture intrinsic to a market society."[34] In an evocatively intermedial move, one could nearly substitute "television" for "music" in the aforementioned quote without a significant change to Lipsitz's characterization of the mental gymnastics required for an audience to disavow its participation in mass culture. Appropriation, then, is as much a spectatorial practice as it is intrinsic to the production of popular culture (or syllabi, for that matter). Because it is a deliberate yet unacknowledged strategy for determining cultural value, it puts into place a set of actions (within the sphere of production, namely writing; within the sphere of reception, namely criticism) that single out individual texts as worthy of praise while eliding their genealogical lineage.

In this particular case, *The Wire* is not thought of as television, nor is the discipline of television studies thought to contain the methodological tools that would be helpful to unpack the series critically. Such a cultural position stems in part from the description of the series and its creative process by its showrunner, David Simon. "If there's anything that distinguishes *The Wire* from a lot of the serialized drama you see," Simon said in one interview with *Vice* magazine, "it was that the writers were not from television" (a curious statement given Simon's previous job as a writer for the police drama *Homicide: Life on the Street* [NBC, 1993–1999]). Similarly, the showrunner contends that the ideal writing atmosphere for TV is one full of "journalists and, to an extent, the novelists who wrote for the show who write in a realistic framework, like researched fiction."[35] This distance is not unique to Simon but endemic to many of the showrunners who have become brand names in this postmillennial golden age; *The Sopranos'* showrunner David Chase has often been characterized as disdainful of the medium, thinking of himself more as a film auteur (a career of artistic integrity) than as a television showrunner (a career for sellouts and hacks).[36] Film (in Chase's case) and journalism (in Simon's) thus offer opportunities for risk-taking and creative license rather than the constraints imposed by institutional Hollywood.

Such an attitude has been rightly critiqued by Newman and Levine for how it renders the televisual text as authored by a single individual, the showrunner, rather than collaboratively, by the showrunner, writers, producers, and occasionally actors.[37] The emphasis on writing is a hallmark of quality TV. It showcases an array of narrative storytelling techniques, described by Jason Mittell as an "operational aesthetic" that presents both a "realistic narrative world" as well as the process behind such delicate narrative construction. In the third golden age, writing is the equivalent of cinematic special effects: techniques that attract audiences who wish to "marve[l] at the craft required to pull off such narrative pyrotechnics."[38] And while the labor required to execute these didactic fireworks has been ultimately recognized in industry awards ceremonies and by some television critics, the showrunner's status as author is never challenged by institutional criticism.

But what is the precise relationship between a showrunner and an author? According to Michel Foucault, the author of a text has been replaced by what he calls the *author-function*, a form of classification that transcends physical subjectivity (an individual as author) to characterize "the mode of existence, circulation, and functioning of certain discourses within a society."[39] Television may be collectively authored, with individual episodes written by individuals or pairs of individuals and then rewritten by a group or by the showrunner. This process varies by series, and showrunners institute different criteria for what constitutes "credit" for an episode. Chase, for example, after feeling frustrated with a perceived lack of industry acknowledgment, gave himself more credit for authoring episodes of *The Sopranos* as the series progressed. Matthew Weiner, the creator and showrunner of *Mad Men*, instituted a policy "that if more than 20 percent of a writer's script remained, he or she would retain sole credit," according to Martin. "If not, Weiner added his name."[40] Within the television industry, credit counts because of residuals and eligibility for trade awards; both the Television Academy and the Writers Guild of America, for example, give 100 percent writing credit to a sole author of an episode, a 50 percent writing credit to each author when the writing credits list two people, and split the writing credit 60 percent for the teleplay and 40 percent for the story writer; Emmy consideration rules specify that only individuals "either by themselves or in conjunction with other story or teleplay writers" with "at least 50% credit-share of the entered program" are eligible for nomination in writing categories.[41] In this context, however, the creator and showrunner of a program become identified as the author through awards programs, regardless of industry credit. The showrunner therefore becomes solidified in the popular imagination as what Foucault calls the result of "a complex operation which constructs a certain rational being which we call author," with the turn toward auteurism in quality television making that "rational being" legible within its industrial reception.[42]

The consolidation of the author-function around the showrunner also results in the calcification of another function: the *novel-function*. Emily Steinlight, writing on the advertising discourse of Charles Dickens's *Bleak House*, uses the term to signal how that novel was presented as an imagined whole in periodicals even when it was in the process of being published over twenty months starting in March 1852. Observing that the serial Victorian novel was always already a commodity situated within the contours of print capitalism but also situated within a matrix of literary narrative, she writes: "If there is

137

something like a text-function, or more particularly, a *novel-function*, it operates as a claim for the unity, singularity and autonomy of the writing. Under the sign of its title, the writing assumes the shape of an imagined totality called a novel long before it is complete."[43]

What is fascinating about postmillennial American quality TV is not only how it has redefined the parameters of broadcast storytelling but how its novel-function produces such an effect. As so many critics persistently remind us, *The Wire* is both the title of the program and an exemplary metaphor for the importance of surveillance culture to late capitalism. Dan Kois, writing in *Salon* in 2004 (prior to the premiere of the third season), notes, "As wiretaps provide the cops in *The Wire* a look into a secret world, so does *The Wire* offer us that same look into places most television viewers never see." (The first three words of Kois's review are, perhaps unsurprisingly at this point, a quote attributed to David Simon: "It's a novel.")[44] The invocation of surveillance shifts the problem of representation and visibility from the industry to the audience; it is not that *The Wire* offers audiences a look into places prohibitively hidden from viewers by Hollywood creatives, after all. Surveillance is thus tied to cultural value as the privilege of looking "into places most television viewers never see" and is figured by Kois as meritorious—although such privilege requires access to a premium cable network. This is not a populist form of surveillance found within CSI or reality television, but one that already exists within audience hierarchies of class: here, Kois's review works to figure the series both as social metaphor and also as artistic totality. In this respect, the novel-function in the case of the third golden age is twofold. It announces the series through its critical legacies—its representation of race relations in a postindustrial urban metropolis, and its documentation of the failure of social institutions, including that from which it borrows its signature style, journalism and the press—at the same time that it brands itself as the successor to the Victorian novel. Yet the novel-function and the author-function are never discrete from one another, since they both precede the scene of production: *The Wire* is shorthand for David Simon, and vice versa.

A 2010 profile on the series and/or Simon in the *New York Review of Books* brings together all these questions about the labor of writing and the novel-function, although it concludes by unwittingly reasserting *The Wire's* televisuality. Lorrie Moore writes: "Certainly the series' creators know what novelists know: that it takes time to transform a social type into a human being, demography into dramaturgy, whether time comes in the form of pages or hours. With time as a medium rather than a constraint one can show a profound and unexpected aspect of a character, and discover what that character might decide to do because of it."[45] Moore positions *The Wire* as a medium of time and not necessarily of television or of literature (although the passage hints at a mixture of both). Her use of time as medium might be read as a larger point about genre, since the increased serialization that promotes such rich character development is primarily found in contemporary drama, though it is also (and has been for decades) present in the daytime soap opera, a genre that receives virtually no attention in journalistic television criticism (save for stories about its impending death). But I would read Moore's attention to time as a reinforcement of the televisual. The oppositional framing of medium and constraint endorses intermedial storytelling: *The Wire* may not be television (or at least not be "TV"), and it may also be novelistic (or at least hail from a shared logographic genealogy), but its temporality encompasses all these forms while also defining the series and giving it its greatness.

An Intermediality That Flexes Its Theoretical Muscles

From the perspective of a territorial television or media studies, a course such as "Storytelling in *The Wire*" might be looked upon antagonistically, as a cannibalization of a medium so easily appropriated into the preeminent cultural medium of university campuses. Such an adversarial claim, however, is not my goal here. While the absence of any media studies texts on the syllabus frames the body of knowledge delineated by *The Wire* as symptomatic of the text's content (race relations in neoliberal urban cities; the incorporation of surveillance technology into everyday life; the corruption within social institutions) rather than its form (serialized premium cable television), the invocation of intermediality as a hermeneutic practice reflexively necessitates this slant.[46] My focus, by contrast, is on the engagement of intermediality as an epistemological practice and on how the deployment of such a practice resonates with the perception of *The Wire* as the archetypal neoliberal novel. In other words, if *The Wire* must be perceived as literature in order to better extract its commentary on the effects of neoliberalism on social institutions (primarily but not exclusively relating to questions of urbanism and race), then these epistemic efforts foreground how intermediality itself is trenchantly a strategy of neoliberal ideology.

To begin, the concept of intermediality itself depends on a certain epistemological flexibility. Intermediality can be thought of as part of a lexicon of media nomenclature that describes the interaction between different media forms. This lexicon has diversified with the advent of digital technologies, as exemplified by Henry Jenkins's coinage of "transmedia storytelling," or by the various terms used to describe the distribution of commercial media across multiple platforms and technologies. Intermediality, as Irina Rajewsky has claimed, might be better thought of as an umbrella term, one that encompasses transmediality, multimediality, plurimediality, crossmediality, remediation, media convergence, and hybridization.[47] While Rajewsky offers a revised definition with which to group and categorize intermediality's various forms, she is not alone. W. J. T. Mitchell has argued that "there are no visual media," with a corollary argument that "*all media are mixed media*," though he does not dismantle medium specificity in such claims but rather permits a "more precise differentiation of mixtures" with respect to a medium's affective and formal language.[48] The racialized overtones of such figurations of intermediality—in which a medium is disseminated as it is "mixed" with other "related" media forms—are evident here, as is the alignment of metaphors of mixture with discourses of universality and "post-"media (or post-race) that resonate with late capitalism.[49] Intermediality is thus figured as stemmatically expansive yet incestuously combinative.

Intermediality also produces what Katie King has called *flexible knowledges* about the role of media today (a term owing a great debt to the work of Donna Haraway and women of color feminists on *situated knowledges*). Emerging in the 1990s with an emphasis on technological innovation and management discourses, flexibility was heralded as an improvement for the labor force, with management attending to the specific needs of individual workers, thus making labor itself mobile, fluid, and tailored to the needs of both company and worker (though, in practice, these flexible labor processes have also resulted in substantial increases in contingent and temporary labor positions). King uses the term as a preferred synonym for interdisciplinarity, and she cites an intellectual project shared with, among others, Haraway and Bruno Latour in which committed scholars "'break the Enlightenment Contract' that requires us to keep separate our purifications and our hybridities as the condition for practicing both."[50]

Rebecca Schneider also finds in the intermediality "a certain slipperiness and imprecision." For her, objects of study and the discipline from which scholars evaluate such objects require a diffuse research topography, and such a landscape refuses the limitations of medium specificity: "That there even should be a discrete 'field' of study of anything, or a medium that can be contained, is to presume a privilege of field over forest, plotting over foraging, agrarianism over nomadism, history over genealogy."[51] Schneider's emphasis on a "certain slipperiness and imprecision," encapsulated by failed performatives, hollow possibilities, and targeted misfires, suggests a particular indeterminateness, one that can be productively harnessed to legitimize lived experience as material, as in the case of feminist, anti-racist, or queer studies. It can also be read to practice a healthy skepticism with regard to medium specificity in general, as in her claim that "to accept uncritically a hard line between binarized divisions in our thinking, and to maintain *confident* distinctions between medial forms, hampers our abilities to expand the conditions of possibility for flexible ways of knowing."[52] Schneider does so out of a disciplinary call for performance studies to attend to its theater history, and she expands her rich body of work to other media forms such as photography, television, and cinema. I will return to the question of theatricality later on in this chapter but focus now instead on the desire for flexible knowledges framed here as a necessarily imperfect approach to opening up new directions in a field or paradigm of study. Tethered together, intermediality and interdisciplinarity expand the boundaries by which the production of knowledge occurs, even in a so-called knowledge economy in which the site of academic knowledge production occurs in an increasingly corporatized environment.

From the disciplinary perspective of literature and film studies, *The Wire* has attracted attention largely as a critique of late capitalism. Just as (following its conclusion in 2008) the series became a celebrity text within cultural criticism, so too has the series attracted attention from titanic figures in critical theory and in the study of the two intermedial forms to which *The Wire* gestures: literature and film. Specifically, a trio of scholars—Marxist cultural theorist Fredric Jameson, psychoanalytic theorist Slavoj Žižek, and feminist film theorist Linda Williams—claim that the series exemplifies artistic mastery while synchronically offering a commentary on social questions, and even on the ontological dimensions of the social itself ("the Real of our times," Žižek declares). While they do not reach similar conclusions about the series, most obviously with respect to its genre, some assumptions govern their inquiries, and these assumptions are not dissimilar to those accepted by journalists who practice a more popular cultural criticism. To be clear: I am not necessarily challenging any of these assumptions but rather documenting them and hoping to demonstrate the way in which the cultural value of both form and content determine each other and shape the affective reception of the series.

First, Jameson, Žižek, and Williams all believe that *The Wire* is innovative storytelling. For Jameson, the series "dramatically unsettles our typological expectations and habits by at once drawing us into an epistemological exploration that greatly transcends the usual whodunit"; through such revision and reinvention it becomes "original and innovative."[53] Žižek contends that *The*

141

Wire's writing room "represent[s] the nascent form of a new collective process of creation," with Simon serving as head "curator."[54] And the first part of Williams's monograph (in which she explores the media forms that are within *The Wire*, namely city desk journalism and television melodrama) is titled "World Enough and Time: The Genesis and Genius of *The Wire*," and she unabashedly owns her position as an adoring fan throughout her analysis.[55]

This, in and of itself, is not surprising; in what might be an analytical version of *Vulture*'s Drama Derby, the contributions of these three authors unquestionably assume the greatness of the series for a bevy of reasons, including its transformative impact on narrative form.[56] What is distinctive about their embrace of the series is its figuration of form as a remainder, an excess that makes *The Wire* so genius. A few sentences into his essay on the series, Žižek proclaims, "It is as if the Hegelian *Weltgeist* had recently moved from the cinema to the TV series, although it is still in search of its form. The inner Gestalt of *The Wire* is in fact *not* that of a series, as Simon himself has referred to *The Wire* as a single sixty-six-hour movie. Furthermore, *The Wire* is not only the result of a collective creative process, but something more."[57] And Jameson pinpoints such excess as Utopia "without [the] fantasy of wish fulfillment," which then "adds something to *The Wire* that cannot be found in most other mass-cultural narratives" (television, of course, is the predominant medium in which "other mass-cultural narratives" can be found).[58] Plot construction is figured primarily in Jameson's and Žižek's readings as "something" in excess of its actual form (serialized television), constituting an ironic disavowal. The arguments read something like this: *The Wire* is technically a television series, and yet is great in spite of this; it is great because of its innovative formal qualities, which may or may not already be present in serialized television, just not in the police procedural, a genre that the series intermittently occupies. As David Simon has said in an interview: "It could have—if we'd done everything wrong—been a cop show."[59]

I do not wish to accuse esteemed theorists such as Jameson or Žižek of being the academic equivalent of the parental activists of TV-Free America. But they—along with Williams, despite her background in film theory and her heightened attention to television's seriality—ascribe to the series yet another uninterrogated claim: that *The Wire* may, in fact, start out as a police procedural but becomes narratively excessive because of the crime story's offender, presented not as an individual criminal but as an institutional social whole. Compounding the "usual whodunit formula," Jameson identifies the ultimate culprit of the series as "a whole milieu, the world of a whole society or subsociety cordoned off from the peace-loving bourgeois civilian public (of whatever color)."[60] For Žižek, this is predictably the totality, which is "*always the ultimate culprit*" within the abstractions of late capitalism.[61] Thus the series is marked as realistic because it represents the complexity of social institutions in the service of capital, and at the same time, it is also in excess of that very realism. Crucially, this remainder falls in between delineated notions of form and content, so that the serial form both determines and is determined by the totality of institutional failure to challenge racialized capitalism.

"Something" More Than a Series: *The Wire*'s Televisual Form

If *The Wire* is a police procedural yet also something more than a police procedural, it becomes important to identify the formal characteristics of this nebulous "something," a something that is also more than television. Three specific features come to mind that contribute to this "something." First, each season of *The Wire* focuses on a social institution or industry: season 1 depicts the Barksdale drug trade; season 2, the trade unions at the Port of Baltimore; season 3, the city's political machinery and its relationship with the police department; season 4, the educational system; and season 5, the *Baltimore Sun,* Simon's former employer. This is not to say there is as a self-contained narrative within each season, but rather to assert that each season sheds light on a microcosm and component of a larger network of social institutions within Baltimore. The majority of the season's plotlines occur within such microcosms, and each season's narrative more-or-less engages with how that microcosm interacts with the other institutions central to the series (and thus to urban modernity).[62] We might speculate that this form is the progenitor of a broader resurgence in "anthology" dramas that tend to blur the generic lines between an ongoing dramatic series and a contained miniseries.[63] The topical emphasis allows for each season to be considered the unit of consumption, rather than individual episodes, which has the added effect of adjusting the series' perceived temporality in addition to contributing to the marketing of the program and the overall brand strategy of the network. Critics often talk about the series in terms of its seasons, ranking or hierarchizing them (the fourth season, in particular, receives the most critical praise). For instance, Jameson and Žižek both cite the second season as an example of the production of a nonphantasmatic Utopia (curiously, the second season is also regarded by critics and fans as the worst of all five seasons). *The Wire*'s second season focuses on the relationship between organized labor and the drug trade, with Frank Sobotka (Chris Bauer), the Polish American leader of the port workers, assuming a pivotal role in the season's narrative. Jameson's mobilization of the second season teases out the series' relationship to race, since the season is the "Whitest" visually (anchored around the White, ethnic, working-class longshoremen and stevedores), but he primarily uses it to illustrate the glimpses and pulses of Utopia that he sees as present within the disintegration of the labor movement. Sobotka's corruption, Jameson argues, is not about money and wealth, which one might expect from a corrupt labor leader, but instead about the promise of the redevelopment of the Port of Baltimore, which would lead to a more secure future for the union. In a version of Lauren Berlant's formulation of "cruel optimism"—in which she interrogates our attachments to objects and situations that ultimately harm us—Jameson frames the revitalization of the Port as the "idle dream that will eventually destroy [Sobotka] and his family"; but this utopian project is unique to the season, as the promise of the port disappears in the third season (replaced by a zone in the projects, called "Hamsterdam," in which a police major experiments with the legalization of the drug trade).[64] In other words, this utopianism is one contained by the temporality of the TV season.

Nowhere do Jameson and Žižek mention the technological and industrial changes to television that might also account for this shift in narrative organization: for example, the release of entire seasons on DVDs and, later on, uploaded to streaming distribution platforms, which helped to create the practice of bingeing discussed earlier. HBO was one of the first networks to pioneer the release of its original programming on DVD. In fact, more viewers saw *The Wire* through these means than when it originally aired; the series has been cited as one that suffered from low ratings yet became rediscovered through these changes in TV distribution in a delayed temporality. Nor do Jameson and Žižek acknowledge the fact that HBO broadcast the series free of commercial interruption, without needing high ratings or commercial sponsors to guarantee renewal. Because it was marked as "creator-centered" programming, the network gave more flexibility to the showrunner, which allowed Simon to develop controversial content that would never have evaded network censors.[65] (This does not mean that *The Wire* is devoid of corporate sponsorship, however: the athletic apparel brand Under Armour, a corporation headquartered in Baltimore, prominently features its logo on the police force's casual wear.) Yet in ignoring such issues, Jameson and Žižek frame the season as an organizational unit as proof of *The Wire*'s innovative storytelling, rather than as enabled by factors specific to its production as a television series.

Another formal feature of the series that contributes to its narrative remainder is its ensemble cast, with screen time devoted equally to the criminal organizations and the police tasked with apprehending them. For Williams in particular, this is significant because "there is no single, central protagonist in *The Wire* and . . . the series' focus on institutions and networks of relations, rather than on unique individuals and their personal will to power is one of its most remarkable features."[66] Such a move renders criminality elastic, as many members of the police force are shown throughout the series violating the law or are referenced as having done so at one point in their pasts, whether in the form of corruption, skimming money on the side, or manipulating the city's crime statistics (called "juking the stats" in the Baltimore vernacular). The blurry line between cop and criminal or between incorruptibility and crookedness is constitutive of the social totality revealed in the program and is the result of late capitalism's reorganization of social institutions in its own service rather than in the service of the law. Again, Žižek: "From the 'absolute standpoint,' it becomes clear that the (legal) system not only tolerates illegality, but indeed requires it, since it is a condition of the system's own ability to function."[67] The boundaries between the contingent subject positions of legal and illegal are flexible throughout the series, and the weight of institutional corruption persistently hangs over Baltimore as the series progresses, becoming a part of the series' atmosphere and thus a body of knowledge in its own right.

Williams goes further, sleuthing around the series' narrative in order to determine the "exact moment when *The Wire* becomes multisited and ceases to be an ordinary police procedural."[68] Through a close reading of the pilot episode, she focuses on the plotline of the mid-level drug dealer D'Angelo Barksdale (Larry Gillard Jr.), whose uncle, Avon Barksdale (Wood Harris), is the kingpin of the largest drug dealing organization in the city. Following D'Angelo's acquittal for shooting another dealer in the lobby of the high-rise project tower that he oversees, he is taken by other members of the Barksdale organization to a strip club for an apparent celebration, but this jubilance at evading the law's grasp is cut short. The function of the "law" is replaced entirely by the criminal organization itself, as lieutenants in the organization as well as Avon himself lecture D'Angelo on his supposed lack of discipline, and Avon subsequently demotes him to a less lucrative public housing complex. Williams recaps the scene to differentiate between a basic police procedural and *The Wire*'s narrative topos, finding the equal time spent on the criminal organization and its characters significant: "The equally important procedures of cops and dealers are thus established, from this moment on in the first season, as the two fundamental 'sites' of the series."[69] Equal time is thus foregrounded by Williams as the entrance into the different ethnographic "sites" of the series, since audiences must follow different narrative threads belonging

145

to a multitude of groups (cops, dealers, politicians, stevedores, journalists) within the institutional labyrinth that is Baltimore. Time is the measure by which character development occurs in serialized television: characters accrue diegetic experiences in successive episodes, opening them up to change. But the impact of *The Wire*'s equal time, I suspect, is not only the opening up of spatial universes but also the examination of criminality as a necessary part of juridical neoliberalism. Put differently, the series documents not only how the legal system requires illegality (in Žižek's terms) but also how these systems of illegality use the same structures of discipline and managerial organization as the legal ones do.

That the series dedicates equal time to cops and criminals and exposes this shared neoliberal logic does not, however, mean that it frames each of these groups in equal fashion. The series has been read as highlighting what Williams calls "networks of relations," or what Patrick Jagoda calls "a distributed system of social relations," that align "with the core insight of social network analysis."[70] The idiom of a network is attractive to any analysis of *The Wire* precisely because of how the series introduces multiple worlds of Baltimore (however temporally organized around the season as a narrative unit) through an impressively large ensemble cast. As a seemingly "networked" serial drama, the program is thus able to focus on the relationships between characters and institutions, as well as on nonhuman agents, primarily embodied through mechanisms of technological surveillance such as the eponymous networks of telephone "wires" that are used by police detectives to solve murders and map out Baltimore's drug trade. A networked optic also fastens the temporality of the series—its serialized complexity and its commensurate focus on social institutions and their criminal counterparts—to the language of spatial imaginaries. A number of readings of the series point to its capacity to "map" social relations: there may be no clear protagonist of the series in its many characters, but the atlas of social interrelationships constructed by the series locates the city of Baltimore itself as such a protagonist.[71] If Baltimore represents an imagined totality, then the series represents an effort to map, cognitively, the network of relations that govern the neoliberal city.

Yet it is difficult to reconcile such a structural grammar with televisual form. As a point of comparison, consider the similarities between *The Wire* and the generic soap opera. In the soap opera, an ensemble cast spanning generations offers multiple points of identification for audiences that hew somewhat closely to the lived experiences of its primarily female viewers. It would not be incorrect to say that soap operas share with *The Wire* the lack of a delineated protagonist in favor of a networked, expansive family. In most feminist work on narrative form, a single protagonist within a series is seen as rendering narrative pleasure as predominantly masculine and orienting the action toward resolution and closure; by contrast, as Tania Modleski has written, soap operas tend to follow more feminine textual strategies through multiple story lines that often resist narrative closure and audience omniscience.[72] The soap opera's commitment to the family (as character) and the home (as setting) can be seen in the metonymic associations between soap opera title and family, since, as any long-standing soap viewer will attest, "General Hospital" does not so much designate an actual hospital as it signifies the families that inhabit and rule the program's diegesis.

The Wire rearranges many of these associations and textual strategies: its characters are overwhelmingly male, offering not a variety of identificatory positions that mirror everyday life (despite their coding as "realistic") but instead figures designed to alienate and unsettle. And while the focus on institutions might share a similar function as that of the family in the soap, The Wire's institutions have narrower charges (for example to educate, to report, or to legislate) that do not have analogs within the structure of the family. The Wire is not a soap opera, despite sharing a number of its formal similarities. Williams proffers serial melodrama as central to the series' genius, as it simultaneously allows for the legacy of serial television while balancing character suffering with demands for a more equitable and just society (fulfilling a similar function to Utopia in Jameson's and Žižek's readings). In her monograph on masculinity and postmillennial television, Amanda Lotz makes scant reference to The Wire despite making a persuasive claim that male-centered serials constitute a mutated version of the soap opera for male audiences.[73] I would maintain that to call The Wire a feminist text (because it plays with this gendered form) or to claim that, through that form, it broaches substantial questions about the role of gender (even intersectionally with race), would be a stretch at best; in fact, its noticeable disinterest in broaching such questions appears to be a calculated attempt at distancing itself from the feminized connotations of serial melodrama. In other words, a networked structure allows the series to appropriate elements of a long-standing and influential televisual form while retaining the cultural prestige of a drama on a premium cable network.

The comparison to soap operas summons the third formal characteristic of The Wire that generates an extratelevisual remainder: the lack of a clear resolution to the series. In the ninety-three-minute series finale, a montage sequence depicts a number of characters making transitions to new careers: the mayor of Baltimore, Thomas Carcetti (Aidan Gillen), becomes the governor of

Maryland; Slim Charles (Anwan Glover) assumes his role as the head of the New Day Co-op and negotiates with the Greek suppliers of overseas drugs; the interracial couple of Cedric Daniels (Lance Reddick) and Rhonda Pearlman (Deirdre Lovejoy), formerly a police lieutenant and (briefly) commissioner and an assistant state's attorney, respectively, are seen in a courtroom in their new roles as a public defender and judge.[74] Younger faces replace the roles with which viewers are familiar, but in a largely cosmetic way, without changing the tenor or the description of social labor. The final montage makes clear that individual characters may come and go and may be promoted or demoted within Baltimore's institutional frameworks, but it is, in essence, business as usual. As Williams remarks, "It is not possible to portray this ending as either happy or unhappy, or even, for that matter, as much of an ending at all, if by that we mean something that does not continue."[75] *The Wire* ends, eerily, not that differently from how it began, thus prompting the question: Can it legitimately be thought of as conclusion? Jameson and Žižek, too, read business as usual through their own emphases. For the former, the television serial is incapable of producing closure, and thus the thrill of the chase endemic to police fiction is preserved in a move that consists of "the appropriations of these dissatisfactions for high culture or high literature."[76] For the latter, the shift from antiquarian tragedy to the tragedy apropos of late capitalism enables television to achieve narrative synchronicity with the rhythms of late capitalism: "The TV series as a *form* also finds its justification in this shift: we never arrive at a final conclusion, not only because we never discover the ultimate culprit (because there is always a new plot behind the current one), but also because the legal system is really striving for its own self-reproduction."[77]

Truthfully, as a scholar trained in television studies, the aforementioned verdicts on the ending that is not quite an ending puzzle me. Because television has traditionally been conceived as having two primary forms, the episodic series and the continuing serial, narrative resolutions have always tended to occur on a "micro" level, through clinches, architectural beats, and repetition. In the case of a serial narrative such as a soap opera, the decentered nature of the narrative and the melodramatic logic of accumulation and crisis resist the imperative to wrap up multiple and complex story lines completely—as if such a task were even possible in the first place!—in favor of concluding *in medias res. The Wire* stubbornly ends in a manner similar to a soap, but again, there is something different about its refusal to provide closure. Here, such a refusal is cited as evidence of the series' televisuality, and yet this comes across without the same polarizing feelings as those elicited

chapter four

by the endings of previous HBO quality series such as *The Sopranos*, in which Tony Soprano sits down with his family in a diner, the screen cuts to black for ten agonizing seconds, and the audience cannot definitively tell whether or not the antiheroic mob boss is alive or dead.[78] The rote criteria by which narrative closure is assessed by viewers boils down to their affective response to a series' final moments. That *The Wire* ends ambivalently, documenting the status quo, testifies to the habitual reorganization of capital in a way that generates pleasure. There is no ambiguity regarding business as usual, and without gestures of radical change, the spectator cannot *not* be disappointed (this is the point, after all, of Jameson's formulation of Utopia without wish fulfillment). The ultimate effect of such inconclusiveness is the status of the text itself; the series ends as formally incomplete, yet this does not feel inherently unsatisfying, and completion is a feeling projected as a totality by the spectator onto the series as a whole.

Taken together, these three formal characteristics mask *The Wire*'s status as a televisual text and position it instead as "something" that escapes the formal restraints of television. This "something" is not easy to define, nor is it given precise form by cultural and scholarly critics. Rather, this "something" is the narrative apparatus by which intermedial appropriation occurs: *The Wire* is always borrowing from police procedurals and from soap operas while branding itself as an improvement over each of these long-standing television genres. This is not to say that *The Wire* has not successfully taken generic, architectural, and temporal tropes of television's past and reincorporated them into a series that elastically accommodates multiple TV iterations, but instead to assert that through this flexibility, it is able to transform itself into the artistic apotheosis of the narratives of networked capitalism.

Dickensian Aspects, Dickensian Affects

I have avoided delving too deeply into the nitty-gritty of *The Wire*'s multiple narratives out of an insistence on treating the discourses about the series as texts in their own right, perhaps even as texts that metanarratively exceed the program itself. Such a treatment, however, risks missing the forest for the trees. While critiquing the discourses surrounding *The Wire* might explain its neoliberal aspects, it does not explain why what is frequently called one of the best television series of all time is oversaturated with graphic depictions of gang violence, institutional racism, drug use, and urban poverty, depictions that would not have been permissible on network television precisely because of their explicit nature. What is it, then, that makes *The Wire* uncomfortable? To

149

the majority of the scholars I have cited, the series does not traffic in affects of discomfort or disgust because of its extratelevisual remainders; as something always greater than the televisual medium, the spectator's attention is drawn to the failure of totality and the totality of failure and not their uncomfortable consequences. If the persistent metaphor of *The Wire* is "the game," originally referring to the drug trade but extending to all social institutions, then game logic might be employed by audiences to shrug off feelings of discomfort, for agonism foregrounds competition and valorizes playing the game at all costs. Just as many characters within *The Wire* express a desire, however momentary or fleeting, to exit "the game" yet find themselves trapped within its circuits or willingly returning to it out of perceived security and comfort, so too might audiences overlook the series' unsavory representations in favor of the game's—that is to say *The Wire*'s—tautological pull.[79]

What are the cardinal affects of *The Wire*? In identifying possible answers, genre emerges as a compelling framework: generic categories can be used as descriptors of a series' formal qualities (e.g., sitcoms are typically shorter than dramatic series) or industrial practices (e.g., reality television programs typically utilize nonunion and freelance production crews), but they also describe how a series *feels*. In Lauren Berlant's words, "Genres provide an affective expectation of the experience of watching something unfold, whether that thing is in life or in art,"[80] Berlant then proceeds to claim that neoliberal culture might suffer from the "waning of genre," which can be corroborated by genre's own flexibility and ability to mutate and mix in order to be transformed into something else (a situation tragedy, a dramedy, a docusoap, among others). The consensus among critics and scholars has been that *The Wire* is a series belonging to realism, overdetermined by the weight of its "whole": the large ensemble cast that liberally borrows from "real" characters and actors (the character of Snoop in particular is cited to this effect).[81] The all-too-real portrayal of street life and a minimalist aesthetic all promote the series' claims to realism, though here the primary metric of what constitutes "realism" is authenticity.

Yet realism is also dependent on affect. In her exploration of televisual realism on *The Wire*'s parental antecedent, *Homicide: Life on the Street*, Bambi Haggins compares that series' "commitment to realism" with the "RealFeel" indexes commonly used in meteorological reports. Even though a thermometer might read one temperature, these indexes take into account other factors such as humidity and wind speed to speculate as to what the temperature "feels like," which often leads to a different number than the "official" temperature.[82] The paradox of realism—that it signifies a direct connection to reality when it actually *simulates* the characteristics of reality—is also present in communication theorist Alice Hall's theory of a continuum of realism, in which a series feels *real* to an audience based on three elements: plausibility (whether the events could have happened), typicality (whether the characters are identifiable), and factuality (whether the plot is based on actual events that occurred).[83] To claim that a series is realistic is to accede that it is on some fundamental level plausible, typical, and factual, even though these criteria are still subject to a large degree of manipulation by producers and to a range of affective responses that help support or subvert the realist form.

The Wire's own reflexivity also contributes to, rather than undermines, a sense of realness. Specifically, the way in which the series frames ethnographic worldviews—networks that require cognitive mapping by the audience— allows for realism as it mimics the detective work performed in the series' narrative. Realism as a generic feeling or as affective category thus signals a process not dissimilar from the mystery structure of the police procedural. Formerly circumscribed by empirical assumptions about the nature of reality, notions of realism's sensorium have depended on the material conditions of the representation's referent. Yet television studies have always argued for the perceptive qualities of realism, as in John Fiske's claim that a program is realist "not because it reproduces reality, but because it reproduces the dominant sense of reality."[84] This reading of realism is one that is without any sort of ontological loyalty to the empirical or the actual conditions of the world; it is instead dependent upon the various discourses that construct a sense of reality. Even before the immense popularity of the genre of "reality television," then, the consensus among scholars of television was that television programs generate, rather than emulate, reality, forcing audiences to interpret texts actively in order to situate themselves in reality's produced effects.

Such an understanding of realism can productively complicate the approach here to both media culture and cultural theory. For example, the study of realism complicates the strand of affect theory that insists on cleanly detaching affect from ideology, as evidenced in the cognitive materialist approaches to affect.[85] If affect is indeed nonsignifying and presubjective, as this strand maintains, it operates on an entirely different level from the processes by which meaning is made. What to do with realism, then, which effortlessly traverses visceral responses and the material conditions that condition our affective expectations? In *The Wire*, realism is often cited as the feeling that the institutional failure endemic to Baltimore is accurate, that the deck is stacked against People of Color, and that, as Williams notes, "the rules are not the same for everyone."[86] The affective dimensions of realism are, in this case,

the spectator plagued by white guilt

a sense of synchronicity but also one of uncertainty, as the affect rests in the space between referent and representation, to some extent asymptotically approximating one another.

Another kind of liminal space also exists in discourses on *The Wire*. Realism may account for the visceral function of totality within the series (its inability to offer viewers Utopia), but the series also includes subject matter that, in other contexts and genres, would attract attention for its ability to cause spectatorial discomfort. *The Wire* is one of the most aesthetically violent series of its time, yet this violence is routinely minimized by audiences, critics, and scholars. One could chalk up such dissonance to the contexts of audience reception, in which a White (male) spectator is presumed, a spectator who carries with him a certain amount of privilege that inoculates him from having to take seriously the visual representations of systematic violence and police brutality against People of Color, the homeless, and the urban poor of Baltimore. In Amanda Lotz's study on the "male-centered serial" dramas that are practically synonymous with original prime-time cable programming, routine and graphic violence is a common, though unexplained, theme, with the vast majority of the antihero protagonists engaging in criminal activity that necessitates violence or in which violent actions lie within the series' narrative path. So much of this violence is highly racialized, yet this, too, becomes disavowed by many of the discourses surrounding the third golden age. That so many of these series aired on HBO, the leader of premium cable content, allows for more explicit content, as Janet McCabe and Kim Akass have demonstrated.[87] Rather than being acknowledged as such, however, violence in postmillennial quality television is recoded as *risk*: it risks both alienation and spectacularization lest programs be accused of being gratuitous. Gang or turf warfare, present in male-centered serials such as *The Sopranos, Breaking Bad, Sons of Anarchy, Oz,* and *The Wire,* highlight interracial tensions that frequently result in gun violence and the death of a crew member, but this occurs through the series' subsumption of the discourse of criminality.

To provide a specific example of this, let us consider an episode from the final season of *The Wire* that negotiates between realism, staged violence, and intermediality. The fifth season of *The Wire* interrogates the role of the press in reporting and manufacturing the events that mediate interactions between the various institutions that the program has explored. As perhaps textual revenge on the newspaper at which David Simon was once employed, the *Baltimore Sun,* the season introduces a reporter, Scott Templeton (Tom McCarthy), who is shown to fabricate stories entirely and repeatedly in order to advance his career. Unassuming yet ambitious, Templeton further lies when suspected of lying by city desk editor Gus Haynes (Clark Johnson), and his prose is consistently described as overwrought and embellished, descriptors that fit well within the purview of critical writing on *The Wire* as a whole—despite its claims to realism. The plotline of Templeton's fictional news stories runs parallel to detective Jimmy McNulty's attempt to secure resources for homicide detectives tasked with solving the row house murders credited to Marlo Stanfield's (Jamie Hector) crew and for the off-books efforts of Lester Freamon (Clarke Peters) to catch Stanfield through an illegal wiretap. McNulty's plan, conceived while intoxicated on the job, is to create a public belief in a serial killer in Baltimore who ostensibly targets the homeless of the Southern District. Through an elaborate code of a red ribbon (the killer's "signature") and the technique of postmortem strangulation, McNulty's fictional serial killer eventually attracts the attention of *Baltimore Sun* reporter Alma Gutierrez (Michelle Paress), but the story is unable to gain serious traction in the press. Then, the fictional killer meets the fabricating reporter in a bizarre bit of synchrony. As McNulty is about to fake a phone call from the killer, Templeton fakes receiving such a call, and the crossed wires and Templeton's resulting story generate the appropriate amounts of media buzz and further the goals of each: McNulty is granted a wiretap, which is then redirected and masked so that he and Freamon can tap Stanfield's phone, and Templeton becomes a cause célèbre among the national press.

Of all the story lines present in *The Wire*, McNulty's fake serial killer is to some extent the most "unrealistic." McNulty occupies an interesting position in the series diegesis insofar as he is figured, problematically, as the protagonist of the series, even when his story line receives little narrative attention.[88] In an episode appropriately titled "The Dickensian Aspect," McNulty finds himself in the position of needing to fake another murder in order to secure his wiretap.[89] To achieve this end, McNulty must change his scheme and alter the serial killer's profile while preserving his signature. So, rather than leaving the bodies to be found by the police with a red ribbon tied around the wrist, the killer announces that he will dispose of the bodies himself, never to be found, while providing the public with a photo of the victim sporting a red ribbon. McNulty uses a mentally ill homeless man, Larry (William Joseph Brookes), as a pawn in this strategy, photographing him with the ribbon and then driving him to Richmond, Virginia, and giving him a stolen identity card and $100 to assume a new life in a local shelter.

Violence, here, functions on a delayed or deferred register as McNulty is merely dressing up and appropriating acts of violence that occurred in the past and that are therefore forgotten. Whereas riddling the men of the street

153

with bullets has been, over five seasons, cast off as quotidian and just a part of the game, the noticeable absence of violence in McNulty's scheme stands out, perhaps, for its affective discomfort. The combination of the homeless man's Whiteness and his recognizable mental illness renders him a completely innocent victim, even if one takes the Žižekian road of seeing the entire ensemble as collective victims to a totality corrupted by late capitalism. McNulty first encounters Larry stumbling down the middle of a traffic-clogged street carrying a sloppy cardboard sign. The camera primarily serves as McNulty's point of view, providing a mid-shot of the busy street with Larry centered yet perspectively distant, and with the camera slightly tilted to the right, emulating the curvature of McNulty's car and its impact on what he is thus able to see. The minor difference in angle situates the shot as realistic, as it establishes a direct identification with McNulty and therefore introduces Larry as mediated through the gaze of the police. But it does more than this, too; it exaggerates Larry's already contorted appearance due to his mental illness, thereby introducing him as unstable on embodied, psychological, and textual levels. From the start, the camera frames Larry as not completely level, rendering him both narratively harmless (his exaggerated gestures signifying his mental illness rather than criminality) yet not narratively irrelevant. He occupies, then, a precarious middle space, one in which he "slips through the cracks" (due to cuts to state-sponsored care) but is harmless (and White) enough not to merit the wrong kind of attention from the police.

Indeed, in subsequent scenes Larry is always positioned at a significant angle, tilted away from the vertical axis that typically structures human posture. On the one hand, the askew body of a mentally ill homeless man triggers the episode's RealFeel index, as nowhere does Larry appear to be stable nor capable of supporting himself. This is a common visual framing technique throughout the series, in which characters who lack the means to improve their situation due to institutional failure are often blocked with their heads and upper bodies inhabiting an ever-so-slight tilt. Compare other shots in which Larry appears—when he accompanies McNulty to the former Major Crimes Unit where Freamon is running the wire; when he rides with McNulty to Richmond, Virginia; and when they arrive at the shelter—with a scene in the same episode in which Detective Bunk Moreland (Wendell Pierce), the "good po-lice" investigating the row house murders, pays a visit to Raylene Lee (Shamika Cotton), the addict mother of Michael Lee, a youth who aspires to become an enforcer in the Stanfield Organization. In every shot, Larry and Raylene are both framed askew, a clear nod to their economic and cultural statuses as broken citizens, asymmetrically excluded from the brief flashes of

4.3 Larry's first appearance. *The Wire*, "The Dickensian Aspect," Season 5, Episode 6.

Utopia that the series may offer. Implying impaired motor skills, the almost-slouching positions of the mentally ill and the addict render these subjects even more abject than the other citizens of Baltimore; they are not even allowed to play the game, and their destinies have already been authored by neoliberal governmentality.

But on the other hand, the positions of Larry's and Raylene's bodies seem to be to be saying much *more* than the mise-en-scène implies. They may boost the RealFeel metrics of plausibility and typicality that signal an authentic representation, but unlike many of *The Wire*'s characters left behind on the social margins, they are types: simplifications of populations that the series attempts to address throughout its five seasons. What is striking about the very minor characters of Larry and Raylene is their lack of complexity, their resolute commitment to inhabiting the execrable spaces of nonresistance. Here, in their *unrealistically* simple forms, they stand out for their total defeat.

Through the incredibly brief introductions to these characters that the series affords us, I suggest there emerges a countertheatricality in their askew realism, a dissonant form of becoming that strikes me as most uncomfortable. Moreover, this countertheatricality relies upon an assumed White guilt on the part of its audience. By *countertheatricality* I mean a theatricality that fails through a stubborn realism, a theatricality that stands out for being *too* real. As entrenched types, Larry and Raylene push realism to its extremes, blind to the glint of the moderated and contained affective impulses of winning

4.4–4.9 Larry and Raylene, side by side. *The Wire*, "The Dickensian Aspect," Season 5, Episode 6.

4.10 *Saturday Night Live*'s skit "How's He Doin'" discusses why White people idolize *The Wire*.

the game through constant hustle. In their landmark study of theatricality, Tracy Davis and Thomas Postlewait position the term as constitutive of the "inevitable 'failure' of mimesis to produce a true likeness."[90] Theatricality cannot pretend that it is anything but artifice, and as scholars of theater and performance have wrestled with its critical purchase, calls to theatricality have emphasized its productive capacity as failure or as a failed performance. A countertheatrical realism can be located in Larry's cameos in *The Wire*'s fifth season, for he barely registers at all, and comprehensive studies of the series (such as Williams's) do not even recognize him by his character name. He is a "failed character" precisely because he indexes realism all too well, making him—as he slips down visually, narratively, and affectively—impossible to root for within the fannish reception of the series.

As Schneider asserts, there is something very infelicitous about intermediality, something that can be gleaned from the slip. "Becoming is in precarious (un)balance," she writes, "tilting not necessarily forward or backward but very possibly falling to the side."[91] We might further clarify that the precarious subjects of *The Wire* are beloved by critics and scholars because they may be the victims of late capitalism; in addition, our melodramatic identifications prop them up, offering a sort of utopic promise through affective investments in the text. And yet, when the series presents us with characters that cannot receive such investments—characters who in fact are deprived of recognition—audiences are jolted from their secure positions as mere witnesses to late capitalism, becoming complicit in the characters' abjection and enabling them to fall to the side.

If I leave the impression of being an unsympathetic reader of *The Wire*, moving beyond a cynical repudiation of its discursive intermediality to exhibiting a hostility toward its ethnographic imaginaries, I can only respond that this is not my intent. According to Alison Landsberg, historical filmic or televisual representations of historical events carry the potential to connect a viewer to some other person while maintaining a sense of difference (as she explores, for example, the way in which a viewer can access a historical figure's memory through representation). Landsberg uses this form of "prosthetic memory" to claim that it is through this unique form of spectatorship that the structuring conditions for empathetic identification may be located. Sympathy, she writes, is different from empathy: it assumes a "preexisting connection between sympathizer and sympathizee."[92] Empathy, by contrast, negotiates compassion and distance, an imagination of another's situation and an approximation of the affects involved while recognizing differences in subjectivity. I read *The Wire* and the discourse surrounding it—a discourse that, as I have hoped to demonstrate, runs dangerously close to assuming the status of a metanarrative about race and neoliberal urbanism—empathetically, cognizant of the difference between myself as a White male spectator and the predominantly minority viewpoints expressed in its story lines and by its characters. To become entangled in *The Wire*, to become lost in its network of characters, risks the distance necessary to understand the racialized spectatorship inherent to the series and its reception.

As an example of this, consider a 2013 *Saturday Night Live* (SNL) sketch, "How's He Doin'?," that parodies a Sunday morning political news program geared entirely toward the political feelings of African Americans. "How's He Doin'?" features ensemble members Kenan Thompson and Jay Pharoah playing the program's host and Ronny Williams, a writer for *Ebony* magazine, respectively, with guest host Kerry Washington as Alice Rogers-Smith, a political science professor at Spellman College who is clearly modeled after former MSNBC commentator Melissa Harris-Perry. The joke of the segment is relatively straightforward: no matter how much Black Americans may disagree with then-president Obama's policies, they will still support him unequivocally. Within the banter typical of political punditry, however, the following exchange occurs (with the 2013 National Security Agency wiretapping scandal as the context):

[RONNY WILLIAMS]: Well personally, I thought White people would be more excited about having their phones being tapped considering how much they like *The Wire*.

[HOST]: I like *The Wire*. They LOVE *The Wire*.

[WILLIAMS]: They love it! I mean White people watch *The Wire* acting like they doing us a favor.

[HOST]: It's like you watch *The Wire*, you ain't volunteering at a school.

[ALICE ROGERS-SMITH]: Have you ever been to a party and a White person approaches you with a smile and you know they just want to talk about *The Wire*?

[HOST]: I had a White friend who wrote episode recaps of *The Wire* on the internet. I mean, can you imagine—he would watch it, write about it, and then other people would read it!

[ROGERS-SMITH]: Did you read it?

[HOST]: I didn't need to read it. I watched it. I mean, that would be like somebody telling me about my day.[93]

How might this innocuous bit, not even the primary joke of the sketch, better inform our understanding of *The Wire* and its reception? The joke implies that White people are the target audience of the series and constitute its most diehard fans. It resonates with George Lipsitz's critique of the series as a magical Uncle Tom story for the neoliberal age, in which White audiences are recruited "to inhabit subject positions as analysts and managers of urban life, not as interactive participants of it."[94] Lipsitz does not contradict the adoration of the series as great television in his reading of the series, yet he criticizes it for operating within neoliberal logics of cultural appropriation; in his words, "the 'otherness' portrayed in *The Wire* remains fully enclosed with a white spatial imaginary" in which the ghettoizing effects of White flight, racial segregation, and the failure of public housing are largely left uninterrogated. If *The Wire* provides viewers with an entrance into its ethnographic imaginaries, the snl sketch appears to imply that its vocal fans and lauding critics are almost always White, and that the ethnography resembles a colonial anthropology in which the social ills of urban life are voyeuristically presented without accounting for their historical causes.

Linda Williams defensively rejects such criticism, claiming that because the series does not pretend to exist in a colorblind world and because the series is generically melodramatic, a Black racial imaginary sits at the series' cultural center. For her, "*The Wire* is too aware of the neoliberal hollowing out of discourses of rights to follow this trajectory of racialized victims and villains."[95] Williams seems to discount Lipsitz's criticism about the progressive capacities of the series because, she argues, his reading relies on an older form of racial melodrama in which White villains oppress Black victims and vice versa. *The Wire*, she believes, undoes this circuit through refusing to keep score in the "game" of racial victimhood. She acknowledges that the series may fall into the trope of "stuff white people like," but because the series depicts a majority-Black world, she is able to dismiss this criticism, as "it makes a big difference if a majority-white audience is invited into a multisited world that is itself majority black."[96] Yet just because the majority of the characters in the series are Black does not mean that the series depicts a "majority-black world," let alone a Black perspective; the fact that the series was created and produced by numerous White men for an affluent premium cable network augurs the selective framing of Baltimore as a metropolis symptomatic of contemporary race relations. The discomfort experienced by a Black person at a cocktail party when approached and asked to talk about *The Wire* remains a blind spot in Williams's otherwise astute observations about the series.

Indeed, if Williams's own reflexively defensive posture is any indication here, it provides the link between intermedial appropriation and cultural appropriation: just as the series is something more than television, so too is it something more than Blackness. Williams's account, along with those of Jameson and Žižek, is a sympathetic account, presuming spectatorial similarities based on a perceived common politics. As a totality, the series presents neoliberal rationality as a given, as having "won" the game, and indeed, as having written the new rules of the game. *The Wire* partially fits the criteria of what Wendy Brown has eloquently described as the left's tendency to cling melancholically to the tenets of liberal democracy, insofar as its tempered realism finds its heroes in characters such as Frank Sobotka (for Jameson) and Omar (for Williams).[97] Instead, I have offered an empathetic reading of the series through characters like Larry or Raylene, who inhabit neither romanticized positions of nostalgia for a Baltimore past nor middle spaces of near-survival under the rules of the late capitalist game. *The Wire* may not, ultimately, be the kind of "television" text that I, as a scholar of television, want it to be, although it approaches this through these alienating characters. Intermediality offers *The Wire* the opportunity for it to be held accountable to the histories of other media forms, genres, and styles, but it also entraps it in the epistemic affects of neoliberal ideology. The final montage of the series, showcasing changes within generations yet also the resistance to overall change, culminates in McNulty driving Larry back to Baltimore from the Richmond shelter. As networked television that is also post–network television, *The Wire* brings Larry home, and in doing so, perhaps, pushes television—and television studies—in new, slippery directions.

the spectator plagued by white guilt

five

the woke spectator

misrecognizing discomfort in the era of "peak tv"

THIS BOOK HAS ADVANCED the argument that in the years immediately following the new millennium, American television's formal, aesthetic, technological, and generic changes helped introduce cultural affects of discomfort into spectatorial lexicons. Throughout, I have emphasized the rather innocuous ways that this transformation of a formerly family-friendly medium was accomplished, a process that enabled viewers to use the discursive language of new televisual structures as a means to understand and process their discomfort, thus turning it into pleasure. Of course, other events from the 2000s to the 2010s also normalized structures of feeling punctuated by precarity and discomfort, such as the attacks of September 11, 2001, and the subsequent enaction of a semipermanent "war on terror," or the Great Recession of 2008–2009 and the subsequent adoption of semipermanent austerity measures. In these examples, discomfort manifests on a scale of intensity while remaining symptomatic of embodied pain; while 9/11 and the Great Recession were certainly paradigmatically impactful, they discursively assume milder forms of discomfort when compared to earlier historical markers such as World War II and the Great Depression or later ones such as the COVID-19 pandemic.

Because of its historical dependence on liveness as a key mode of address, television is thought to be a medium of the present; this temporal self-styling combined with its mass reach and assumed audience allows for a certain affective seduction, with the medium frequently serving as a preferred and perhaps fetishized object for generalizing and registering changes to national moods and cultural expressions of citizenship. Television's commitment to seasons-long storytelling all but guarantees a certain messiness when constructing a historiography. For example, while the 1980s are remembered in popular and academic histories of television for the cultural dominance of the prime time soap (and with Ewing and Carrington fashions aesthetically symbolizing the decade's glamour and indulgent consumption), it is important to remember that *Dallas* was on the air for fourteen seasons overall, and it premiered almost three years before the start of Ronald Reagan's presidency, which metonymically designates that decade's political, cultural, and economic values. Similarly, in Jane Feuer's periodization of televisual Reaganism, she reads the 1993 corporate takeover of *Metropolitan Home* magazine as the stylistic end of the "Reagan era" five years after he left office.[1] The work of periodization appears messy and contradictory, especially when television is involved, since the medium inherently holds an ambivalent commitment to historical specificity. Episodes of television, even those disseminated digitally, have specific broadcast dates that immediately date them in television's chronology, yet long-running and popular series inevitably complicate such easy historical framings. (To reiterate a point made in this book's introduction, many popular programs of the 2000s—sitcoms such as *Friends* and medical procedurals such as *ER*—do not approach discomfort in the same way as do the collection of programs and genres read in my subsequent chapters.) In his own slightly self-deprecating introduction to periodization (in which he declares it to be "theoretically unfashionable"), Fredric Jameson refers to Raymond Williams's idea of the "'residual' or 'emergent,'" or what Jameson calls the "full value of the exceptional": the moments of rupture within "the sharing of a common objective situation" definitive of a historical period.[2] I take Jameson's larger point to mean that socially shared structures of feeling serve as barometers for understanding the work of periodization, which requires the keen abilities of differentiation as it plays out across technological, cultural, political, and economic registers. Periodizing postmillennial television is messy work in part because multiple emergences twist, combine, and cluster in ways that resemble television's own sprawling narratives that now constitute the norm for telling a story.

163

In one sense, this is a question of scale: television has simply gotten bigger with respect to screen size, narrative complexity, and choice in programming. In *Television Scales*, Nick Salvato astutely states that the "central, unresolved, and finally irresolvable challenges for television studies are indeed scalar ones."[3] Salvato is interested here in using scale as a methodological framework for approaching television's historicity, the glut of content in the contemporary television landscape, and "the many different scales at which one may investigate the ontologically dense and variegated field that is 'television.'" His rigorous and admittedly weird fascination with scale opens up a rich deviation from the traditional categories of classification within television studies—scales of genre, industry, medium of transmission, series, and so on—and explodes television's energetic intertextuality and television studies' interventions into association, remix, and flow in the service of what he describes as "partial constellations" of televisual objects and texts reflective of "messy medial complexities." Periodization is one such scalar problem, and the discomfort risked in asserting the changes to television and in reading those changes as I have throughout this book has not gone unnoticed. Moreover, writing and revising this manuscript during the late 2010s made the act of periodization even more scalarly complex, as it became clear that televisual discourses have been changing dramatically again. This shift might be registered through a more honest reflection on my own research methods; analyzing discomfort—even in the playful way this book projects—requires watching so-called uncomfortable content over and over again, thus enacting its own self-fulfilling hermeneutic of acculturating discomfort. This was not, however, a dulling feeling, one that foreclosed empathetic identifications with the *Girls* or *Intervention* seasons watched on screen, but rather something that resembled its opposite: a hyperawareness of discomfort and its cultural and political effects. What happens when spectators suddenly perceive the crystallization of structures of feeling despite television's vast fragmentation? Is recognizing this state of emergence akin to an awakening to television's uncomfortable affects?

While the work of periodization is inherently imperfect, the television of the latter part of the 2010s *feels* radically different from that at the beginning of the decade. I end this book therefore by considering the changes to television throughout this decade and by describing how viewers' relationship to discomfort has changed as well. Put differently, if for most of the early twenty-first century what I have called postmillennial television acculturated its audiences to the rhythms of discomfort common to late capitalism, I argue here that toward the later part of the 2010s, television and its audiences began to become aware of the debilitating effects of televisual discomfort: in short, that TV became *woke*. I explore several factors that precipitated such an awakening: the transformation of streaming services into Hollywood studios, a dramatic increase in the number of original series for viewers to consume, and the presidency of businessman and reality television host Donald Trump. Together, these factors allowed cultural minorities (as well as their allies) more access to television as a storytelling platform while empowering them to politicize the medium through renegotiating the affective parameters of televisual representation itself. This emphasis on the political is intentional and requires assessing the capacity of television to serve as an instrument of meaningful political change. And thus, television's thorny problems of scale rear their hydra-like heads yet again: scales of pleasure in relation to those of discomfort, or scales of entertainment in relation to those of politics.

Hence, I turn to woke TV as an affective corollary to what has been called the era of "Peak TV" that helps to produce a woke spectator. The former uses wokeness in primarily discursive and aesthetic ways, while the latter refers to a process by which viewers watch a television program and, due to that program's politics of representation, feel an investment in social justice. Woke spectatorship thus describes an affective mood that conceives of political action primarily in terms of awareness and shifts in perception. The benefits of woke spectatorship appear in its orientation toward, rather than its explicit intervention in, social issues: for many reasons, woke spectatorship will not generally motivate viewers to turn to the streets, most obviously because that would require those viewers to look up from their screens. This system places faith in the interpretative work of decoding—amplified by postmillennial television's fan cultures and discursive platforms—as a crucial part of social and political change, although some forms of interpretation clearly do more work than others. Woke TV announces an engagement with social justice partially as a result of the intense strategies of narrowcasting brought on by cable and premium cable broadcasting systems as well as by streaming platforms. Woke TV generally depicts the politicized and intersectional narratives of young People of Color, women, queers, and persons with disabilities with a certain level of financial backing and celebrity status previously bestowed by Hollywood on straight White males. As an extension of, and perhaps as the inheritor to, what Mary Beltrán has defined as "meaningful cultural diversity," woke TV has the capacity to capture on a representational level the nuance and complexity of prejudice.[4]

But it equally has the capacity to become commodified by the media industries—such as in MTV's casual definition of the term as "being aware"— in a branding move reminiscent of broadcast networks' aggressive attempts to court Black viewers in the late 1980s and early 1990s, which led to record numbers of sitcoms featuring Black casts and increased opportunities for Black

165

creative talent, as Kristal Brent Zook and Herman Gray have historicized.[5] Gray's work on Black television of this time in particular invites a comparison to television's wokeness of the late 2010s. In *Watching Race*, he identifies many Black sitcoms of the late 1980s and early 1990s as pluralist, noting that these programs emphasize how Black families often have the same problems as White families. Broadcast networks such as NBC and Fox developed these programs as part of a larger branding and marketing strategy to court Black viewers instead of pursuing equitable representation.[6] But Fox then switched its strategy in the mid-1990s and replaced those programs with live sports broadcasts and animated programming that targeted young White males, a move that is symptomatic of what Gray terms a refusal to acknowledge Black viewers as an enduring or significant market demographic. In the following characterizations of woke TV and woke spectatorship, I note that what holds these series together are not the formal, stylistic, or narrative structures common to our understanding of genre or even the explicit attempt at courting audience demographics consisting of cultural minorities, but instead the production of a woke structure of feeling demonstrative of a shared cultural politics of televisual representation.

While identifying the contours of woke TV and woke spectatorship should make apparent television's explicit acknowledgment of discomfort in the name of political change, naming wokeness actually does little to enact meaningful political change. As Elizabeth Davis asserts, "the logic now, at an increasingly mainstream level, suggests a cultural politics of wokeness is (sometimes clumsily) supplanting previous schematizations of racial feeling among the politico-cultural center/left."[7] Wokeness is thus premised on an affective misrecognition, in which the framing devices that yoke together media consumption, social and cultural expression, and political change are often mistaken for each other, encouraging a slipperiness of scale. In particular, it allows for White spectators to participate in conversations about social justice and to claim affective pleasure through this participation and commentary. "Misrecognition" thus describes a number of assumptions about the television of the late 2010s: that the rapid increase in content (commonly referred to as Peak TV) necessarily leads to more meaningfully diverse representations of cultural minorities, that this television indexes political associations and actions in ways that it had not previously, and that wokeness can be applied to a number of performative viewing positions and across a variety of televisual texts, fandoms, and discourses.

I first assess the capacity of Peak TV—the period following the third golden age dissected in the previous chapter—to satisfy audiences by analyzing its invocations of food and consumption metaphors, before interrogating its capacity to represent cultural minorities through a sustained examination of wokeness as a viewing position. I then note the ways in which, following the 2016 election of Donald Trump to the presidency, woke TV both minimized and emphasized discomfort as a form of political expression and protest, drawing from examples such as *Queer Eye* (Netflix, 2018–present) and *The Handmaid's Tale* (Hulu, 2017–present). Finally, I end this conclusion by turning to the example of transracial performance in two satirical (and metafictionally surreal, though in very different ways) comedies—*30 Rock* (NBC, 2006–2013) and *Atlanta* (FX, 2016–present)—in order to consider what, exactly, is uncomfortable about televisual wokeness, and how this discomfort is shaped by further aesthetic, technological, and generic changes to the medium. Focusing this last part on comedies that frequently wield racial satire, allegedly in order to expose the persistent structures of white supremacy, allows me to close this book's study of televisual discomfort by examining television's capacity to represent racial counterpublics, building on earlier historical legacies of the 1970s (as in historical miniseries such as *Roots*) and the 1990s (as in the "multicultural" programming found on new broadcast networks such as Fox and, later, UPN and the WB). Thinking about both the possibilities and limitations of such an affective construction of wokeness, I ask how this engagement with the political—even when appropriated by the media industries that produce it to attract audiences—reacts to the questions of alienation and resistance that are central to minoritarian survival under late capitalism, tracing scales of discomfort and pleasure throughout television's multiple emergences.

Misrecognizing Peak TV for Quality

One way in which TV changed again during the mid and late 2010s is through a substantial increase in its content. By August 2015, FX president John Landgraf notoriously announced the era of Peak TV at a Television Critics' Association (TCA) press tour, provocatively claiming that there was "simply too much television" on air.[8] The famously outspoken executive based his diagnosis on the number of original scripted series in the United States for the 2015–2016 programming season, which for the first time exceeded four hundred, and he predicted that as more and more players entered the SVOD (subscription video on demand) market, the deluge of programming would stretch the attention spans of audiences thin, leading to a bursting of the so-called content bubble. Landgraf's speech made waves throughout the trade press for acknowledging something of an open secret within Hollywood: that with the

167

entrance of streaming players such as Netflix, Hulu, and Amazon, "television" (defined here through its content) became much bigger. Audiences not only had many more options to choose from, but they were also expected to invest more time outside of watching programs, both through the immersive and complex diegetic worlds enacted by many serialized programs and through participation in television fandoms, now normalized throughout nearly all of TV's genres and forms. While Landgraf's predictions did not necessarily come to fruition in the years immediately following his comments (for the 2019–2020 season, the last full season before the global COVID-19 pandemic upended the media industries, an estimated 532 programs aired, double the number from ten years earlier), I find his periodization of Peak TV striking for the metaphors and logics he deploys in his projections for the future.

Landgraf's comments emphasize size and scale within not only media consumption but also appetite. Audiences have normalized binge-watching across convergent platforms while generating massive amounts of big data in the process. Of course, to "consume" media is not only to acknowledge its exchange-value but also to bring it from the public into the private sphere, ingesting it in distinctly personalized rituals of watching and making meaning. Landgraf defined Peak TV in terms of glut and affluence, telling audiences a few weeks later at the Edinburgh TV Festival, "It's like winning a pie-eating contest every day . . . in some ways, we're choking on our own abundance."[9] Such a metaphor clearly recalls the logics of bingeing-and-purging discussed in chapter 2. Here, according to Landgraf, spectators would presumably gorge on SVOD content until they reached a limit, when mediated storytelling would cease to pique any interest at all. (Following this logic, cord-cutting could evolve into cutting out television entirely.) The reliance on metaphor was naturally amplified by television critics, who applied it to other noticeable patterns across the industry. Writing in 2016, television critic James Poniewozik noted, "Today's great fattening, like so many trends in TV now, is in part the influence of streaming TV. The only thing limiting the length of a Netflix or Amazon binge show is your ability to sit without cramping. The menu is bigger, and so are the portions."[10] Poniewozik's rant against television's "case of gigantism" is essentially one of quality versus quantity, with too many "plus-size" individual episodes stretched out in ways that feel "bloated," imperiling the health of the story. He channels the descriptors of debility common to so many parodies of television spectatorship, calling back, like intertextually constructed muscle memory, to the example of *Portlandia*'s Doug and Claire in pain on their couch as they binged DVDs of *Battlestar Galactica*, as discussed in chapter 1. Taken together, "too much TV" would seem to incapacitate both television's content (since good story suffers from "excess fat") and its audience (who thus cannot get a full night's sleep).

This incapacitation hinges on the trope of the couch potato, which links the overconsumption of television with unproductivity and poor health. Michael Litwack has incisively argued for the "centrality of obesity to the status of television in an age of accelerated convergence among various media forms," reading obesity television as both a cultural technology and an ideological apparatus in ways similar to this book's theorization of addictive spectatorship.[11] Both approaches wield television's representational and analogical capacities to pressure its excesses, investing in this excess as a way to displace obesity and addiction in nontelevisual registers. For Litwack, this displacement illuminates the biopolitical imperatives that scaffold the structural excesses identified by critics like Poniewozik, with television's "cross-platform facility and increasingly promiscuous flows across various media forms" amounting to a televisual "workout plan." Yet despite such digital attempts at making viewing time productive through the empowering rhetoric of participatory culture, Peak TV temporally endangers its audiences through its abundance. This application of Lauren Berlant's theory of "slow death"—in which systemic and racialized inequities wear out the obese subject, making it impossible for them to recoup interruptive agency—emphasizes the entanglement between the routine and the enfeebling, making the obesity crisis principally a temporal crisis, insofar as the unproductive and ordinary time of daily life becomes life-wasting and debilitating time as well.[12] And while it may appear to be a facetious stretch to weave the phenomenon of Peak TV together with the brutally difficult social and physical consequences faced by obese people every day, press accounts already have made such a comparison. In 2018 *Vanity Fair*, for example, ran the flippant headline "Is Peak TV Slowly Killing TV Critics?," with Nicole Sperling's story accompanied by a graphic depicting an exhausted TV critic on her bed surrounded by screens.[13] While Sperling allows for readers to roll their eyes in mock sympathy for the critic unable to watch all of the fall season's pilots on time, she also reveals the language with which television critics understand their labor, likening the glut of content to emergency room triage or, in one bizarre comparison (courtesy of then-*Variety* critic Maureen Ryan), to water torture. And while much discursive space exists between the overworked critic falling behind on new programs and the couch potato aimlessly channel-surfing in a vegetative state, they share enough metaphorical signifiers that make clear the effects of televisual excess.

While Peak TV's quantity of content summons to mind a never-ending buffet of options that overwhelm and ultimately debilitate its audiences, other

169

5.1 *Vanity Fair*'s overworked Peak TV critic. Illustration by Zohar Smith.

food metaphors are at work here as well. Peak TV represents the televisual equivalent of junk food, hastening the viewer's descent into obesity. Implicit in this argument is the relation between quantity and quality: the excesses of Peak TV have come to replace the period formerly known as television's golden age. The signature characteristics of golden-age television as described in earlier chapters—such as the prevalence of antiheroes, intense serialization, and increased production budgets for higher-quality aesthetics—still remain a vital part of the television landscape for both producers and audiences. But they no longer represent the medium's attempt for artistic legitimation and no longer depend upon intermedial comparison (as in claims to a "cinematic" or "novelistic" television) in quite the same ways. By the end of the 2010s, for example, the industry's penchant for comic book adaptations and popular TV reboots added many more programs to television's roster without necessarily focusing on previously powerful metrics of quality, including those associated with diversity and representation. This resonates with Aymar Christian and Khadijah Costley White's trenchant demands for more "organic representation," defined by them as "when systems and institutions empower those who have been historically marginalized not only to appear in their stories but also to own and fine-tune narratives, marketing, and distribution."[14] Christian and White tie these metaphors to the status of cultural minorities, refusing to allow quantity to dictate quality; following this logic, Peak TV's expansion of original programming does not necessarily lead to more authentic representations of cultural minorities, which have been often categorized through the unproductive binary of "good" or "bad" representation. Gleaned from the authors' call for organic representation is a transformative overhaul of production culture, an infrastructural investment in local production communities that also grants ownership to creators. While Christian and White's description of "locally sourced" representation mirrors those within gastronomic culture that claim organic diets as inherently healthier (while also being significantly and often prohibitively more expensive), it opens up the space for the excesses of Peak TV to be recuperated through the lens of representation—or through an awakening that requires changing one's habits of consumption entirely.

Misrecognizing a Buffet of Diversity: From Peak TV to Woke TV

Peak TV's deployment of food metaphors makes sense only in light of the technological changes and subsequent changes to television form and industry practices enabled by SVOD. The massive investments in original programming by new Hollywood players Netflix, Hulu, Amazon, and Apple (as well as by existing studios Disney and Warner Bros., social media companies such as Meta, and smaller outlets such as Sundance Now) constitute the main growth in the number of original scripted series. Following Landgraf's declaration of the phenomenon of Peak TV, his own network, FX, shared research on this statistic during its TCA press tours; however in 2019, Landgraf told reporters that because streamers are so intertwined with the traditional television ecosystem, it would no longer measure this volume by distributor (evidenced by Disney's announcement that, following its 2019 acquisition of 21st Century Fox, it would make Hulu the official broadcast home for FX).[15] The 2018 data, however, showed a 385 percent increase in the number of original scripted dramas, comedies, and limited series distributed by SVOD platforms between 2014 and 2018, while those distributed by basic cable actually declined over the same time period (by 17 percent); this made 2018 the first year that streamers comprised a plurality of all original scripted series.[16] Importantly, this exponential growth did not wholly represent attempts by streamers to legitimize their presence within Hollywood through traditional means such as awards. In 2013, for example, Netflix's first three original scripted dramas were designed to attract industry recognition through established Hollywood names such as David Fincher and Kevin Spacey (*House of Cards*) and Eli Roth (*Hemlock Grove*). These names bestowed legitimacy on the Silicon Valley corporation gone to Hollywood, perhaps as a way to distract skeptical critics from its Big Tech roots, since the corporation has famously promoted its massive use of data collection and algorithmic analysis in its development process, enabling it to manufacture an audience for a particular series based on previous indicators. Writing in *Salon* at the time, Andrew Leonard outlined the differences between Netflix's business strategy and legacy TV, finding that "unlike the traditional broadcast networks or cable companies, Netflix doesn't have to rely on shoveling content out into the wild and finding out after the fact what audiences want or don't want. They believe they already know."[17] Over the following few years, audiences appeared to want the streaming corporation to act more like television, and Netflix added partnerships with Marvel and reboots of nostalgic series to its programming strategy, replacing traditional metrics of quality (which became applied to only a fraction of its original scripted series) with mass production. That Netflix and other SVOD platforms could quickly attract writers, actors, and other creative talent across multiple genres—from Oscar-nominated documentary films to telenovela-inspired melodramas—spoke to these corporations' seemingly unlimited pockets and a financial imperative to spend intemperately in the name of growth—just like their contemporaries throughout the technology sector.

chapter five

While this "more is best" strategy has been read by many for its effects on spectatorial agency, I wish to focus here on two of its ideological and discursive effects. On the one hand, the aggressiveness by which SVOD services fused data analytics with traditional mass fare (some of Netflix's aforementioned reboots included legacy TV staples such as multi-cam sitcoms, for example) emphasizes the logics of personalization and predictability across the increasingly homogenous metrics of lifestyle and generic taste present in late capitalism. Much attention on the digital economy's structure has focused on its replication of Deleuzian control societies, in which individuation serves as a marker of user expression and the aesthetic and affective promise of customization is sold to the customer in exchange for increased data surveillance. SVOD services that make primary use of this surveillance can then offer tailored guides to assist their users in navigating their massive catalogs, in the process suggesting to the user that they have unique tastes in media content, when, in fact, the opposite is true: a user is just one of many subscribers whose tastes, these companies believe, can be manipulated.[18] This strategy of personalization and control manifests at the level of individual user through an experience of comfort, either through predictability (in which the SVOD introduces the user to a series that they then like) or through familiarity (in which genres and forms previously liked are again emphasized). Moreover, it also leverages the affective intimacy engendered by customization to equalize various viewing experiences despite their interchangeability; consider, for instance, the Peak TV resurgence of the prestige limited series, which is based on its perceived viewer accessibility (for audiences intimidated by long-form serialization) and its flexibility (for A-list movie stars who can "do" television—and possibly win an Emmy—without a multiyear series commitment). Combined with interface design, this simulation of the gig economy's larger characteristics proffers Peak TV not strictly as a buffet of content for the gluttonous consumer but as a personalized experience of consumption, not unlike the individually packaged ready-made meal plans devised by nutritionists. Yet as prescient work by Neta Alexander has suggested, in pursing both content and aesthetic design that emphasizes the comfort of the audience, SVOD platforms can actually be quite restrictive on the level of taste and, importantly, on the level of the formation of taste, denying "the importance of contingency, serendipity, and potentiality."[19] What interests me most about Alexander's analysis of the linkages between algorithmic development within streamers and the focus on subscriber "comfort zones" is the idea that watching more content in fact inhibits the viewer's taste, or the possibility of growing one's taste. While this model might approximate

173

the woke spectator

cynical and hostile attitudes toward mass culture that hearken back to the Frankfurt School, it also carries some hints of what Anna Watkins Fisher has elegantly formulated as the "coercive hospitality" projected by corporations in which the appearance of openness and choice disguises user manipulation and exploitation through the appealing rhetoric of virtualization.[20] Of course, mass culture has always been exceptionally successful at advertising itself as the cure to the problems that it creates. But SVOD platforms' careful construction of a comfort predicated on the uniqueness of predictability also masks the increasing amount of audience investment and labor required to sustain such levels of comfort.

On the other hand, a common discourse about streaming-driven Peak TV is that it has led to more stories told by cultural minorities. This diversity comes from the fact that programs made by SVOD services are not beholden to the same standards of accountability—both in terms of content and in terms of securing commercial sponsorship—as those on broadcast or pay cable networks. Taking great caution to note that most of the time corporate streamers behave like legacy media companies in their appropriation of diversity, Aymar Christian advances such a discourse through the analytic of "open TV," or the ways in which digital and networked distribution practices allow independent voices to be heard: "The Internet brought innovation to television by opening mass distribution to those excluded from legacy development processes, fostering new ways of creating and marketing series."[21] Christian takes corporate streamers to task for their window-dressing invocations of "diversity," exhaustively noting the discrepancies between how streaming original series portray certain identities and the composition of their casts and crews, finding these new studios on par with legacy broadcasting. This argument can be read alongside a growing body of work that crystallizes and explodes the concept of televisual representation in the 2010s, at a time in which technological change has radically changed common understandings of both television and representation. Kristen Warner's useful term "plastic representation," or representation defined by its artificiality and malleability, is surprisingly transparent about its dependence on cultural appropriation, which serves as the extraction process in her geochemical analogy. "An operational definition of plastic representation," she proffers, "can be understood as a combination of synthetic elements put together and shaped to look like meaningful imagery, but which can only approximate depth and substance because ultimately it is hollow and cannot survive close scrutiny."[22] Warner's antidote to plastic representation is an aspirational strategy of cultural specificity that refuses to conceive of representation in binary terms of positive (through respectability politics) and negative (through pernicious stereotypes), and that requires attention to the degree of complexity and nuance contained within characters and plotlines. Like Christian, Warner wants audiences to engage differently with their televisual content by rejecting forms of television that feel mass-produced and artificial (and both follow this purging with desires for more "organic" television). While Warner's cursory manifesto on plastic representation casts a broad net, focusing on Hollywood writ large rather than on specific segments of the media industries (such as broadcast networks or SVODs), its very emphasis on mass production requires the structures of Peak TV enabled by digitization. The artificiality of Peak TV can also be gleaned in Taylor Nygaard and Jorie Lagerwey's tropological clustering of "Horrible White People" programs, which represent specific images of liberal Whiteness on TV throughout the 2010s that sport credibility within mainstream feminism and that incorporate occasional nods to racism or racial dynamics. Nygaard and Lagerwey identify two ways in which "Horrible White People" series reflect Peak TV: first, they tend to be the select programs within Peak TV that aspire to the quality designation by critics and that win awards for their aesthetic and formal innovation; and second (and more importantly), they "reflect Peak TV's insatiable demand for and attempt to use those quality aesthetics to appeal to ever-diminishing audiences of White, relatively affluent, tech-savvy, educated, urban viewers described by traditional discourses of quality audiences."[23] This self-reflexive feedback loop, in which White audiences watch well-made series about extreme stereotypes of White people who fail despite their privilege, reinforces white supremacy by creating a kind of White echo chamber that affirms the exceptional experience of being White.

Both the notion of plastic representation and the figures of "Horrible White People" evoke a strained relationship to discomfort. Both are openly transparent about their ability to be condensed into the language of cultural stereotypes and thus can easily trigger spectatorial discomfort (wincing at the appearance of yet another sassy gay or Black friend, for example) while using the fact of their hyperawareness as a protective shield from that discomfort. Indeed, plastic representation is insidious because it prioritizes artificial affects full of false comfort; representations of cultural minorities with the saccharine taste of aspartame might be delicious to some palettes, but their surface-level comforts evade accountability in their simplicity. Yet pleasure or comfort are themselves evasive terms in this work on representation. Warner is clear that in rejecting plastic representation she does not want "to disparage the joyous effect and identification that arise from seeing a version of one's self on screen; to the contrary, I believe the desire should be expanded, not only to

175

see a version of one's self on screen but for that identification to resonate and connect with the histories and experiences of the culture that the character's body inhabits."[24] Since plastic representations are capable of generating pleasure within audiences through their quality aesthetics and high production values (as Nygaard and Lagerwey also note), they are eminently enticing, and their capacity to distract or to maintain surface-level criticism—to dupe the viewer into a state of mere contentment—is what ultimately sustains their artificiality. This calls in Sianne Ngai's sharp observation that "gimmicks are fundamentally one thing . . . overrated devices that strike us as working too little (labor-saving tricks) but also as working too hard (strained efforts to get our attention)."[25] Having identified plastic representation as one of Peak TV's primary gimmicks, Warner's solution is twofold: for audiences to "demand more" from the content they consume, which would then presumably lead to producers investing more in complex representations imbued with cultural specificity; and for audiences to demand more from pleasure itself, raising their standards when it comes to what is considered comfortable, uncomfortable, and in between. Nygaard and Lagerwey are equally as transparent about how, for many White audiences, the act of categorizing a cycle of "Horrible White People" programs requires a betrayal of the identifications at the heart of such pleasure, pointing to the endurance of Robin DiAngelo's schema of "white fragility"—itself invoked in many woke television programs—as a psychic obstacle that may prevent such betrayals from occurring. Nygaard and Lagerwey therefore evince a sincere desire for (White) readers to renegotiate the pleasurable attachments they may have to "Horrible White People" series in order to identify and eventually dismantle their attending structures of white supremacy.

All the approaches toward representation described here so far make an implicit (and aspirational) assumption about the audiences of Peak TV: that viewers have a moral imperative to seek out meaningful representation that neither artificially renders the complexities of minoritarian life nor participates in the gimmicky faux dismissal of White privilege. These approaches thus rely on a shared temporality in which audiences consume problematic content (presumably because Peak TV makes such consumption so easy) up until they realize that these representations are unhealthy or unsatisfying, at which time they will change their consumption habits, such as by seeking out "organic" or locally produced content. These inquiries into the challenges of representation in Peak TV anticipate a spectator who becomes "woke," and who will be mobilized as an audience member accordingly. Such a strategy that emphasizes viewer agency is reminiscent of public campaigns promoting environmentalism in the 1990s, which encouraged individual consumers to reduce their energy consumption and to recycle, rather than holding larger corporate actors accountable for pollution. The end result is primarily affective: a sense of feeling good about one's consumer practices.

As numerous dictionary definitions attest, "wokeness" denotes a state of alertness to surrounding examples of injustice while also asking its receivers to take action, even if through the mere incitement of a political consciousness within the individual subject or viewer. Yet this action is also one of continuity and persistence, as in the term "stay woke," which emerged in early twentieth-century political writing and music to signify the need for Black people to be aware of the dangers of Jim Crow, including physical harm and death by lynching. In their useful history on the term, Aja Romano notes its instability—especially when used by audiences of varying political ideologies, such as in right-wing media ecosystems—and spreadability, tracing the phrase's integration into the mainstream cultural imaginary across direct actions such as the 2014 Black Lives Matter protests in Ferguson, Missouri, and the 2017 Women's Marches and across popular culture, from Erykah Badu's 2008 song "Master Teacher" to Jordan Peele's 2017 film *Get Out*.[26] Wokeness describes a moment of transformation, implying a forward-looking present of maintained vigilance, since the term itself presumes the occlusion of its opposite (after all, outside of Fox News one never hears of someone becoming "unwoke" and thus presumably less sympathetic with respect to issues of racial justice). At the same time, however, it also describes a shorthand for a liberal politics reflexively focused on social justice. Following the Ferguson protests, Romano asserts, "woke" began to be associated with social justice movements specifically concerning group identity (such as Black Lives Matter and #MeToo), and as it assimilated into the vernacular, it was easily critiqued for being an empty signifier, used ironically to refer to the ways in which well-meaning White folks consume cultural difference in mostly problematic ways. This use of wokeness becomes deployed pejoratively, often mediated through modes of address that call attention to its own construction. Lena Dunham and White people who love *The Wire* (to name two examples from this book) may indeed be "woke," but often occupy such positions insincerely and awkwardly, with a calculated political brand aimed at maximizing revenue or soliciting industry acceptance. Like plastic representation, this sort of wokeness elicits within spectators a hollow feeling, a pleasure that is really not any pleasure at all. This construction mirrors that of former president

177

Obama's paternalistic comments about the oversized importance of woke-ness to college-age youth, in which he defined being woke as the feelings of pleasure that come from calling out someone's actions on social media.[27]

But if wokeness has a certain flippant orientation and an increasingly cyni-cal or nihilistic attitude toward structural inequalities, it is in part because of the term's polyvalence. As a mode of attentiveness signifying vigilance to forms of injustice, "wokeness" is also an irreducibly past tense of "wake," an experience of sudden consciousness or an awakening. In her masterful theorization of Black subjectivity and cultural production, Christina Sharpe explodes the polysemy of the "wake" to reposition "Black being in the wake as form of consciousness" rather than abjection as a means to better understand Black modes of resistance.[28] For Sharpe, the wake refers simultaneously and aggregately to the track left on the water's surface by a ship, the vigils held beside the bodies of the recently deceased, and the lines of flight emanating from a firearm, in addition to the aforementioned state of sudden conscious-ness. Because Sharpe is writing beside and occasionally against Afropessimist schools of thought in her deconstruction of the term, all definitions inevitably return to slavery and the ways in which Black life persistently makes meaning from the social in the wake of Black death. While I do not wish to minimize her overall argument in my comparisons to the popular cultural texts of Peak TV, I am interested in how, for Sharpe, the wake represents the after currents or specters of slavery and its many brutalities, containing, regulating, and punishing Black lives often in ethereal and immaterial ways. The wake an-nounces itself as affective atmosphere, one coalescing somewhat predictably following moments of rupture and crisis, and one that makes visible the forms of oppression that capitalism wants forgotten.

I want to hold onto Sharpe's important formulation of waking, of being awake, and of staying woke as affective atmosphere. While this element of wokeness appears to conform to Raymond Williams's definition of a structure of feeling, Sharpe's rejoinder links the condition to the culturally specific past histories of Black people; to "stay woke" is to acknowledge the existence of those who previously were not woke or of those who did not wake up to protect themselves adequately from the threat of racial injustice. If televi-sion's present-day temporality, its insistence to be consumed in the present as a chronicle of the present, allows it to "thrive on its own forgettability" (as Mary Ann Doane famously asserted), in what ways does television's own woke awakening in the late 2010s carry the ghostly traces of TV's past within?[29] Moreover, how is televisual wokeness presented as a form of viewer resis-tance? To answer these questions, I now turn to two readings of the political

chapter five

possibilities of woke TV: first, its engagement with the ideological politics of the Trump administration, and second, its engagement with the racial politics of its past.

Misrecognizing Woke TV as Political Resistance

If American audiences began to get woke toward the end of the 2010s, it was because the national political culture emphasized discomfort on all levels of political participation. While the technological changes to television that have enabled a diverse and fragmented Peak TV undoubtedly changed the audience's relationship to discomfort throughout the decade, for Americans, larger affective forces spurred by the 2016 presidential election elevated national levels of anxiety, dread, and abject irritation, often regardless of party affiliation. While mental health discourses and resources (both pharmacological and cultural) increased significantly throughout the decade, for many Americans the election and the subsequent Trump presidency exacerbated already challenging and semipermanent states of agitated stress. Media outlets picked up on this as early as six months before the election, with *Time* magazine running an article with the headline "Stressed? Blame the 2016 Election" and featuring tips on how to exercise political engagement without the expected burnout.[30] One interesting recommendation was to avoid watching the presidential debates, in part because they could not be fact-checked in real time; yet those audiences who did not heed author Elizabeth King's advice and who tuned in to the second presidential debate witnessed a tableau of extreme discomfort, with Trump pacing around the stage (there were no lecterns, as it was a town hall–style debate) and presenting aggressive posturing in an attempt to disrupt his opponent, Hillary Clinton. Following that debate, in which Trump responded to the infamous leak of the *Access Hollywood* tape in which he fantasized about nonconsensually assaulting women by inviting many of the women who accused former president Bill Clinton of sexual misconduct to sit prominently in the town hall audience, television critics and political pundits emphatically commented on the discomfort of the spectatorial experience, with CNN enlisting a quote from an anonymous "senior TV executive" that "people are repulsed by [the election] now."[31] Repulsed by the election, or by its mediation? It appeared that live news coverage of political events—an exemplary TV genre that has long manufactured gravitas in the name of propping up the stability of the family and nation—had become unwatchable.

One could write an entirely separate book theorizing Trump and the mediations of his presidency as "uncomfortable television," but that is not my task here. Instead, I am interested in tracing how television responded to this transparent amplification of toxic affects. Lynne Joyrich has incisively analyzed the ways in which Trump harnessed the "logic of reality televisualization" in his quest for the presidency, foregrounding the importance of the genre's emphasis on branded celebrity, melodrama, and tribal individualism to contemporary political culture.[32] This appropriation of reality television to the political realm—invited by many pundits and journalists who observed that Trump equated governing the country with hosting a reality series—changed the public's relationship to reality television: if turning on the news meant that the viewer would be exposed to the excessive affects of reality television (with the former president regularly shaming and confronting others in melodramatic spectacle), why watch Simon Cowell do the same on *America's Got Talent*? As some forms of discomfort began to feel all too real in the Trump era, reality television thus began to feel less uncomfortable. For example, in the popular Netflix series *Tidying Up with Marie Kondo* (2019–present), the eponymous host and organizing consultant begins each makeover process by blessing each house in a respectful ritual rather than by taking homeowners to task for having too much unneeded stuff and diagnosing them with a psychological condition, as in *Hoarders*. Gamedocs still aggressively promote strategies of entrepreneurial labor, but the substantive discussions of intersectional oppression and adversity now common to award-winning series such as *RuPaul's Drag Race* (Logo/vH1, 2009–present) result less and less in the contestants' sensationalized breakdowns and more and more in reconciliation, solidarity, and praise, utilizing rhetorical tropes traditionally found in the after-school special to address some forms of cultural difference.

To me, this shift in discomfort is best adumbrated through a cursory examination of the makeover program *Queer Eye for the Straight Guy* (Bravo, 2003–2007) and its streaming reboot *Queer Eye* (Netflix, 2018–present), both of which feature a team of queer male–assigned individuals who make over those in need of stylistic help. The original series, which aired during the reality boom's experimental period, often underscored the difference between the lack of style of heterosexual masculinity and the aspirational style of the "metrosexual" to structure its narrative. Each episode would open with the collective generation of shame from the "Fab Five"—each of whom was responsible for an element considered key to well-rounded style: grooming, fashion, food and wine, decor, and "culture" (haphazardly defined throughout the series' original run)—as they ransacked the sad apartments, closets, and refrigerators of Tri-State–area straight men, frequently piling up aesthetically displeasing objects as if they were building bonfires. To some extent, the desexualized and comic affects of the Fab Five mitigated this typical deployment of shame in the reality makeover, as many scholars have pointed out.[33] Yet while the program was lauded for normalizing the presence of queerness (here mostly defined by White gay men) on television through promoting a subculture of gay and metrosexual style in the mainstream, that did not necessarily precipitate making over the project of conventional masculinity, as Brenda Weber has astutely noted, since the program's use of shame extended to the women who failed to prevent the straight guy's slovenly habits.[34] And while the sin of heterosexual style was not rendered in explicitly life-threatening terms—unlike the viscerally gross and dangerous forms of decay and clutter in other makeover programs such as *Hoarders*—*Queer Eye for the Straight Guy* used the same aesthetic practices as *Hoarders* in its opening sequences, employing surveillance-style overhead shots and quick cuts to belabor the incompetence of its subjects. The series premiere, for instance, opens with the Fab Five in their suv, pouring over the dossier of their first makeover subject, Butch, whose style elicits the kind of casual insults found in the queer subcultural practices of reading and throwing shade. The makeover subject is introduced to the audience solely through his stylistic flaws even before he appears within the camera's frame.[35] Once the Fab Five arrive at Butch's apartment, they spend over eight minutes picking apart everything, but in most of this sequence Butch himself is edited out of the frame or only shown very briefly, allowing the camera to dwell on these markers of scummy straightness. The cumulative effect of these early reality TV aesthetics is to cement these identifications and to remind Butch of his inadequacies—the Fab Five repeatedly yell how "ugly" and "disgusting" Butch's taste is as they examine dirty jockstraps and bathtub hair—but both Butch and the viewer are able to displace these identifications onto the larger social target of heterosexual masculinity.

By contrast, the Netflix reboot has been praised by critics specifically for being more inclusive and diverse, since the recipients of makeovers have been broadened beyond straight men to include women and other queer people. This difference is highlighted immediately in the opening credits: "The original show was fighting for tolerance, our fight is for acceptance," fashion savant Tan France explains, while food and wine guru Antoni Porowski states, "My goal is to figure out how similar we are, as opposed to how different we are."[36] In so doing, the reboot also participates in making over the makeover form itself: rather than shaming the heterosexual subject for their unfortunate lifestyle (and demanding that they conform to a gay-inflected metrosexuality), the reboot highlights stylistic failure as a barrier to one's sense of self, such as

181

through an individual's emotional vulnerability and mental health. While this transformation at the level of program form more clearly allies the makeover subgenre's discourse of self-improvement with standard neoliberal ideologies, it also uncannily internalizes discomfort as the source of individual obstacles to optimization rather than heterosexual masculinity writ large.

Indeed, *Queer Eye*'s opening sequence begins not with the on-the-go (and lesser image quality) shots of an SUV interior but with a sequence that takes place on a studio set. Here, in documentary close-up, the new Fab Five comment on what an honor it is to be a part of the series and on the reification of reality television's power of celebrification in the wake of mainstream cultural LGBT acceptance. We are two minutes into the series before the episode introduces its makeover subject, Tom, and this is not even done through the original series' segments of confrontation and critique, as Tom appears to the audience not at his presumably messy residence but at a colorful and bright Mexican restaurant where he is a regular. Rather than immediately shaming Tom for his bad style, *Queer Eye* asserts itself foremost through the metrics of queer celebrity, reminding its audience that the new Fab Five are not only experts in their respective lifestyle areas but that they are also gay icons. Michael Lovelock has read in this expansion the indexing of a compulsory authenticity that displaces "the heteronormativity of traditional broadcasting" with "a world view in which a shared investment in the value and importance of authenticity, of being true to one's apparently true, essential self, binds publics and people, over and above any formal criteria of sexuality, gender, or identity."[37] Lovelock is correct in noting this shift within television broadcasting and in tying it to the acceptance of queer subjects into the cultural mainstream. I would modify his analysis by emphasizing how the difference between the two series stems from its intervention into the practices of reality television as much as through compulsory authenticity's alignment with late capitalism's strategies of media brand management. As social media branding became the primary locus of self-expression throughout the 2010s (and as Trump emerged as both online troll- and commander-in-chief), it perfected the process by which individual expression became absorbed into mass consumption. *Queer Eye* differs most from its counterpart through the cultivation of its "woke" sensibility—one review of the reboot dubbed it "Queer Eye for the Woke Guy"—that filters out shame and humiliation in favor of blandly inoffensive stagings of self-empowerment.[38] Like an Instagram feed that repackages individuality to conform to the tastes of the digital marketplace, *Queer Eye* marshals this sensibility as a comfort to viewers, a distraction from the affective chaos that marked the consumption of news and political programming during the late 2010s. Wokeness, therefore, becomes not a wary call to guard the viewer from potential harm but acts here instead as a security blanket that invites viewers to dissociate into perfunctory performances of allyship.

Another way in which television used wokeness to comment on the Trump presidency was by deploying discomfort as a political call to oppose the administration. I am thinking here of how the figures at the heart of *The Handmaid's Tale* (Hulu, 2017–present), the oppressed child-bearing handmaids who are kept as subordinate slaves in a hyperpatriarchal religious society called Gilead, emerged as an aesthetic symbol for the feminist resistance to Trump. First appearing on television in 2017, the series attracted instant attention for its graphic depictions of brutal rape and violence, with stylized sequences in particular depicting the monthly rituals when the men belonging to the privileged caste within Gilead, called Commanders, rape their handmaids while their wives watch (and during which the wives occasionally participate by holding down the handmaid). Brenda Weber has compared *The Handmaid's Tale* to torture porn—in part through exhaustively listing the types of violence within the series' first season—but makes a crucial clarification: that the systemic rape and violence is not gratuitous but in fact central to the series' narrative.[39] Weber ends her brief assessment of the series' reception, which so far consciously avoided any invocation of the Trump presidency, by enumerating a number of important questions about how spectators receive such uncomfortable scenes of brutality: "Why, I wonder, do viewers need to see all these atrocities before they might take the patriarchy seriously? Absent these visceral dystopic horrors, does quotidian patriarchy also seem less horrible? Do you have to drown before you can be woke? . . . Perhaps the excesses of torture porn are the only way to shock ennui into empathy and to truly make America great again." Here, Weber aligns the experience of watching the series, of being exposed to scene after scene of gruesome violence, with the explicit purpose of being politicized. Again, wokeness is the end product of the spectator's renegotiation of discomfort, an empathetic attitude that slyly references Trump's campaign slogan (itself appropriated from Ronald Reagan's successful 1980 presidential campaign). Under this logic, spectatorial discomfort has a purpose: it is generated not just for the sake of advancing the narrative but for the possibility of promoting structural political change.

As a symbol of the oppression of women, the handmaid also quickly came to stand for resistance to the Trump administration's attempts, in concert with those of conservative state legislatures, to enact further restrictions on choice and access to reproductive healthcare. Within a month of the series'

5.2 "Handmaids" protesting in Washington, DC. Photograph by Aaron P. Bernstein for the *New York Times*.

premiere on the streaming service Hulu, activists clad in red robes and white bonnets protested the attempted congressional repeal of the Affordable Care Act in Washington, DC, as well as the efforts to allow employers in Missouri to discriminate against women who take birth control and to restrict the availability of abortions in Ohio. Caroline Bayne has read in these protests and in the increased popularity of tattoos featuring the phrase *nolite te bastardes carborundurum* (a spotty Latin translation of "Don't let the bastards get you down," and a signal of resistance within the text) a form of feminist self-publishing that surreptitiously comments on political action through its integration of the private into public space.[40] While *The Handmaid's Tale* therefore easily lent itself to popular forms of feminist activism (that could also easily become whitewashed and commodified digitally—and here it is instructive to remember the series' complicated relationship to race), the surreal scenes of fictional characters becoming real-life political actors evoked uncomfortable acts of mimicry.[41] This was corroborated by Atwood's own endorsement: "Because it's a visual symbol," she said in one press interview, "women can use it without fear of being arrested for causing a disturbance, as they would be for shouting in places like legislatures."[42]

chapter five

While Atwood's comments reveal the utility of audiovisual media to direct action, they also reaffirm the quality aesthetics of *The Handmaid's Tale*'s televisual adaptation, since the silence of the handmaids is situated against higher production budgets that emphasize the handmaid as a visual symbol. Yet this framing also had the effect of placing the symbolic value of the handmaid in the streets on the same plane as its televisual representation and its subsequent digital circulation, with images of protesting silent handmaids uncannily resembling their own memeification. This example of what Nicholas Kelly has called the "hacktivist cultural archive"—in which symbols from speculative and dystopic television series and video games are reappropriated for digital political protest—serves a primarily affective function, empowering members of online subcultures to make visible specific political messages and to disseminate these messages among one another and to the broader public.[43] While the handmaids' silent protests did not necessarily prevent certain state legislatures from enacting restrictive measures with respect to reproductive choice, the appropriation of the costume enhanced media coverage of the protests, with the images of the protests serving to inspire others to engage in the struggle for women's reproductive freedom. Although it is impossible to know the extent to which the protestors identified as fans of the series or of the book, the protests reified the handmaid as a visible yet silent symbol of political resistance—a sort of politicized cosplay—that stitched together the affective benefits of belonging to a TV fandom with those of belonging to a political group or cause.

Is donning the robe and bonnet of the handmaid and silently protesting outside a state capitol building an effective form of political action? Moreover, is it woke? The transformation of the handmaid into a real-life political symbol has the eerie effect of appearing as reenactment, with lines of protestors emulating the choreographed formation of the handmaids as they appeared within the series. The registers of performance, however, appear to exceed the neat composition of the TV series: on one level, the protestors were playing the role of handmaids by remaining silent, but on another level, their status as protestors who were afforded the freedom to protest (and importantly, who could remove their robes and bonnets whenever they wished) delimited the usefulness of the handmaid as a political symbol. Yet the costume still functioned as an affective portal to the status of women within the text. One Irish protestor noted, "The bonnet [made] you feel very vulnerable, because your hearing [was] cut off"; others observed that the size and angle of the bonnet circumscribed each protestor's range of vision.[44] In this sense, by assuming the figurative dress of the handmaid, a protestor also assumed the handmaid's own sensory limitations, which extended to the act of protest itself. The images of lines of protestors call to mind a scene from the tenth episode and finale of the first season, "Night," after the handmaids have refused to stone one of their own and demonstrated their exceedingly limited capacity to resist through collective action. As they return to their homes (and to their domestic scenes of submission), they march down a snowy residential street to the sounds of Nina Simone's cover of the jazz standard "Feeling Good."[45] The camera focuses directly on series' protagonist Offred (Elisabeth Moss) at the front of the line, which has the effect of making the handmaids appear as one gigantic red-and-white organism. This juxtaposition of tonal triumph with the violence of the series was ridiculed by critics such as Angelica Jade Bastién, who wrote that the scene functioned as "the kind of moment of empty sisterhood and girl-power faux feminism that has continually undone other episodes in their final moments."[46] Compared to conventionally raucous and loud protests outside of government buildings, the noiseless handmaids did not disrupt the status quo so much as they unnerved it through their woke presence.

Here, the protests embodied the contradictions of woke spectatorship through their expressive limitation and collective silence, which could be visually misrecognized as docility and compliance. The protesting handmaids used the images of television as a protective armor against actual retaliation from police: indeed, they were just dressed up as television characters, so how could they be an actual threat to the legislative process? Yet even this act of (cos)play contained signifiers of television's increased legitimization and formal evolution in storytelling. *The Handmaid's Tale* leveraged its industry acclaim—it was the first original series from a SVOD platform to win the Emmy Award for Outstanding Drama Series—and its literary roots to grant the protests of the silent handmaids some degree of authenticity and credibility. Furthermore, the handmaid could function as a political symbol in part because of the series' use of serialized narrative, which allowed for the handmaids to be fleshed out both as individual characters and as a social caste. Both these considerations augmented the series' reception as a text resisting the Trump administration's attacks on reproductive freedom and its perceived hostility toward women's issues. It is difficult to imagine, for example, the victims of sexual assault that populated television screens throughout the 2000s and early 2010s (such as the countless college co-eds who were raped on series such as *Law & Order: Special Victims Unit* or across the many CSI franchises) as similarly inspiring political symbols. The episodic nature of those series afforded their victims little interiority, and submission to the formulaic genre

5.3 Handmaids returning to their homes after refusing to stone one of their own. *The Handmaid's Tale*, "Night," Season 1, Episode 10.

of the police procedural ultimately curtailed their ability to be recuperated as symbols of misogynistic violence. The images of protesting handmaids thus indexed a form of woke spectatorship insofar as they demanded to be *looked at*, a visual reminder of the ways that televisual fandom can gesture toward political change—or at least toward the aesthetics of political change.

Misrecognizing the Past for the Present: On the Impossibility of Racial Performance

In the summer of 2020, as the Black Lives Matter movement spurred uprisings across the world following the murders of George Floyd, Breonna Taylor, and many others, Hollywood, like others across corporate America, was called upon to act. In addition to the expected statements of support posted on social media, some gestures stood out. Some, like Viacom CBS, focused on the present: the media conglomerate paused programming across its networks for eight minutes and forty-six seconds (the length of time that Floyd was choked by a White police officer's knee), counting down the time as the slogan "I Can't Breathe" flashed on screen.[47] Others focused on the past: HBO temporarily pulled the landmark epic *Gone with the Wind* from its streaming platform before later re-releasing it with an introduction featuring film scholar Jacqueline Stewart, who added historical context about the racism depicted within the film. Others focused on the more recent past: streaming

187

platforms pulled episodes of popular series *The Golden Girls*, *Community*, *Scrubs*, and *It's Always Sunny in Philadelphia* and cut a scene from an episode of *The Office* for featuring characters appearing in blackface.[48] And Tina Fey, the creator of *30 Rock* (NBC, 2006–2013), requested that four episodes of the critically acclaimed series be pulled (with parent company NBCUniversal's blessing) from streaming platforms, digital rental, and TV syndication for featuring characters in blackface.

Fey's statement accompanying this request acknowledged that *30 Rock*, a surreal metacomedy that satirizes NBC corporate and television production cultures, fell short in its rationalization of blackface as ironic, stating "that 'intent' is not a free pass for white people to use these images."[49] Unlike the media coverage of her request, Fey's statement notably does not use the term "blackface" to describe *30 Rock*'s transgressions; Fey chose instead to use the more neutral language "actors in race-changing makeup," a euphemism that elides the relations of power inherent to such an act. While the request was certainly apologetic and highlights Fey's own Whiteness, this curious substitution reveals a renegotiation of the boundaries of accepted comic satire. One episode pulled, for example, the third season's "Believe in the Stars," uses "actors in race-changing makeup" not as an incidental throwaway gag (as in some of *30 Rock*'s other incidents) but as the episode's main plot: cast members Tracy (Tracy Morgan) and Jenna (Jane Krakowski) enter into an argument over whether Black men or White women are subject to more prejudice, and the characters decide to swap identities for a day "in a *Freaky Friday* experiment" to settle the debate.

I will return to "Believe in the Stars" momentarily, but for now, it is important to note that the broadened descriptor of "actors in race-changing makeup" implies that Fey believed that having Tracy dress up as a White woman (primarily to exaggerate White privilege) could function as an ugly trope, raising the question of how whiteface assimilates into the scope of contemporary television satire. While I take for granted the obvious limitations of blackface, whiteface has been used differently to comment on television's relationship to race, most prominently in the lauded episode "Teddy Perkins" from *Atlanta* (FX, 2016–present), Donald Glover's surrealist comedy about Black millennial life. In "Teddy Perkins," the multimedia auteur donned whiteface to play the episode's titular character, a mysterious wealthy recluse who lives in a mansion that serves as the episode's setting. Unlike "Believe in the Stars," "Teddy Perkins" does not use whiteface to make a broader and more declarative point about race or racial prejudice; instead, the episode's use of racial misrecognition as well as its attendant discourses and acclaim reanimate questions about the possibilities of using racial performance to articulate new insights about televisual discomfort and racial satire. In his own examination of blackface performance in early histories of animation, Nicholas Sammond asks a prescient question about the limitations of racial satire: "If you perform racist behaviors and stereotypes in order to demonstrate their absurdity, do you deflate them or invest them with new life by destigmatizing them?"[50] I situate this question and these televisual examples against the broader claims of "wokeness" that have permeated postmillennial popular culture, though my interest is less in assessing whether or not *30 Rock* or *Atlanta* are indeed "woke" and more in considering the effectiveness of woke aesthetics and affects in spurring social change. By tracing the use of racial performance in these two programs, woke spectatorship becomes fundamentally premised around a misrecognition that speaks to specific anxieties about the changing status of representation in Hollywood and the changing status of television.

The claim that "actors in race-changing makeup" might be used satirically in order to exaggerate the ridiculousness of visual representation persists— even if Tina Fey correctly acknowledged that "'intent' is not a free pass for white people to use [such] images." This is to say that Fey presumably *intended* for the episode to serve as an ironic commentary on the act of racial transformation or that she *intended* for the episode to "demonstrate its absurdity" in Sammond's words. What was Fey trying to say about this absurdity—what else can even be said about this absurdity—and what was the intended effect of such a demonstration? The question of intent asks *how* spectators receive satirical texts, *how* they recognize the layers of satire within a particular text, and *what* that knowledge then empowers them to do (or not do) after viewing the performance of such texts. On the one hand, watching television has not historically been considered a political act in and of itself, and the medium's persistent deployment of cultural stereotypes—let alone the fact that most of Hollywood is still run by straight White males—gestures to the limitations of claiming television as a powerful force for restorative justice (as in the famous Gil Scott-Heron phrase "The revolution will not be televised"). On the other hand—and as the legacy of cultural studies underscores— representations within popular culture still matter very much in terms of changing public opinion about personal and group identity. Reading between the lines of Fey's *mea culpa* reveals an ambiguous desire for racial performance to have some sort of effect on the viewer: it presumes that viewers will understand the absurdity of *30 Rock*'s use of racial performance (because irony and satire define the program's comedic style), and it presumes that after watching the episode, audiences will somehow become less racist (because they would place less cultural weight on the visual representation of racial identity). While these are two already-problematic presumptions (complicated by the changing culture of reception as *30 Rock* moved from its scheduled broadcast on NBC to distribution on streaming platforms), one more presumption exists as well: that audiences trust the *intent* of the producer rather than the polysemy enabled by the dissemination of a text. Indeed, this last point elicits debates within television history extending back to Eddie Murphy, Archie Bunker, and others on how audiences respond to stereotypes in mass culture (debates again indebted to the work of cultural studies) and on whether they endorse or resist the stereotype.[51]

I suggest that Fey is projecting a structure of woke spectatorship onto her work that does not quite actually exist—at least in part because of the changes to both television and social attitudes on race that occurred between 2008 (when "Believe in the Stars" aired) and 2020 (when Fey requested that the episode be pulled). "Believe in the Stars" balances a plot in which the series lead and producer of TGS (a *Saturday Night Live* knockoff) Liz Lemon (Fey) flies to Chicago for jury duty and, while under the strong influence of narcotics, hallucinates a conversation with Oprah Winfrey, in addition to the argument between Tracy and Jenna that culminates in their respective uses of whiteface and blackface.[52] Their argument emerges in a scene in which Jenna is mad at Tracy for not compensating her properly for her voice-over work in his profitable videogame. In order to seek recompense, she turns to mediation, here misrecognized through the recurring character of Jeffrey Weinerslav (Todd Buonoparte), who works in General Electric's human resources department.[53] Within seconds of the mediation's beginning, the fight escalates, with each member asserting one way in which they face prejudice:

> [JENNA]: Do you know women still get paid less than men for doing the same job?

> [TRACY]: Do you know it's still illegal to be Black in Arizona?

> [JEFFREY]: Do you have any idea how hard it is to be an overweight transgender in this country?

Here, Jenna's factually correct statement is placed on the same comic register (as well as in the same visual frame) as Tracy's incorrect statement (though his is a statement that accurately highlights the presence of white supremacists in Arizona), with Weinerslav's follow-up occupying an uncomfortable ambiguity between the real and the parodic.[54] The scene thus reinforces *30 Rock*'s mode of address that privileges the White female viewer, most commonly shown via its protagonist, Liz. (Viewers learn from this scene and others that one cannot really identify with Tracy, as he exists far too much in the realm of the absurd.) Misrecognition structures the entire episode, which is amplified by Liz's later hallucination of Oprah (played here by herself) while under the influence of pills given to her by her boss, Jack Donaghy (Alec Baldwin), to calm her stress while flying. Liz unloads on the iconic talk-show host with her problems, at one point asking Oprah if she knows Tracy before realizing the silliness of such a query; but again, even Liz's incoherent sharing rests on assumptions that Black celebrities would indeed know one another. Much of the episode, and of *30 Rock*'s comic style more broadly, indulges in such verbal and visual misrecognitions, but the episode attempts to signal to the viewer that its lead characters (Liz and Jack) do not approve of Tracy and Jenna's social experiment, even if such resistance is overwhelmed by the episode's use of traditional comic gags, such as characters switching bodies à la *Freaky Friday*, or even by the sitcom form itself, which requires conflict in order to restore stability by the episode's conclusion.

This signaling is asserted in the scene in which Liz, Jack, and TGS writer James "Toofer" Spurlock (Keith Powell) confront Jenna and Tracy in their respective alternate racial states. Toofer (whose nickname, Jack explains in another episode, stems from the fact that "with him you get a two-for-one; he's a Black guy and a Harvard guy") calls out the offensiveness of the experiment by stating, "You realize blackface makeup reignites racial stereotypes African Americans have worked for hundreds of years to overcome." Toofer punctuates this statement with didactic frustration, but its target lies within the episode's already-established matrix of misrecognition. Toofer's "you" is, on one level, aimed very directly Jenna in blackface, but on another level, it is also directed at the audience, who must be reminded that *30 Rock* itself is a work of satire. Toofer's "you" is *not*, however, directed at Tracy in whiteface, as the scene's blocking separates its cast by gender. On aesthetic grounds, the episode portrays Jenna's blackface as more morally dubious than Tracy's whiteface in part because she uses better quality theatrical makeup and styling, which echoes Bambi Haggins's description of televisual whiteface as delineating a "cartoon version of whiteness."[55] The episode thus slyly encourages the viewer to identify with a character in blackface while simultaneously granting the viewer enough space to disavow such an identification: after all, *30 Rock* is a satire about television, and the viewer should not be taking it that seriously in the first place. Sammond reminds us that "Believe in the Stars" appeared shortly after the 2008 election of Barack Obama to the presidency, a moment that "somehow generated permission for media producers to more freely

5.4 & 5.5 Jenna's and Tracy's blackface/whiteface experiment. *30 Rock*, "Believe in the Stars," Season 3, Episode 2.

express racist stereotypes and sentiments under the dictum that a forthright acknowledgement of racism also provides for its ironic absolution."[56] Whatever feelings of discomfort summoned by viewers at the sight of Jenna in blackface are, like the earlier scene that triggered the social experiment, mediated and ultimately self-contained by the techniques of ironic metacomedy.

"Teddy Perkins," by contrast, refuses metacomedic strategies in its deployment of racial performance, borrowing instead heavily from the aesthetics and pacing of horror films and surrealist dramas (Glover has cited *Twin Peaks* as an inspiration for the series).[57] In the episode, Darius (Lakeith Stanfield) is planning to pick up a free piano from Perkins, but he stops first at a hardware store to purchase supplies in the episode's opening scene. Impulsively adding a red hat with a Confederate flag and the phrase "Southern Made" and a marker while checking-out, Darius heads to Perkins's house by altering the hat so it reads "U Mad" next to the image of the flag. The episode thus opens with the same kind of ironic misrecognition in which *30 Rock* frequently indulges, as immediately prior to the titles flashing on screen, viewers see the image of a Black man wearing a hat sporting the image of the Conference flag to the sounds of Stevie Wonder (heard diegetically on the radio of Darius's rented U-Haul). (And here, too, it is unclear who the "U" really is—who is supposedly getting mad or being made to feel uncomfortable by the image of Darius.) But once Darius arrives at Perkins's mansion, the episode's tone shifts dramatically: Darius removes his hat and an eerie silence sets in as he meets Perkins, who has pale skin and a mask-like face (Darius later implies that Teddy bleached his skin to look like "Sammy Sosa if you ran him through a dryer"). Teddy claims that the piano belongs to his brother Benny Hope, a once-famous jazz pianist, but as the plot unfolds, Darius suspects some sort of misrecognition at play: that Teddy is actually Benny. This diegetic misrecognition is also an intertextual misrecognition for viewers, as Teddy exhibits a number of characteristics shared by pop icon Michael Jackson: both are extremely pale, have high-pitched voices, and sit secluded in mostly-empty estates.[58] But this set of visual references does not present itself as satire insofar as it has any relevant narrative value; rather, the ghost of Jackson appears to accentuate Darius's (as well as the viewer's) own disorientation and inability to make sense of Teddy's appearance.

Critics have mostly read the use of whiteface in "Teddy Perkins" less as a commentary on White people and more as a commentary about the status of the Black artist—who becomes celebrified through the Whiteness of Hollywood, as in the case of Jackson—so that in donning whiteface (and in channeling Jackson), Glover narrates a "discussion of pain and hidden failure tied to artistic success," to quote one review.[59] But this discursive association between Glover and Jackson misrecognizes its own misrecognition, insofar as Glover's whiteface signals the power of Whiteness without granting it any other power vis-à-vis Darius. Is it really whiteface, or is it MJ-face? The prosthetics worn by Glover shape Teddy's face as mask-like, but does this make the character, or *Atlanta* more broadly, *plastic*, in Warner's sense of the term? Here, whiteface does not function in some of the ways that Marvin McAllister has outlined in his comprehensive study of the practice; it neither parodies Whiteness to undermine racial inequalities nor uses the trappings of White

193

5.6 Teddy Perkins. *Atlanta*, "Teddy Perkins," Season 2, Episode 6.

privilege to articulate Black style. Rather, whiteface serves, albeit perversely, as what McAllister calls the exposure of "systematic white terror in order to warn and potentially transform Afro-America" and to move "black audiences to personal or political action, be it long-term psychic healing or figurative nationalist jihads."[60]

To warn and transform in the name of change, to spur to personal and political action: such functions echo my earlier framing of wokeness as an affective call, despite its self-circumscription. What exactly is uncomfortable about these figurations of wokeness? Within the world of *30 Rock* (including Fey's *mea culpa*), Fey is a symbol of the extensions of woke culture that are a favorite target among far-right conservatives. The discomfort that comes with discussing structural formations of white supremacy, for example, has reanimated the culture wars of the late twentieth century to privilege the comfort of a White spectator. This spectator is not a sophisticated viewer who uses television to explore new worlds and in particular new racial imaginaries (as in Fey's imagined enlightened ironic White spectator of "Believe in the Stars"), but a White viewer insistent in her right not to be made uncomfortable, her right not to be reminded of television's legacy of racial caricature. Indeed, in the wake of the George Floyd uprisings and subsequent debates around the role of so-called critical race theory in public education (itself misrecognized from its original context in Black feminist legal studies and sociology), the Tennessee state legislature passed a law regulating what can

chapter five

be taught and not taught in schools receiving public funding. (Other states followed in passing similar laws, including Idaho, Iowa, and Oklahoma.) Also prohibited from Tennessee state curricula are the following acknowledgments: "This state or the United States is fundamentally or irredeemably racist or sexist" and "An individual should feel discomfort, guilt, anguish, or another form of psychological distress solely because of the individual's race or sex."[61] Here, the discomfort of White students is privileged not as an opportunity to understand histories and experiences of racial difference but as something to be avoided; following such far-right advocacy, Fey would have been right to erase "Believe in the Stars" from public view, since it spares its younger White audiences from having to confront the awkward unease of the flatness of that episode's attempt at racial satire. Now politicized to the point of its very legislation—the legislature tellingly provides no metrics by which one could presumably objectively test and regulate a student's discomfort—discomfort is a weapon in the ongoing conservative war against public education.

To regulate discomfort, even in a transparent effort to preserve the fragility of the White conservative, grants it power. Might televisual wokeness, then, and the acknowledged discomfort that accompanies it, possibly serve as a form of viewer resistance? *30 Rock* does not meet this claim, despite Fey's desperate attempts to read in the series' self-reflexivity a (White) liberal progressiveness. A woke spectator could view "Believe in the Stars" as a lame metacomedic attempt at pointing out the challenges of commenting on race in a seemingly postracial society, but such a recognition would only have been possible at an earlier moment in time, when attitudes about the status of Black life in America were less progressive. Perhaps cynically, Fey pulled episodes featuring blackface from future broadcast while leaving up numerous episodes of *30 Rock* that contained examples of racial satire that would seem offensive a decade later (with Fey herself escaping cancellation by the media industries). "Teddy Perkins," by contrast, is read as woke through a number of aesthetic signifiers, including the high production value ascribed to quality cable programming, the centering of Black characters and production, and the fact that FX originally broadcast the episode without commercial interruption, as well as through a number of intertextual and relational signifiers, such as the association between Perkins and Jackson. Some of these signifiers speak, quite obviously, to the changed status of Black talent within Hollywood, with *Atlanta* one of a number of critically acclaimed series created by millennials of color. (In this sense, Donald Glover represents a newer archetype of the television showrunner than Tina Fey.) But these signifiers also speak to the changed status of television, which has in the period between 2008

195

and 2018 allowed for its series to experiment more explicitly with televisual genre and form. "Teddy Perkins" thus uses whiteface to awaken within its spectator the acknowledgment that not all artists (including, perhaps, Tina Fey) are perfect, and that audiences, like Darius, should "stay woke" as they watch, cutting through the layers of misrecognition to attest to the formal and narrative possibilities and limitations of satire. Juxtaposing these two texts allows us to understand the way that discomfort became desirable through-out twenty-first-century television, repackaged first as ironic sophistication and then rebranded as political awareness. Both texts creepily emphasize how television may let its audience down when it comes to commentary in the name of racial change, but only one of them provides the formal space for audiences to unpack that commentary: the other, after all, has been pulled from our screens and uncomfortably relegated to the past.

chapter five

notes

Introduction

1. Spigel, "Introduction," 2. Spigel characterizes television "after TV" as a "reinvention" of the medium in the period 1994–2004, noting how the following changes resulted in the merging of television's commercial and public-service imperatives: "The demise of the three-network system in the United States, the increasing commercialization of public service/state-run systems, the rise of multichannel cable and global satellite delivery, multinational conglomerates, internet convergence, changes in regulation policies and ownership rules, the advent of HDTV, technological changes in screen design, the innovation of digital television systems like TiVo, and new forms of media competition all contribute to transformations in the practice we call watching TV" (2). It is this book's contention that these changes do not begin to impact relations of televisual discomfort and pleasure until *after* the period Spigel describes.

2. Throughout this book, I capitalize terms such as *White* and *Whiteness* in order to underscore their influence as a racial category. Because American television has assumed a White audience for most of its history (even while targeting non-White audiences with specific programming), I use these forms of capitalization as a way of making visible television's role in making Whiteness invisible through its normalization. I consciously do not capitalize the term *white supremacy*, however, as it refers not to a socially constructed racial category and more to an ideological system that rewards Whiteness.

3. *Louie*, "Come On, God," Season 2, Episode 8.

4. Seresin, "On Heteropessimism."

5. Sedgwick, *Tendencies*, 111. See also Lacquer, *Solitary Sex.*

6. R. King, "Powers of Comedy," 306.

7. Ryzik et al., "Detailing Lewd Acts," A1.

8. Tellingly, C.K. bought back the rights to *I Love You, Daddy* in full from its distribution company, agreeing to pay for all future distribution and marketing costs.

9. *Seinfeld*, "The Contest," Season 4, Episode 11.

10. In a 1993 article in *Rolling Stone*, the four castmates argue over who won the contest. Here, sitcom form tames the act entirely: "Always it comes back to masturbation: There remains a major controversy, thus a need for resolution." See Zehme, "Jerry & George & Kramer & Elaine," 46.

11. Around the same time as "The Contest," a sixth-season episode of *Roseanne* (ABC, 1988–1997), "Homeward Bound," also dealt with the topic of masturbation, though from the perspective of Dan and Roseanne discovering that their teenage

son DJ had begun masturbating. Contained within the episodic confines and kinship structures of the domestic family sitcom, the episode's humor is similarly inoffensive to that in "The Contest."

12. Sepinwall and Zoller Seitz, TV (The Book), 105. Sepinwall and Seitz's short chapter on *Louie* is notable for how it excuses the series' uncomfortable subject matter, stating only that "some of the portrayals of female sexuality have a touch of bitter-white-guy misogyny" (107). They also analogize C.K.'s formal influence on television with that of another notable auteur accused of sexual misconduct, Woody Allen.

13. Goodman, "When TV Brands Go Off Brand."

14. As Rob King astutely notes of C.K., "self-exposure, it seems, was the engine of his comedic art." See R. King, "Powers of Comedy," 292.

15. Sedgwick, *Touching Feeling*, 8. For Sedgwick, critical work on identity and performance often undertheorizes space while privileging temporality, though for her, no clear hierarchy exists within or between the two terms. We might extrapolate from her reading of the beside a logic of mutual constitution, in which the spatial is already temporal and vice versa.

16. Dienst, *Still Life in Real Time*, 141–142.

17. On this, see Spigel, "From Domestic Space to Outer Space," 205–235.

18. J. Dean, *Democracy and Other Neoliberal Fantasies*, 133.

19. Sedgwick, *Touching Feeling*, 12.

20. Villarejo, *Ethereal Queer*, and Ahmed, *Cultural Politics of Emotion*, especially chapter seven.

21. Hall, "Encoding/Decoding."

22. See, for example, the commentary revisiting some of *Louie*'s more controversial episodes following the revelation of C.K.'s misconduct: VanDerWerff, "Most Controversial Episode." See also Brennan, "Reconsidering *Louie*." For other responses to *Louie*, see Robinson, "What on Earth Is Louis C.K. Trying to Say about Rape?"; and North, "Louis C.K.'s Self-Deprecating Comedy." See also Karen Petruska's examination of the gender politics of recappers in the larger media industries, "Recappables."

23. Poniewozik, "Decency Police."

24. In writing about a similarly-lit *Time* magazine cover—a 1995 issue that introduced "cyberporn" into the public eye through the image of a young boy illuminated by the glow of a computer screen—Wendy Chun notes that the spectator "literaliz[es] his enlightenment/exposure" at the expense of the young boy's innocence, interpellating the magazine reader into the "position of the intruding pornographic image. Or else he serves as our mirror image, his surprise and invasion mirroring our own." In Chun, *Control and Freedom*, 90–91. The cyberporn cover is from *Time* 146, no. 27 (July 3, 1995).

25. The distinction between indecent content and obscene content as defined by the FCC matters here. Indecent content on television generally contains "serious literary, artistic, political, or scientific value," while obscene content does not and thus would be subject to censorship. See Federal Communications Commission, "Obscene, Indecent, and Profane Broadcasts."

26. While the literature on the confluence of neoliberal governmentality and reality television is extensive, two key examples are Ouellette and Hay, *Better Living through Reality TV*; and Weber, *Makeover TV*.

27. Boltanski and Chiapello, *New Spirit of Capitalism*.

28. Uricchio, "Television's Next Generation," 180.

29. See Blake Hallinan and Ted Striphas's important essay that pressures the cultural assumptions present in the notion of "algorithmic culture." Hallinan and Striphas, "Recommended for You."

30. Harvey, *A Brief History of Neoliberalism*. Harvey's book is probably the most well-known "history" of neoliberal policy, though by no means is it the only history.

31. Povinelli, *Economies of Abandonment*, 17. As the subtitle of her monograph suggests, she prefers the term "late liberalism" to highlight the role of tense in defining these social struggles, using the phrase to denote "the shape that liberal governmentality has taken as it responds to a series of legitimacy crises in the wake of anticolonial, new social movements, and new Islamic movements" (25). My own use of the term *neoliberalism*, while registering these crises, is not dependent upon them, and my geographic focus on the United States limits me from addressing, for example, how these new social movements might complicate the transmission of affect in global popular cultures.

32. Brown, *Undoing the Demos*, 34.

33. Beasley-Murray, *Posthegemony*, 115.

34. Deming, "Locating the Televisual," 127; Beasley-Murray, *Posthegemony*, 115.

35. See Mittell, *Complex TV*.

36. Nussbaum, "When TV Became Art.".

37. Newman and Levine, *Legitimating Television*, 47–48.

38. The scholarship discussed here includes: Caldwell, *Televisuality*; Joyrich, *Re-viewing Reception*; Dienst, *Still Life in Real Time*; and Feuer, *Seeing Through the Eighties*.

39. Caldwell, *Televisuality*, vii.

40. Dienst, *Still Life in Real Time*, 4; Joyrich, *Re-viewing Reception*, 23.

41. Caldwell, *Televisuality*, 5.

42. Dienst, *Still Life in Real Time*, 60.

43. Feuer, *Seeing Through the Eighties*, 12

44. Joyrich, *Re-viewing Reception*, 38–40.

45. Caldwell, *Televisuality*, 337. Both Joyrich and Caldwell, in fact, share a common textual example to make this point: the avant-garde children's program *Pee Wee's Playhouse* (CBS, 1986–1991).

46. Feuer, *Seeing Through the Eighties*, 1.

47. Joyrich, *Re-viewing Reception*, 4.

48. Dienst, *Still Life in Real Time*, 179n68.

49. Dienst, *Still Life in Real Time*, 33–35.

50. Jameson, *Postmodernism*, 271, 33.

51. Ventura, *Neoliberal Culture*, 5–6.

52. See Mittell, "A Cultural Approach to Television Genre Theory."

53. Linda Williams's foundational work on "body genres" is instrumental to thinking through this point. See Williams, "Film Bodies." See also Snyder and Mitchell, "Body Genres."

54. Bernstein, "Dances with Things," 70.

55. Bernstein, "Dances with Things," 83.

56. Dienst, *Still Life in Real Time*, x.

57. On this, see Alvey, "'Too Many Kids and Old Ladies'"; and Lentz, "*Quality* versus *Relevance*."

Chapter One. The Irritated Spectator

1. Variants of this index have also been used to assess realism in contemporary dramatic television. See Haggins, "*Homicide*: Realism," 13–14.

2. Freeman, "Hopeless Cases," 336.

3. J. V. Fuqua has described, for example, how TV emerged as a consumer appliance in the late 1940s and 1950s while simultaneously being integrated into the interior architecture of hospitals, allowing hospitals to brand themselves as rehabilitative spaces for the patient-consumer. See Fuqua, *Prescription TV*.

4. *Portlandia*, "One Moore Episode," Season 2, Episode 2.

5. See, most famously, White, "Crossing Wavelengths," 55.

6. Lowry, "Onion News Network, Portlandia." Reviews both of the series in its infancy and at its completion noted this affective trait. See Humphrey, "Paradox of *Portlandia*,"; Les Chappell, "*Portlandia* Suffers the Disability,"; and Armstrong, "TV Comedy *Portlandia*." Chappell's categorization of irritation as a "disability" particularly stands out here.

7. Russo, "Many Copies," 451.

8. Brinkema, *Forms of the Affects*, xii.

9. Hemmings, "Invoking Affect."

10. Deleuze and Guattari, *Thousand Plateaus*, 270; and Massumi, *Parables for the Virtual*, 28.

11. Massumi, *Parables for the Virtual*, 27–28.

12. Ahmed, *Cultural Politics of Emotion*, 40n4.

13. Shaviro, *Cinematic Body*, 26.

14. Shaviro, "Cinematic Body REDUX," 52.

15. Shaviro, "Cinematic Body REDUX," 53. Emphasis mine.

16. Brinkema, *Forms of the Affects*, 29.

17. See Marks, *Skin of the Film*; Barker, *The Tactile Eye*; Richmond, *Cinema's Bodily Illusions*; Thain, *Bodies in Suspense*. One exception to this direction can be found in Laine, *Feeling Cinema*.

18. Sandy Flitterman-Lewis once tried to sketch a psychoanalytic theory of television, but she ended up concluding that longstanding theories of cinematic identification such as the male gaze and its critiques cannot directly be applied to TV, which relies instead upon multiple and fractured glances. See Flitterman-Lewis, "Psychoanalysis, Film, and Television."

19. Joyrich, "Going through the E/Motions," 24. Like Shaviro, Joyrich is motivated polemically, writing in part to refute Fredric Jameson's claim that postmodernism entails the "waning of affect" and to lay the foundation for a broader feminist critique of postmodernism.

20. Modleski, "Rhythms of Reception,"

21. Schneider, *Performing Remains*, 35.

22. R. Williams, *Television*, 92.

23. R. Williams, *Television*, 93.

24. R. Williams, *Television*, 118, 119, 119, 120.

25. R. Williams, *Marxism and Literature*, 132

26. R. Williams, *Marxism and Literature*, 131, 129.

27. R. Williams, *Marxism and Literature*, 131.

28. R. Williams, *Marxism and Literature*, 134.

29. See Muñoz, *Sense of Brown*.

30. Bordowitz, *The AIDS Crisis Is Ridiculous*, 49.

31. Berlant, *Cruel Optimism*, 65.

32. R. Williams, *Marxism and Literature*, 131.

33. Dienst, *Still Life in Real Time*, 33. Dienst in particular draws this critique from the final line of Williams's chapter on flow: "In all these ways, and in their essential combination, this is the flow of meanings and values of a specific culture" (R. Williams, *Television*, 120).

34. K. Stewart, *Ordinary Affects*, 27.

35. R. Williams, *Television*, 92.

36. Leys, "Turn to Affect," 451.

37. Feuer, "Concept of Live Television," 12.

38. Van Es, "Liveness Redux," 1248.

39. Van Es, "Liveness Redux," 1247.

40. This is not to devalue a category like race from the history of television studies; studying the early domesticity of the medium, for example, requires an attentiveness to the racialization of domestic and sub/urban space, as work by Herman Gray, George Lipsitz, and Lynn Spigel has demonstrated.

41. M. Dean, "The Internet's Toxic Relationship with HBO's *Girls*."

42. M. Dean ascribes the series' mediocrity to the style of Dunham's mentor, television and film auteur Judd Apatow, also an executive producer of the series and famous for television series such as *Freaks and Geeks* (NBC, 1999–2000) and films such as *The 40-Year-Old Virgin* (2005) and *Knocked Up* (2007).

43. *Oxford English Dictionary*, s.v. "Think Piece."

44. Quoted in Haglund, "Why 'Think Piece' Is Pejorative."

45. Echoing Ward, Johannah King-Slutzky provides one acerbic definition of the term: "That short, poorly researched form of essay that exists to criticize recent cultural phenomena on usually disingenuous political or moral grounds." King-Slutzky also argues, not unconvincingly, that the emergence of the think piece is concomitant with the concept of the problematic, which she writes "whines" but "does not act." King-Slutzky, "The Internet Has a Problem(atic)." See also North, "'Think Pieces Were Made for Millennials,'"

46. Coleman, "Phreaks, Hackers, and Trolls," 113.

47. See Johnston, "Introducing the Trollgaze Index."

48. Chen, *Animacies*, 191–192.

49. Daum, "Lena Dunham Is Not Done Confessing." MM30. See also Gay, "Lena Dunham,"

50. See Coates, "On Being Your Authentic Self." Also see Berman, "'I'm a White Girl'"; and Nussbaum, "Hannah Barbaric."

51. *Girls*, "I Get Ideas," Season 2, Episode 2.

52. Abdul-Jabbar, "*Girls* Just Wants to Have (*White*) Fun,"

53. NPR, "Lena Dunham Addresses Criticism Aimed at *Girls*."

54. Als, *White Girls*, 81.

55. See Cardenas, "Feminism and Flawed Women." See also D. Stewart, "Why We Need to Keep Talking"; Holmes, "White *Girls*"; and Caramanica, "Broadcasting a World of Whiteness."

56. Wortham, "Where (My) Girls At?" See also K. James, "Dear Lena Dunham."

57. This is most clear from hooks, *Black Looks*; and Fleetwood, *Troubling Vision*, especially 12–21.

58. Keeling, *The Witch's Flight*, 2.

59. Gill, "Afterword," 230.

60. Griffin, *Feeling Normal*, 128.

61. On this, see many of the essays in Nash and Whelehan, *Reading Lena Dunham's "Girls,"* especially Whelehan, "Hating Hannah"; and McCann, "'A Voice of *a* Generation.'"

62. Nygaard, "Girls Just Want to Be 'Quality,'" 373.

63. See Nygaard and Lagerwey, *Horrible White People*.

64. Havas and Sulimma, "Through the Gaps of My Fingers," 82.

65. Rebecca Wanzo, "Precarious-Girl Comedy," 36. Importantly for Wanzo, the abjection present within Hannah is a different form of abjection than that found within her non-White peer Issa Rae (through her webseries *Awkward Black Girl*). According to Wanzo, Rae's use of the term *awkward* in her title (and, one would infer, her title in her HBO series *Insecure*) "becomes a synonym for abjection and also a modification of it, lessening its power to wound" (30).

66. Ngai, *Ugly Feelings*, 184.

67. Nussbaum, "It's Different for *Girls*" and "Hannah Barbaric."

68. Ngai, *Ugly Feelings*, 182.

69. Ngai, *Ugly Feelings*, 181.

70. *Girls*, "Beach House," Season 3, Episode 7.

71. Ahmed, *The Promise of Happiness*, 65.

72. Again, a comparison between Dunham and Issa Rae merits mention here: in *Insecure*'s first-season finale ("Broken as Fuck"), Issa—the character played by series creator Issa Rae—and her friends go to Malibu for a birthday weekend. The weekend is for celebrating, not necessarily for healing, even though Issa and her best friend, Molly (Yvonne Orji), are fighting, and the episode finds the four

friends deconstructing Molly's and Issa's respective love lives. The difference between these similarly structured episodic conceits (four female friends emotionally processing their friendship on a weekend trip) is again, perhaps, due to what Wanzo identifies as "Rae's embrace of black awkwardness in her performance." Whereas Shoshanna's calling out in "Beach House" comes from a position of exhaustion—in many respects sitting outside of the diegetic world of the series and assuming the position of the irritated spectator—the embrace of awkwardness within *Insecure* keeps the characters affectively connected, internalizing rather than externalizing negative affect. This may, in part, be because Rae has stated in numerous interviews that she did not create *Insecure* for White or for male audiences. See *Insecure*, "Broken as Fuck," Season 1, Episode 8; and Wanzo, "Precarious-Girl Comedy," 45.

73. Whelehan, "Hating Hannah," 37. For more on anticathartic comedy and millennial feminism, see Jenzen, "A Queer Tension."

74. *Girls*, "Goodbye Tour," Season 6, Episode 9.

Chapter Two. The Addicted Spectator

Epigraphs: Derrida, "The Rhetoric of Drugs," 16; comment from "mel," on Varone, "Linda from *Intervention*."

1. *Intervention*, "Linda," Season 7, Episode 1.

2. The best known of these is Ouellette and Hay, *Better Living through Reality TV*.

3. See McCarthy, "Reality TV."

4. McNamara, "Critic's Notebook," D1.

5. Boskind-Lodahl, "Cinderella's Stepsisters," 352.

6. Newman, "TV Binge." Newman, too, is guilty of drinking the novelistic Kool-Aid, observing at one point that "watching all of a serial drama like [HBO's *Six Feet Under*] on a binge is like tearing through a thick novel in a week at the beach."

7. Boskind-Lodahl, "Cinderella's Stepsisters," 351.

8. Netflix, "Netflix Declares Binge Watching is the New Normal."

9. Writes McCracken, "We don't just *watch—Arrested Development, Battlestar Galactica, Game of Thrones, Lost, Mad Men, The Wire*—we *occupy*. We inhabit it." See McCracken, "From *Arrested Development* to *Dr. Who*."

10. Sanneh, "Reality Principle."

11. Greenfield, "Netflix Is Making Both Cable and Internet Television Better," Indeed, Greenfield's use of the word "better" in the article's title should already make clear the anxieties that programs and platforms had over their signification as "quality" texts.

12. For more on the comparison between reality television and sports programming, see Hill, "Reality TV Experiences."

13. See many of the essays in Vice, Campbell, and Armstrong, *Beyond the Pleasure Dome*.

14. Fan, "Poetics of Addiction," 44.

15. Kubey and Csikszentmihalyi, *Television and the Quality of Life.*

16. Kubey and Csikszentmihalyi, "Television Addiction Is No Mere Metaphor."

17. Mittell, "Cultural Power of an Anti-television Metaphor," 217.

18. See Spigel, *Make Room for TV*, esp. 50–60.

19. See de Valck and Hagener, *Cinephilia*; and Jullier, "Philistines and Cinephiles."

20. See Scott, "Who's Steering the Mothership?"; and Jenkins, "Guiding Powers That Be."

21. Mittell, "Cultural Power of an Anti-television Metaphor," 218. Adopting his position from the foundational work of Janice Radway (with respect to metaphors of consumption) and Jimmie Reeves and Richard Campbell (with respect to 1980s televisual representations of crack/cocaine), Mittell particularly petitions the discipline of television studies to rally around this political position, claiming that "as critical scholars of media and culture, we must engage with this metaphor and refuse to yield it any more ground of our collective common sense" (235).

22. Boothroyd, *Culture on Drugs*, 5.

23. Eve Sedgwick has also pointed to the elasticity of the concept "drug," noting how substances can straddle cultural and geographic associations from the exotically foreign to the domestically banal. See Sedgwick, "Epidemics of the Will," in *Tendencies*, 130–142. Craig Reinarman has also reached the same conclusion through a sociological perspective. See Reinarman, "Addiction as Accomplishment."

24. Boothroyd, *Culture on Drugs*, 24. Emphasis in original.

25. Ronell, *Crack Wars*, 51–52.

26. Benson-Allott, *Stuff of Spectatorship*, 171–213.

27. Friedman, "Prohibition and Drugs," 104.

28. Sedgwick, "Epidemics of the Will," 132.

29. Sedgwick, "Epidemics of the Will," 131.

30. The trope of sickness is evident in psychological profiles of addiction, as in the title of one recent study that constructs addiction as a "disorder of choice." See Heyman, *Addiction.*

31. Sedgwick, "Epidemics of the Will," 131. It should be noted that this thesis of addiction—in which addiction is caused neither by a toxic substance nor by an imperiled body, but rather exists beside each of these—architecturally expresses the "third way" emblematic of Clintonian economic policy, corroborating the affinities between addiction's textual and economic guarantees.

32. On this, see Berlant, "Subject of True Feeling"; and Harkins, *Everybody's Family Romance*, particularly chapter 2.

33. See Leerhrsen, "Sex, Death, Drugs, and Geraldo," 76.

34. See White, *Tele-advising*; Shattuc, *Talking Cure*; Gamson, *Freaks Talk Back*; Dovey, *Freakshow*; and Glynn, *Tabloid Culture*. For a different perspective on these programs, see Grindstaff, *Money Shot.*

35. White, *Tele-advising*, 11. She extends this argument further, noting how "therapeutic and confessional modes of discourse have frequently been affili-

ated with female audiences, especially in forms of melodrama and women's fiction" (171).

36. Murray and Ouellette, "Introduction," 3.

37. Conlin, "America's Reality-TV Addiction."

38. Ronell, *Crack Wars*, 19.

39. Recovery television, as a cousin to the makeover subgenre, falls uncomfortably between the second and third generations of reality television as outlined by Misha Kavka. See Kavka, *Reality TV*, 9–10.

40. Weber, *Makeover TV*, 29–30.

41. Weber, *Makeover TV*, 22.

42. On the addicted subjects of reality television and gender, also see Pitts-Taylor, *Surgery Junkies*; and the essays in Weber, *Reality Gendervision*.

43. Moreover, this list does not even begin to cover the wide assortment of ideological apparatuses that comprise drug abuse prevention, such as community-, government-, and education-based programs that target youth.

44. *Intervention*, "Allison," Season 4, Episode 18.

45. Ronell, *Crack Wars*, 74.

46. *Good Morning America*, "When Does Passion Become a Problem?"

47. Douglas, "*Jersey Shore*: Ironic Viewing," 149.

48. Ang, *Watching "Dallas,"* 99.

49. Room, "Cultural Framing of Addiction," 225.

50. Heyman, *Addiction*, 44.

51. Reinarman, "Addiction as Accomplishment," 315.

52. Quoted in Lynch, "How A&E Got Rich Off of Recovery."

53. Murray, "'I Think We Need a New Name for It,'" 78. See also Corner, "Afterword: Framing the New."

54. Nichols, *Introduction to Documentary*, 250.

55. Contrast the documentary's discourse of sobriety with the genre of narrative cinema most frequently read narcoanalytically, a kind of "techno-cinema" in which the film's narrative privileges embodied sensation as experienced by the viewer. Representation is important to these films only insofar as it becomes a vehicle for multiple distributions of movement and affect. A film such as *Requiem for a Dream* (dir. Darren Aronofsky, 2000), for example, can position spectators to consume narrative as if it were a drug, through what Skye Bianco calls "intensive affects" that give the spectator access to the experience of being, for example, on heroin without any actual consumption of the drug. These affects emerge from a number of narcoanalytic techniques, including the speed between cuts and the close-ups of the consumption of drugs via different modes such as injection and snorting. See Bianco, "Techno-cinema."

56. Reality television can get "too real," however, in instances that make space for (literal) sober reflection. These are moments of death, when the subject of reality television who occupies a less desirable moral and cultural position (the hot mess, the redneck, the addict) strays too far from the boundaries of acceptability. This also comes across in the moments in which producers and crew must

negotiate their own degree of involvement with respect to potentially dangerous situations (such as when an alcoholic gets behind the wheel of a car). See Wallace, "Diamond in the Mud"; and Peters, "When Reality TV Gets Too Real."

57. Dehnart, "*Intervention*'s Success Rate Is High."

58. See Chua, *Battle Hymn of the Tiger Mother*, for the best illustration of the "tiger mom" bestialization.

59. Kavka, *Reality Television, Affect, and Intimacy*, 100. Emphasis in original. Kavka also draws our attention to how affect theory has approached the topic of believability and performance, reminding us of how Brian Massumi mines Ronald Reagan's presidency to show how Reagan's lack of concern with the difference between acting and not acting carried severe ideological effects (96–97).

60. McFarland, "On TV: 'Addiction,'" C1.

61. Wegenstein and Ruck, "Physiognomy, Reality Television and the Cosmetic Gaze," 29. See also Kavka, *Reality Television, Affect, and Intimacy*, 103.

62. I should clarify, though, that Wegenstein and Ruck's terminology—and their use of the term "gaze" specifically—only somewhat applies to recovery television. This is because of the rich tradition within television studies (stemming from the work of John Ellis) that privileges scopic logics of the "glance" rather than those of the "gaze," which has been traditionally associated with cinematic spectatorship. While the gaze sets the boundaries for uninterrupted spectating (and could thus be applied to the phenomenon of binge-watching), I want to hold onto the glance for how the distracted nature of TV spectatorship both speaks to the medium's gendered history as well as its emphasis on bodily movement and speed. On distraction and intoxication, see Benson-Allott, *Stuff of Spectatorship*, 183–193.

63. Wegenstein and Ruck, "Physiognomy, Reality Television, and the Cosmetic Gaze," 46.

64. Silverman, *Threshold of the Visible World*, 135.

65. Elswit, "*So You Think You Can Dance* Does Dance Studies."

66. McCarthy, "Reality TV," 33.

67. McCarthy, "Reality TV," 33. Emphasis mine.

68. Funny or Die, "*Intervention Intervention* with Fred Armisen."

69. On makeover television as fairy tale, see Bratich, "Programming Reality"; and Palmer, "*Extreme Makeover: Home Edition*: An American Fairy Tale."

70. Sedgwick, "Epidemics of the Will," 133.

71. Derrida, "Rhetoric of Drugs," 11.

Chapter Three. The Aborted Spectator

1. Hendershot, *Saturday Morning Censors*, 97–98.

2. *Oxford English Dictionary Online*, s.v. "queer."

3. Johnson, "Apostrophe, Animation, and Abortion," 38.

4. Parks, "Flexible Microcasting," 135.

5. This is a slightly different definition from the one proffered by Jay David Bolter and Richard Grusin in their landmark study *Remediation*, in which

"convergence is the mutual remediation of at least three important technologies—telephone, television, and computer" that "means greater diversity for digital technologies in our culture." Both Jenkins and Bolter and Grusin agree, however, that the movement between individual media forms is neither unidirectional, as the corporations that produce these technologies often claim, nor directed toward a single hybrid media apparatus. See Bolter and Grusin, *Remediation*, 224–225.

6. Jenkins, *Convergence Culture*, 175.

7. Jenkins, *Fans, Bloggers, and Gamers*, 41. Jenkins first used the term "participatory culture" in his 1992 book *Textual Poachers* to describe the cultural production and social dynamics of fan communities, thus creating the signifying chain between participatory culture and "fandom" that, while modified to reflect the changes to media consumption and technology since, still remains intact.

8. Organization of Transformative Works, "FAQs."

9. *Campbell v. Acuff-Rose Music.*

10. Bacon-Smith, *Enterprising Women*, 276, 292.

11. Grossberg, "Is There a Fan in the House?," 56. In the same paragraph, he writes that "affect is what gives 'color,' 'tone' or 'texture' to our experiences," perhaps foregrounding Eve Sedgwick's own gloss on texture/texxture.

12. Grossberg, "Is There a Fan in the House?" 57. Brian Massumi responds to this definition of affect dismissively, claiming that "Grossberg slips into an equation between affect and emotion" despite his claims to the contrary; as "unformed and unstructured" and as outside of conscious awareness, affect "is not fundamentally a matter of investment." See Massumi, *Parables for the Virtual*, 260n3. See also Hills, *Fan Cultures*, 60–64.

13. Grossberg, *We Gotta Get Out of this Place*, 255.

14. Felski, "Context Stinks," 587.

15. Russo and Coppa, "Fan/Remix Video (A Remix)."

16. Navas, *Remix Theory*, 1–8.

17. Yet this is not always the case. For example, a remixer named "Sherclop Pones" created *Friendship Is Witchcraft*, a remix of the cult animated series *My Little Pony: Friendship Is Magic* (The Hub, 2010–2019) that, similar to *Jiz*, sets recut visual footage to darkly humored dialogue and music, first appearing on YouTube and Dailymotion in 2011. In 2013, Hasbro successfully removed some episodes of the remix from these platforms, claiming that although the remixes should have been protected under the "fair use" copyright clause afforded to transformative works, images from the remixes were trademarked and thus not legal for reuse. See Romano, "Hasbro Halts Production of Unauthorized *My Little Pony* Video Game."

18. Feuer, "Concept of Live Television," 16. Mimi White samples both Williams and Feuer in her own early interventions onto televisual form, citing the phrase "from Feuer, offered as a reworking and refinement of Williams's introduction of the term." This is yet another example of television studies mimicking the very logic of segmentation as its object of study. See White, "Crossing Wavelengths," 64n6.

19. Lessig, *Remix*, see especially chaps. 5 and 6.

20. Lessig, *Remix*, xviii.

21. Lessig, *Remix*, 114.

22. For a helpful gloss of these critiques, see Neves, *Underglobalization*, 20–22.

23. See Said, *Culture and Imperialism*, especially chap. 4.

24. Manovich, "What Comes after Remix?"; and Wark, "Spectacles of Disintegration," 1129.

25. De Certeau, *Practice of Everyday Life*, xi.

26. De Certeau, *Practice of Everyday Life*, xi-xii. Emphasis in original.

27. Booth, "Mashup as Temporal Amalgam."

28. Kreisinger, "Queer Video Remix and LGBTQ Online Communities.".

29. Both characters were rivals for the ring of SATC's Mr. Big, with Carrie playing the role of homewrecker to Big and Natasha's marriage while herself cheating on her current boyfriend during SATC's third season.

30. Christian, "Fandom as Industrial Response."

31. "It Gets Worse" is also the name of a short article by Jack Halberstam in a special issue of *Periscope* on queer suicide. In it, Halberstam eviscerates Savage and Hecker's campaign for its bourgeois sensibility, though without *Jiz*'s trademark profanity: "The touchy feely notion embraced by this video campaign that teens can be pulled back from the brink of self destruction by taped messages made by impossibly good looking and successful people smugly recounting the highlights of their fabulous lives is just PR for the status quo, a way of patting yourself on the back without changing a thing, pretending to be on the front lines while you eat caviar and sip champagne in the VIP lounge. By all means make cute videos about you and your boyfriend, but don't justify the self-indulgence by imagining you are saving a life."

While Halberstam's critique about the project's enabling narcissism is certainly justifiable, it also implicates participatory culture as equally self-indulgent: "real" grassroots activism, it would seem, cannot be disseminated as a "cute video" online. See Jack Halberstam, "It Gets Worse."

32. *Jiz*, "It Gets Worse."

33. Berlant and Warner, "Sex in Public," 565.

34. *Jem and the Holograms*, "Adventures in China," Season 1, Episode 10.

35. Jenkins, *Convergence Culture*, 62.

36. Here I should note the obvious: advertising executives, unlike scholars in the humanities, do *not* by and large differentiate between affect and emotion.

37. Ahmed, *Cultural Politics of Emotion*, 45. Drawing from feminist philosophers Alison Jaggar and Elizabeth Spelman, Ahmed, too, resists a distinction between affect and emotion, believing principally that such distinctions inevitably lead to hierarchies in which emotion is epistemologically subordinated in concert with the feminine. Ahmed directly engages this debate in a footnote, arguing that a model that separates affect from emotion "creates a distinction between conscious recognition and 'direct' feeling, which itself negates how that which is not consciously experienced may itself be mediated by past experiences" (40n4). Here, the notion of the body emerges as an archiving machine beyond the realm

208

of conscious signification, similar to theories of embodiment and subjectivity offered by Michel Foucault and Judith Butler in continental philosophy and by Carrie Noland and Rebecca Schneider in performance studies. It is also important to note here that while Ahmed and Jenkins use similar phrasing, they do not engage with each other's work directly.

38. O'Dwyer, "A Capital Remix," 323–332.

39. Ahmed, *Cultural Politics of Emotion*, 46.

40. On this, see Alexis Lothian's groundbreaking framing of queer pleasure and perverse reading practices in *Old Futures*, 160–162.

41. Coppa, "A Fannish Taxonomy of Hotness," 109. Emphasis in original.

42. Sedgwick, *Epistemology of the Closet*, 22.

43. Freeman, "Introduction," 161.

44. The series *Got 2B Real* (2011–2015) can be found online at https://www.youtube.com/playlist?list=PLfKWL-GKl8DPdes_wsfIRinmtwTX5iSiN.

45. Monk-Payton, "#LaughingWhileBlack," 17.

46. Christian, "Netflix's 'Arrested Development' Will Not Change TV."

47. Jameson, *Postmodernism*, 20. Linda Hutcheon has addressed this contradiction by noting how many accounts of nostalgia modeled after Jameson overlook it as an affective response, and my reading of televisual remix here is in response to her call for "transideological" approaches to the study of nostalgia. In Hutcheon, "Irony, Nostalgia and the Postmodern," 193.

48. Ehrenhalt and Srivastava, "*Jem and the Holograms*." See also Ehrenhalt, "Truly Outrageous!"

49. Quoted in Lapin, "Barbie Takes Up Rock 'n' Roll."

50. For a recuperative reading of the Misfits' bad-girl feminism, see Chaney, "Requiem for a Jem," 5. Ehrenhalt also frames the musical and style differences between the two groups by drawing comparisons to existing female 1980s pop bands, with the Holograms occupying the position of a "squeaky-clean, just-wanna-have-fun image of the sanitized Go-Go's, Bananarama, and the Bangles," and the Misfits occupying that of the "ultimate bad-girl band the Runaways." See Ehrenhalt, "Truly Outrageous!," 86.

51. Mattel returned the favor, creating a line of dolls called "Barbie and the Rockers" in order to compete with the *Jem* merchandise. While the dolls sold well—better than Hasbro's line of *Jem* dolls—Barbie had far less success on television. See Lapin, "Barbie Takes Up Rock 'n' Roll"; and Gellene, "Barbie Prevails."

52. The original commercial can be found on YouTube: "80's Jem Toy Commercial + Cassette Offer." Note, too, how in this particular example, a title card for the *Transformers* appears at the beginning of the commercial.

53. Joyrich, *Re-viewing Reception*, 41. See also Swindle, "Feeling Girl, Girling Feeling."

54. *Jiz*, "The *Jiz* Commercial."

55. Swindle, "Feeling Girl, Girling Feeling," 24.

56. Treichler, *How to Have Theory in an Epidemic*, 75.

57. Grusin, "YouTube at the End of New Media."

58. *Jiz*, "The Abortion Episode."

59. Joyrich, *Re-viewing Reception*, 101–102. Joyrich makes this point in a larger argument about the reproductive politics of *Moonlighting* (ABC, 1985–1989) that assumes a similar structural weight to the argument I offer here: reading the miscarriage of its protagonist at the beginning of its final season as a crucial form that television frequently takes up, such that what appears to be creative and progressive self-reflexivity ultimately ends up neatly containing feminine excess, allowing for the reassertion of the patriarchal sphere as in control of the TV family and that of its viewers.

60. On abortion and television documentary, see D'Acci, "Leading Up to *Roe v. Wade*."

61. Some episodes during the decade involved women reflecting on their own histories with abortion (*Cagney & Lacey, thirtysomething*), while others covered the politics surrounding privacy and access to reproductive health (*The Facts of Life, Hill Street Blues*). Only in a few isolated instances did characters undergo the procedure: in a 1986 episode of the daytime soap *The Young and the Restless*, for example, and in a 1989 episode of the teen drama *Degrassi High*.

62. Lee, "*Friday Night Lights* Tackles Abortion."

63. This is repeated as the conditions for penetration in general in another episode, in which the Mammograms rehearse a new song with the following refrain: "If you wanna get with me, there are things that you should know / If I knock a bitch up, then the baby's gotta go."

64. Berlant, *Queen of America Goes to Washington City*, 116.

65. Gournelos, "Puppets, Slaves, and Sex Changes," 272.

66. Marx, "*Family Guy*: Undermining Satire," 180.

67. Johnson, "Apostrophe, Animation, and Abortion," 29.

68. Johnson, "Apostrophe, Animation, and Abortion," 33.

69. Johnson, "Apostrophe, Animation, and Abortion," 34.

70. A. James, "I F*cking Hate @RuPaul."

71. Johnson, "Apostrophe, Animation, and Abortion," 38.

72. Freeman, *Time Binds*, xi.

73. Johnson, "Apostrophe, Animation, and Abortion," 39.

Chapter Four. The Spectator Plagued by White Guilt

Epigraph: Fry, RUA/TV, 13.

1. Examples of these programs include the *The United States Steel Hour* (ABC/NBC, 1945–1953), *Kraft Television Theatre* (NBC, 1947–1958), *Philco TV Playhouse* (NBC, 1948–1955), Westinghouse Studio One (CBS, 1948–1958), *Robert Montgomery Presents* (NBC, 1950–1957), *Playhouse 90* (CBS, 1956–1960), and *Goodyear TV Playhouse* and *Alcoa Theatre* (NBC, 1957–1960).

2. Thompson, *From "Hill Street Blues" to "ER,"* 30. Thompson lists programs such as *Hill Street Blues* (NBC, 1981–1987), *St. Elsewhere* (NBC, 1982–1988), *Cagney & Lacey* (CBS, 1982–1988), *Moonlighting* (ABC, 1985–1989), *thirtysomething* (ABC,

1987–1991), and *China Beach* (ABC, 1988–1991) as examples of this second golden age (although Jane Feuer has pointed to the MTM-produced comedies of the 1970s as also worthy of such a designation). See also Feuer, "Quality Drama in the US."

3. See Newman and Levine, *Legitimating Television,* esp. chap. 2.

4. Martin, *Difficult Men,* 13.

5. Fleissner, "Objecting to Novelty," 12.

6. Sontag, *Against Interpretation,* 31.

7. By "critical assumptions" I signal the primary objects that this chapter will interrogate: the writings of critics themselves, as well as the structural and institutional features inherent to the industry of television criticism, both along nonacademic (best-of lists, recaps, and journalistic meditations on the medium) and academic (syllabi) registers.

8. Martin, *Difficult Men,* 21.

9. Smith, *Contingencies of Value,* 52.

10. While the institutionalization of fan communities online have increased the degree to which these lists can be "crowd sourced"—in which fans or users collectively author the best-of list through online voting—the single-critic format is still widely used across all platforms of journalistic criticism. I would argue, moreover, that the language differs in these different contexts of reception: fan-authored lists utilize more subjective terms such as "favorite," while critic-authored lists utilize more objective terms such as "best."

11. Raferty, "What's the Best TV Drama of the Last 25 Years?"

12. Raferty is a regular contributor to *Vulture*; like most online media periodicals, he is a freelancer and thus his position of critic becomes instantiated by the fact that he writes for several different publications.

13. Seitz, "Greatest TV Drama of the Past 25 Years, the Finals."

14. McGrath, "Triumph of the Prime-Time Novel," 29–30.

15. See Fehrman, "Channeling of the Novel," BR35. Also see Kirsch and Hamid, "Are the New 'Golden Age' TV Shows the New Novels?" BR31; and Maciak, "Who's Afraid of Serial TV."

16. O'Sullivan, "Broken on Purpose," 65.

17. Newman and Levine, *Legitimating Television,* 5. Emphasis mine.

18. In his monograph *"Breaking Bad" and Cinematic Television,* Angelo Restivo uses the term "cinematic"—defined as "a kind of interruptor within the regime of images"—to interrogate how that quality series manipulates image and sound to produce affective encounters between audience and neoliberal everyday life. While Restivo's use of "cinematic television" overlaps somewhat with how other scholarly and cultural critics use the term (and how I use it here), his alignment with autonomous theories of affect erases any productive attempt at reading social relations of race and gender within the series—a curious effect, given the importance of white supremacy to that particular series as well as to its habitual representations of violence against women and People of Color. See Restivo, *"Breaking Bad" and Cinematic Television,* 6–7.

19. These boundaries are, of course, unstable, as a number of critics point to how a series such as *The X-Files* constitutes, in Jeffrey Sconce's words, "performative exercises in character, style, and narration . . . vacillating between stand-alone 'ghoul of the week' episodes and programs devoted to the ongoing conspiracy arc of alien invasion." See Sconce, "What If," 107.

20. As Ian Goode has pointed out, British television critics have largely read *CSI* as *quality* television, with such quality coming through in the visual effects that showcased forensic technology. See Goode, "*CSI: Crime Scene Investigation*."

21. Poniewozik, "Decency Police," 30.

22. *CSI: Crime Scene Investigation*, "King Baby," Season 5, Episode 15.

23. Kompare, *CSI: Crime Scene Investigation*, 5. See also Cohan, *CSI: Crime Scene Investigation*.

24. Much of the literature on the so-called CSI effect simply tests its validity—such as its measured effect on criminal juries—employing quantitative methodologies like the ones found within the series itself (and thus legitimizing scientific analysis further). For a summary and counteranalysis of this work, see the essays in Byers and Johnson, *CSI Effect*.

25. Here, the lab technician is a woman of color, Mia Dickerson (Aisha Tyler).

26. Pierson, "Evidential Bodies."

27. Gever, "Spectacle of Crime, Digitized," 447. Steven Cohan, too, sees in the series a totalizing faith in analysis that produces affective pleasures for the academic spectator, since the investigators "look for the same in the evidence they gather, in effect treating a crime scene as if it were a text." See Cohan, *CSI: Crime Scene Investigation*, 6.

28. *Law & Order: Special Victims Unit*, "Hooked," Season 6, Episode 15.

29. Cuklanz and Moorti, "Television's 'New' Feminism," 311, 312.

30. See Projansky, *Watching Rape*.

31. Newman and Levine, *Legitimating Television*, 159.

32. "Storytelling in *The Wire*," syllabus at Brown University, Peter Saval, instructor (Spring 2013).

33. Lipsitz, *Possessive Investment*, 119.

34. Lipsitz, *Possessive Investment*, 122.

35. Quoted in Pearson, "David Simon." *Vice*.

36. In one interview, Chase is quoted as saying: "Look, I do not care about television. I don't care about where television is going or anything else about it. I'm a man who wanted to make movies. Period." Brett Martin, in a generously hagiographic move, frames Chase's antipathy as "one of the small tragedies: that the Reluctant Moses of the Third Golden Age, the man who, by example, opened the door for so many writers, directors, actors, and producers to work in television gloriously free of shame, was unable himself to enter the Promised Land" (*Difficult Men*, 34–35). For more on Chase's obsession with cinema, see Newman and Levine, *Legitimating Television*, 46–47.

37. See also Banks, "*I Love Lucy*." Simon has mentioned in interviews that he found the process of writing for television to be "very communal," going out

of his way to single out the other writers on staff for their contributions to the program. TV critics, however, nearly universally attribute *The Wire*'s greatness to Simon's vision. See Pearson, "David Simon."

38. Mittell, "Narrative Complexity," 35.

39. Foucault, "What Is an Author?, 172.

40. Martin, *Difficult Men*, 258. Martin does not offer any evidence for this in his book, and as a work of general nonfiction, he is under little obligation to provide citations for his sources. He writes in his "Notes on Sources" that "Matthew Weiner declined, politely, to sit for interviews specific to this book. I was, however, able to draw on our multiple conversations in other contexts and on the truly heroic amount of talking he's done on behalf of *Mad Men* elsewhere" (294).

41. Taken from the Television Academy, "73rd Primetime Emmy Awards."

42. Foucault, "What Is an Author," 213.

43. Steinlight, "'Anti-*Bleak House*,'" 153.

44. Kois, "Everything You Were Afraid to Ask about *The Wire*."

45. Moore, "In the Life of *The Wire*."

46. Linda Williams makes a compelling counterreading to this effect, claiming that race is produced as a serial problem through the serial form. I explore her claims in greater detail shortly. See L. Williams, On "*The Wire*."

47. Rajewsky, "Intermediality, Intertextuality, and Remediation," 44.

48. Mitchell, "There Are No Visual Media," 260.

49. Though she does not employ the language of mixture, Jodi Melamed's work on "neoliberal multiculturalism" is useful here, as is Daniel McNeil's contribution to the inaugural issue of the *Journal of Critical Mixed Race Studies*, in which he makes a persuasive call against the co-optation of mixed-race metaphors (and, by extension, mixed-race subjectivity) by neoliberal institutions. See Melamed, "Spirit of Neoliberalism"; and McNeil, "Slimy Subjects and Neoliberal Goods."

50. K. King, "Historiography as Reenactment," 460.

51. Schneider, "Intermediality, Infelicity, and Scholarship on the Slip," 258.

52. Schneider, "Intermediality, Infelicity, and Scholarship on the Slip," 258. Emphasis in original.

53. Jameson, "Realism and Utopia in *The Wire*."

54. Žižek, *Year of Dreaming Dangerously*, 91.

55. Williams, On "*The Wire*," 11.

56. On form, see O'Sullivan, "Broken on Purpose"; and Harris, "A Return to Form?"

57. Žižek, *Year of Dreaming Dangerously*, 91.

58. Jameson, "Realism and Utopia in *The Wire*," 371.

59. Quoted in Lorrie Moore, "In the Life of *The Wire*."

60. Jameson, "Realism and Utopia in *The Wire*," 363.

61. Žižek, *Year of Dreaming Dangerously*, 101. Emphasis in original.

62. Žižek reads the order of the seasons as a larger narrative system, with "each successive season taking a further step in the exploration," though his own

summary of the seasons does not follow such a linear trajectory (*Year of Dreaming Dangerously*, 95). Indeed, he never clarifies exactly what such "further steps" entail nor the larger significance of having each season constitute a unit for analysis.

63. An example of this would be FX's popular series *American Horror Story* (2011–present), in which each season is a self-contained narrative set in a different temporal and spatial location (though one part of a larger shared diegetic universe) that features many of the same actors.

64. Jameson, "Realism and Utopia in *The Wire*," 371.

65. See Leverette, Ott, and Buckley, *It's Not TV*.

66. Williams, *On "The Wire*," 194.

67. Žižek, *Year of Dreaming Dangerously*, 107.

68. Williams, *On "The Wire*," 16.

69. Williams, *On "The Wire*," 17.

70. Jagoda, "Wired," 193.

71. Yet when pressed, critics and fans of the series generally offer two characters as approximate protagonists: Detective Jimmy McNulty (Dominic West) and the criminal vigilante Omar Little (Michael K. Williams). In many ways McNulty, through his Irish American swagger and his drinking problem, corresponds to stereotypes of East Coast working-class White policemen, whereas Omar, a gay Black stick-up man, is often described as "enigmatic" and "intriguing" because he has no cultural antecedent in either detective fiction or the police procedural. Indeed, Omar's relative uniqueness has attracted many fans, including Barack Obama, whose admiration of the character has been widely cited in reviews of *The Wire*.

72. See Modleski, "Rhythms of Reception."

73. See Lotz, *Cable Guys*, especially chapter 2.

74. *The Wire*, "-30-," Season 5, Episode 10

75. Williams, *On "The Wire*," 212.

76. Jameson, "Realism and Utopia in *The Wire*," 362.

77. Žižek, *Year of Dreaming Dangerously*, 100.

78. *The Sopranos*, "Made in America," Season 6, Episode 21.

79. Writes Williams: "The point of the 'game' metaphor as it operates throughout the series is that the rules are not the same to everyone" (*On "The Wire*," 192). Paul Allen Anderson has thoughtfully critiqued the metaphor of the game for functioning as a tautology that allows those in power to maintain it. See Anderson, "'The Game Is the Game.'"

80. Berlant, *Cruel Optimism*, 16–17.

81. The character of Snoop, who is muscle for the Stanfield drug organization, was played by Felicia "Snoop" Pearson, who herself was a drug dealer in her teens, serving six and a half years in prison for second-degree murder. She later appeared on the VH1 reality docusoap *Love & Hip Hop: New York* from 2016 to 2018.

82. Haggins, "*Homicide*: Realism," 13–21.

83. A. Hall, "Reading Realism," 634.

84. Fiske, *Television Culture*, 21.

85. Lynne Joyrich makes a similar point much prior to the "affective turn" without drawing from cognitive materialism: "The dispersal of affect and positions of identification may itself be seen as ideological, cut to the demands of the power divisions and hierarchies that define today's society." See Joyrich, "Going through the E/Motions," 32.

86. Williams, On "The Wire," 192.

87. McCabe and Akass, "Sex, Swearing, and Respectability."

88. Jameson and Williams differ on this point: Jameson accedes that the idealist McNulty fulfills the function of a protagonist even as the series destabilizes the distinction between lead and supporting characters; Williams, by contrast, reads the character as one who once inspired heroism yet whose poor behavioral choices force the audience to "become increasingly disenchanted with [his] cocky, self-destructive, alpha-male Irish cop character" (On "The Wire," 195).

89. The Wire, "The Dickensian Aspect," Season 5, Episode 6.

90. Davis and Postlewait, "Theatricality," 6.

91. Schneider, "Intermediality," 258.

92. Landsberg, Prosthetic Memory, 156.

93. Saturday Night Live, "Kerry Washington/Eminem," Season 39, Episode 5.

94. Lipsitz, How Racism Takes Place, 120.

95. Williams, On "The Wire," 188.

96. Williams, On "The Wire," 190.

97. Brown, "Resisting Left Melancholy."

Chapter Five. The Woke Spectator

1. Feuer, Seeing Through the Eighties, 149.

2. Jameson, "Periodizing the 60s," 178.

3. Salvato, Television Scales, 14.

4. Beltrán, "Meaningful Diversity."

5. Zook, Color by Fox; and Gray, Watching Race.

6. Gray, Watching Race.

7. E. Davis, "Beside(s) Love and Hate," 577.

8. Rose and Guthrie, "FX Chief John Landgraf on Content Bubble."

9. Tartiglione, "The Too-Much-TV Debate."

10. Poniewozik, "Forget Too Much TV," C1.

11. Writes Litwack: "Within the couch potato idiom, though, it is not merely that TV makes viewers obese but that television itself is obese with its stylistic excesses, its cult of consumption and production of celebrity, and its overidentification with the commodity form." In Litwack, "Making Television Live," 51.

12. Berlant, Cruel Optimism, 101–103.

13. Sperling, "Is Peak TV Slowly Killing TV Critics?"

14. Christian and White, "Organic Representation as Cultural Reparation," 144.

15. Goldberg, "Peak TV Update" (2020). Within industry parlance, "original scripted series" excludes many genres such as daytime soap operas, single-episode specials such as stand-up comedy, and children's programming.

16. Goldberg, "Peak TV Update" (2018). FX Networks Research bases this information on data "culled from Nielsen, Online Services, Futon Critic, Wikipedia, Epguides, et al."

17. Leonard, "How Netflix Is Turning Its Viewers into Puppets."

18. This also extends to the way in which the SVOD browsing experience is designed (and interfaces are not uniform across different streamers); for example, Kevin Sanson and Gregory Steirer have read the aesthetics of Hulu's interface to argue that the streamer presents its programming "not as non-linear binging opportunities but as long-term, quasi-linear consumption opportunities, each with its own inherent rhythm of engagement" in a way to differentiate itself from its competitors. See Sanson and Steirer, "Hulu, Streaming, and the Contemporary Television Ecosystem," 1219–1220.

19. Alexander, "Catered to Your Future Self," 90.

20. Fisher, *The Play in the System*, 51–56.

21. Christian, *Open TV*, 4.

22. Warner, "In the Time of Plastic Representation."

23. Nygaard and Lagerwey, *Horrible White People*, 48. Nygaard and Lagerwey, like Christian, Warner, and myself, all find that SVOD services assimilated easily into the logics and business practices of legacy television on the level of representation.

24. Warner, "In the Time of Plastic Representation."

25. Ngai, *Theory of the Gimmick*, 1.

26. Romano, "A History of 'Wokeness.'"

27. See Chiu, "Obama Finds Rare Bipartisan Support."

28. Sharpe, *In the Wake*.

29. Doane, "Information, Crisis, Catastrophe," 222.

30. E. King, "Stressed? Blame the 2016 Election."

31. Stelter, "Second Clinton-Trump Debate."

32. Joyrich, "TV Trumps."

33. See, for example, the short essays contained in "Queer TV Style," especially those essays by Sasha Torres, José Muñoz, and Gustavus Stadler.

34. Writes Weber: "When the Fab 5 goes through dirty refrigerators and piles of soiled laundry, when they laugh at baggy clothes and poor eating habits, they are critiquing both the men they will make over and the failed women who share those men's lives. The underlying logic of the show contends that men need environments of like-to-like in order to improve." In Weber, *Makeover TV*, 201–202.

35. *Queer Eye for the Straight Guy*, "Hair Today, Art Tomorrow: Brian S," Season 1, Episode 1.

36. *Queer Eye*, "You Can't Fix Ugly," Season 1, Episode 1.

37. Lovelock, *Reality TV and Queer Identities*, 189.

38. Fallon, "'Queer Eye' for the Woke Guy."

39. Weber, "Torture Porn in Dystopic Feminism," 192–194.

40. Bayne, "#nolitetebastardescarborundorum."

41. On this, see Phoenix, "From Text to Screen."

42. Beaumont and Holpuch, "How *The Handmaid's Tale* Dressed Protests."

43. Kelly, "The Hacktivist Cultural Archive."

44. In Beaumont and Holpuch, "How *The Handmaid's Tale* Dressed Protests."

45. *The Handmaid's Tale*, "Night," Season 1, Episode 10.

46. Bastién, "*The Handmaid's Tale* Season 1 Finale."

47. Brandy Monk-Payton has situated Viacom's corporate activism against its construction of televisual flow, since MTV's pause in programming was immediately followed by a Pop Tart commercial. As she writes, "Laid bare are the contradictions in American television's desire to be relevant, to *matter* in this moment ('Black storytelling matters,' Netflix tweets), to be part of the revolution." In Monk-Payton, "Tele-visionary Blackness."

48. See Alter, "Every Blackface Episode and Scene." As Alter reports, global television properties also faced harsh scrutiny, with streaming platforms removing several popular British and Australian television comedies that frequently featured White actors playing characters of Color.

49. Quoted in Thorne, "'30 Rock' Blackface Episodes Pulled." Fey's statement to the press is as follows: "As we strive to do the work and do better in regards to race in America, we believe that these episodes featuring actors in race-changing makeup are best taken out of circulation. I understand now that 'intent' is not a free pass for white people to use these images. I apologize for pain they have caused. Going forward, no comedy-loving kid needs to stumble on these tropes and be stung by their ugliness. I thank NBCUniversal for honoring this request."

50. Sammond, *Birth of an Industry*, 17.

51. Stuart Hall's seminal "Encoding/Decoding" comes to mind here, as does Racquel Gates's trenchant interrogation of seemingly "negative" representations of Blackness. See S. Hall, "Encoding/Decoding"; and Gates, *Double Negative*.

52. *30 Rock*, "Believe in the Stars," Season 3, Episode 2.

53. At the time of the episode's airing, NBCUniversal was owned by General Electric. It was later sold to cable corporation Comcast in 2011, an event which was heavily spoofed in *30 Rock*'s fourth season.

54. While overweight transgender individuals certainly face much discrimination on a day-to-day basis, it is unclear to me after much Internet research whether or not Buonoparte identifies as transgender. If not, *30 Rock* is thus also a series that misrepresented transgender individuals from the present-day standards of Hollywood casting culture.

55. Haggins, *Laughing Mad*, 76.

56. Sammond, *Birth of an Industry*, 16. Eric Lott also notes the curious resurgence of blackface in media representations following Obama's election; see Lott, *Black Mirror*, 1–3.

57. *Atlanta*, "Teddy Perkins," Season 2, Episode 6.

58. Tim Molloy lists many other intertextual references to the King of Pop throughout the episode, including nods to Dionne Warwick, a shared chin cleft, and abusive fathers. See Molloy, "'Atlanta.'"

59. Dennis Jr., "The Second Season of 'Atlanta.'"

60. McAllister, *Whiting Up*, 14. McAllister's framing of whiteface here is indebted to Daphne Brooks's notion of "Afro-alienation acts," which relies upon theatrical techniques of alienation and estrangement to represent the atrocities of the past. See Brooks, *Bodies in Dissent*.

61. Tennessee State Legislature, Senate Bill 0623 (June 1, 2021). https://wapp .capitol.tn.gov/apps/BillInfo/Default.aspx?BillNumber=SB0623.

Notes to chapter five

bibliography

Abdul-Jabbar, Kareem. "*Girls* Just Wants to Have (*White*) Fun." *Huffington Post,*
    April 2, 2013. http://www.huffingtonpost.com/kareem-abduljabbar/girls
    -review_b_2593756.html?utm_hp_ref=tw.
Ahmed, Sara. *The Cultural Politics of Emotion.* New York: Routledge, 2004.
Ahmed, Sara. *The Promise of Happiness.* Durham, NC: Duke University Press,
    2010.
Alexander, Neta. "Catered to Your Future Self: Netflix's 'Predictive Personaliza-
    tion' and the Mathematization of Taste." In *The Netflix Effect: Technology
    and Entertainment in the 21st Century,* edited by Kevin McDonald and
    Daniel Smith-Rousey, 81–97. New York: Bloomsbury, 2016.
Als, Hilton. *White Girls.* San Francisco: McSweeney's, 2014.
Alter, Rebecca. "Every Blackface Episode and Scene That's Been Pulled from
    Streaming So Far." *Vulture,* June 29, 2020. https://www.vulture.com/2020/06
    /blackface-tv-episodes-scenes-removed-streaming.html.
Alvey, Mark. "'Too Many Kids and Old Ladies': Quality Demographics and 1960s
    Television." *Screen* 45, no. 1 (Spring 2004): 40–62.
Anderson, Paul Allen. "'The Game Is the Game': Tautology and Allegory in *The
    Wire.*" In *"The Wire": Race, Class, and Genre,* edited by Liam Kennedy and
    Stephen Shapiro, 84–109. Ann Arbor: University of Michigan Press,
    2012.
Ang, Ien. *Watching "Dallas": Soap Opera and the Melodramatic Imagination.*
    New York: Routledge, 1992.
Armstrong, Jennifer Keishin. "TV Comedy *Portlandia*: Liberal Self-Mockery as
    Art." *BBC,* January 31, 2018.
Bacon-Smith, Camille. *Enterprising Women: Television Fandom and the Creation
    of Popular Myth.* Philadelphia: University of Pennsylvania Press, 1991.
Banks, Miranda. "*I Love Lucy:* Showrunner." In *How to Watch Television,* edited
    by Ethan Thompson and Jason Mittell, 260–268. 2nd ed. New York: NYU
    Press, 2020.
Barker, Jennifer. *The Tactile Eye: Touch and the Cinematic Experiences.* Berkeley:
    University of California Press, 2009.
Bastién, Angelica Jade. "*The Handmaid's Tale* Season 1 Finale: Resistance."
    New York Times, June 15, 2017. https://www.nytimes.com/2017/06/15/arts
    /television/the-handmaids-tale-recap-season-finale-night.html.
Bayne, Caroline. "#nolitetebastardescarborundorum: Self-Publishing, Hashtag
    Activism, and Feminist Resistance." *Communication, Culture and Critique* 11
    (2018): 201–205.

Beasley-Murray, Jon. *Posthegemony: Political Theory and Latin America*. Minneapolis: University of Minnesota Press, 2011.

Beaumont, Peter, and Amanda Holpuch. "How *The Handmaid's Tale* Dressed Protests around the World." *Guardian*, August 3, 2018. https://www.theguardian.com/world/2018/aug/03/how-the-handmaids-tale-dressed-protests-across-the-world.

Beltrán, Mary. "Meaningful Diversity: Exploring Questions of Equitable Representation on Diverse Ensemble Cast Shows." *Flow*, August 27, 2010. https://www.flowjournal.org/2010/08/meaningful-diversity/.

Benson-Allott, Caetlin. *The Stuff of Spectatorship: Material Cultures of Film and Television*. Berkeley: University of California Press, 2021.

Berlant, Lauren. *The Queen of America Goes to Washington City: Essays on Sex and Citizenship*. Durham, NC: Duke University Press, 1997.

Berlant, Lauren. "The Subject of True Feeling: Pain, Privacy, and Politics." In *Left Legalism/Left Critique*, edited by Wendy Brown and Janet Halley, 105–133. Durham, NC: Duke University Press, 2002.

Berlant, Lauren. *Cruel Optimism*. Durham, NC: Duke University Press, 2013.

Berlant, Lauren, and Michael Warner. "Sex in Public." *Critical Inquiry* 24, no. 2 (1998): 547–566.

Berman, Judy. "'I'm a White Girl': Why *Girls* Won't Ever Overcome Its Racial Problem." *Atlantic*, January 22, 2013. http://www.theatlantic.com/entertainment/archive/2013/01/im-a-white-girl-why-girls-wont-ever-overcome-its-racial-problem/267345/

Bernstein, Robin. "Dances with Things: Material Culture and the Performance of Race." *Social Text* 27, no. 4 (Winter 2009): 67–94.

Bianco, Jamie "Skye." "Techno-cinema: Image Matters in the Affective Unfoldings of Analog Cinema." In *The Affective Turn: Theorizing the Social*, edited by Patricia Ticiento Clough, 47–76. Durham, NC: Duke University Press, 2007.

Boltanski, Luc, and Eve Chiapello. *The New Spirit of Capitalism*. New York: Verso, 2005.

Bolter, Jay David, and Richard Grusin. *Remediation: Understanding New Media*. Cambridge, MA: MIT Press, 2000.

Booth, Paul J. "Mashup as Temporal Amalgam: Time, Taste, and Textuality." *Transformative Works and Cultures* 9 (2012). https://doi.org/10.3983/twc.2012.0297.

Boothroyd, Dave. *Culture on Drugs: Narco-cultural Studies of High Modernity*. New York: Manchester University Press, 2007.

Bordowitz, Gregg. *The AIDS Crisis Is Ridiculous and Other Writings: 1986–2003*. Edited by James Meyer. Cambridge, MA: MIT Press, 2004.

Boskind-Lodahl, Marlene. "Cinderella's Stepsisters: A Feminist Perspective on Anorexia Nervosa and Bulimia." *Signs* 2, no. 2 (Winter 1976): 342–356.

Bratich, Jack. "Programming Reality: Control Societies, New Subjects, and the Powers of Transformation." In *Makeover Television: Realities Remodelled*, edited by Dana Heller, 6–22. New York: I. B. Tauris, 2007.

Brennan, Matt. "Reconsidering *Louie*—and Myself." *Paste*, November 13, 2017. https://www.pastemagazine.com/articles/2017/11/louis-ck-louie-sexual -misconduct-fx-critics.html.

Brinkema, Eugenie.*The Forms of the Affects*. Durham, NC: Duke University Press, 2014.

Brooks, Daphne. *Bodies in Dissent: Spectacular Performances of Race and Freedom, 1850–1910*. Durham, NC: Duke University Press, 2006.

Brown, Wendy. "Resisting Left Melancholy." *boundary 2* 26, no. 3 (1999): 19–27.

Brown, Wendy. *Undoing the Demos: Neoliberalism's Stealth Revolution*. Cambridge, MA: MIT Press, 2015.

Byers, Michele, and Val Marie Johnson, eds. *The CSI Effect: Television, Crime, and Governance*. Lanham, MD: Lexington Books, 2009.

Caldwell, John. *Televisuality: Style, Crisis, and Authority in American Television*. New Brunswick, NJ: Rutgers University Press, 1995.

Campbell v. Acuff-Rose Music, 510 U.S. 569 (1994). https://supreme.justia.com /cases/federal/us/510/569/case.html.

Caramanica, Jon. "Broadcasting a World of Whiteness," *New York Times*, April 29, 2012, AR20.

Cardenas, Kerensa. "Feminism and Flawed Women in Lena Dunham's *Girls*." *Ms. Magazine* (blog), April 14, 2012. http://msmagazine.com/blog/2012/04/14 /flawed-women-and-feminism-in-lena-dunhams-girls/.

Chaney, Keidra. "Requiem for a Jem." *Bitch Magazine* 63 (2014): 5.

Chappell, Les. "*Portlandia* Suffers the Disability of Being Annoying Instead of Funny." *AV Club*, February 25, 2016.

Chen, Mel Y. *Animacies: Biopolitics, Racial Mattering, and Queer Affect*. Durham, NC: Duke University Press, 2013.

Chiu, Allyson. "Obama Finds Rare Bipartisan Support by Bashing 'Woke' Shaming." *Washington Post*, October 31, 2019.

Christian, Aymar Jean. "Fandom as Industrial Response: Producing Identity in an Independent Web Series." *Transformative Works and Cultures* 8 (2011). https://doi.org/10.3983/twc.2011.0250.

Christian, Aymar Jean. "Netflix's 'Arrested Development' Will Not Change TV. Web TV Is Already TV." *Televisual*, January 11, 2013. http://tvisual.org/2013/01 /11/netflixs-arrested-development-will-not-change-tv-web-tv-already-did/.

Christian, Aymar Jean. *Open TV: Innovation beyond Hollywood and the Rise of Web Television*. New York: NYU Press, 2018.

Christian, Aymar Jean, and Khadijah Costley White. "Organic Representation as Cultural Reparation." *Journal of Cinema and Media Studies* 60, no. 1 (2020): 143–147.

Chua, Amy. *Battle Hymn of the Tiger Mother*. New York: Penguin, 2011.

Chun, Wendy Hui Kyong. *Control and Freedom: Power and Paranoia in the Age of Fiber Optics*. Cambridge, MA: MIT Press, 2006.

Coates, Ta-Nehisi. "On Being Your Authentic Self." *Atlantic*, January 14, 2013. http://www.theatlantic.com/entertainment/archive/2013/01/on-being-your -authentic-self/267128/.

221

Cohan, Steven. *CSI: Crime Scene Investigation*. London: Bloomsbury Academic, 2008.

Coleman, Gabriella. "Phreaks, Hackers, and Trolls: The Politics of Transgression and Spectacle." In *The Social Media Reader*, edited by Michael Mandiberg, 99–119. New York: NYU Press, 2012.

Conlin, Michelle. "America's Reality-TV Addiction." *BusinessWeek*, January 29, 2003. http://www.businessweek.com/stories/2003-01-29/americas-reality-tv -addiction.

Coppa, Francesca. "A Fannish Taxonomy of Hotness." *Cinema Journal* 48, no. 4 (2009): 107–113.

Corner, John. "Afterword: Framing the New." In *Understanding Reality Television*, edited by Su Holmes and Deborah Jermyn, 290–299. New York: Routledge, 2004.

Cuklanz, Lisa M., and Sujata Moorti. "Television's 'New' Feminism: Prime-Time Representations of Women and Victimization." *Critical Studies in Media Communication* 23, no. 4 (2006): 302–321.

D'Acci, Julie. "Leading Up to *Roe v. Wade*: Television Documentaries in the Abortion Debate." In *Television, History, and American Culture: Feminist Critical Essays*, edited by Mary Beth Haralovich and Lauren Rabinovitz, 120–143. Durham, NC: Duke University Press, 1999.

Daum, Meghan. "Lena Dunham Is Not Done Confessing." *New York Times*, September 10, 2014, MM30.

Davis, Elizabeth. "Beside(s) Love and Hate: The Politics of Consuming Black Culture." *Theory and Event* 22, no. 3 (2019): 576–594.

Davis Tracy C., and Thomas Postlewait. "Theatricality: An Introduction." In *Theatricality*, edited by Tracy C. Davis and Thomas Postlewait, 1–39. New York: Cambridge University Press, 2003.

Dean, Jodi. *Democracy and Other Neoliberal Fantasies: Communicative Capitalism and Left Politics*. Durham, NC: Duke University Press, 2009.

Dean, Michelle. "The Internet's Toxic Relationship with HBO's *Girls*." *The Nation*, January 28, 2013. http://www.thenation.com/blog/172481/internets-toxic -relationship-hbos-girls#.

de Certeau, Michel. *The Practice of Everyday Life*. Berkeley: University of California Press, 1984.

Dehnart, Andy. "*Intervention*'s Success Rate Is High, but Has Dropped." *Reality Blurred*, September 7, 2015. https://www.realityblurred.com/realitytv/2015 /09/intervention-success-rate-sobriety/.

Deleuze, Gilles, and Félix Guattari. *A Thousand Plateaus: Capitalism and Schizophrenia*. Minneapolis: University of Minnesota Press, 1987.

Deming, Caren. "Locating the Televisual in Golden Age Television." In *A Companion to Television*, edited by Janet Wasko, 26–141. Norton, MA: Blackwell, 2010.

Dennis, Jr., David. "The Second Season of 'Atlanta' Has Been a Chilling Tour of Broken-Down Heroes." *Uproxx*, April 12, 2018. https://uproxx.com/tv/atlanta -season-2-broken-heroes-donald-glover-teddy-perkins-katt-williams/.

Derrida, Jacques. "The Rhetoric of Drugs: An Interview." *differences* 5, no. 1 (1993): 1–25.

de Valck, Marijke, and Malte Hagener, eds. *Cinephilia: Movies, Love, and Memory.* Amsterdam: Amsterdam University Press, 2005.

Dienst, Richard. *Still Life in Real Time: Theory after Television.* Durham, NC: Duke University Press, 1994.

Doane, Mary Ann. "Information, Crisis, Catastrophe." In *Logics of Television: Essays in Cultural Criticism,* edited by Patricia Mellencamp, 222–239. Bloomington: Indiana University Press, 1990.

Douglas, Susan. "*Jersey Shore:* Ironic Viewing." In *How to Watch Television,* edited by Ethan Thompson and Jason Mittell, 148–156. New York: NYU Press, 2013.

Dovey, Jon. *Freakshow: First Person Media and Factual Television.* London: Pluto Press, 2000.

Ehrenhalt, Lizzie. "Truly Outrageous!: Towards a Defense of *Jem and the Holograms.*" *Bitch Magazine* 33 (2006): 82–87.

Ehrenhalt, Lizzie, and Prachi Srivastava. "*Jem and the Holograms.*" In *Girl Culture: An Encyclopedia,* edited by Claudia A. Mitchell and Jacqueline Reid-Walsh, 371–373. Westport, CT: Greenwood Press, 2007.

Elswit, Kate. "*So You Think You Can Dance* Does Dance Studies." *TDR: The Drama Review,* 56, no. 1 (2012): 133–142.

Fallon, Kevin. "'Queer Eye' for the Woke Guy: Netflix's Reboot Struggles to Be Fabulous." *Daily Beast,* February 7, 2018. https://www.thedailybeast.com /queer-eye-for-the-woke-guy-netflixs-reboot-struggles-to-be-fabulous?ref =scroll.

Fan, Victor. "The Poetics of Addiction: Stardom, 'Feminized' Spectatorship, and Interregional Business Relations in the *Twilight* Series." *Camera Obscura* 27, no. 1 (2012): 31–67.

Federal Communications Commission, "Obscene, Indecent, and Profane Broadcasts." January 13, 2021. https://www.fcc.gov/consumers/guides/obscene -indecent-and-profane-broadcasts.

Fehrman, Craig. "The Channeling of the Novel." *New York Times Sunday Book Review,* December 16, 2011. BR 35.

Felski, Rita. "Context Stinks." *New Literary History* 42 (2011): 573–591.

Feuer, Jane. "The Concept of Live Television: Ontology as Ideology." In *Regarding Television: Critical Approaches—An Anthology,* edited by E. Ann Kaplan, 12–24. Frederick, MD: University Publications of America, 1983.

Feuer, Jane. *Seeing Through the Eighties: Television and Reaganism.* Durham, NC: Duke University Press, 1995.

Feuer, Jane. "Quality Drama in the US: The New 'Golden Age'?" In *The Television History Book,* edited by Michele Hilmes, 98–102. Los Angeles: British Film Institute, 2003.

Fisher, Anna Watkins. *The Play in the System: The Art of Parasitical Resistance.* Durham, NC: Duke University Press, 2020.

223

Fiske, John. *Television Culture*. New York: Routledge, 1987.

Fleetwood, Nicole. *Troubling Vision: Performance, Visuality, and Blackness*. Chicago: University of Chicago Press, 2011.

Fleissner, Jennifer. "Objecting to Novelty: The Objectivity of the Novelistic." *Novel* 44, no. 1 (2011): 11–13.

Flitterman-Lewis, Sandy. "Psychoanalysis, Film, and Television." In *Channels of Discourse, Reassembled*, edited by Robert C. Allen, 203–246. Chapel Hill: University of North Carolina Press, 1992.

Foucault, Michel. "What Is an Author?" In *The Essential Works of Foucault, 1954–1984*. Vol. 2, *Aesthetics, Method, and Epistemology*, edited by James D. Faubion, translated by Robert Hurley et al., 205–222. New York: The New Press, 1998.

Freeman, Elizabeth. "Introduction." In "Queer Temporalities," edited by Elizabeth Freeman. Special issue, *GLQ: A Journal of Lesbian and Gay Studies* 13, nos. 2–3 (2007): 159–176.

Freeman, Elizabeth. *Time Binds: Queer Temporalities, Queer Histories*. Durham, NC: Duke University Press, 2010.

Freeman, Elizabeth. "Hopeless Cases: Queer Chronicities and Gertrude Stein's 'Melanctha.'" *Journal of Homosexuality* 63 no. 3 (2016): 329–348.

Friedman, Milton. "Prohibition and Drugs." *Newsweek* 79, no. 18 (May 1, 1972), 104.

Fry, Tony. *RUA/TV: Heidegger and the Televisual*. Bloomington: Indiana University Press, 1993.

Fuqua, J. V. *Prescription TV: Therapeutic Discourse in the Hospital and Home*. Durham, NC: Duke University Press, 2012.

Gamson, Joshua. *Freaks Talk Back: Tabloid Talk Shows and Sexual Nonconformity*. Chicago: University of Chicago Press, 1998.

Gates, Racquel M. *Double Negative: The Black Image and Popular Culture*. Durham, NC: Duke University Press, 2018.

Gay, Roxane. "Lena Dunham: A Generation's Gutsy, Ambitious Voice." *Time*, September 24, 2014. http://time.com/3425759/lena-dunham-a-generations -gutsy-ambitious-voice/.

Gellene, Denise. "Barbie Prevails: 'Jem' Singing Her Swan Song; Hasbro Doll Being Pulled as Mattel Beats the Band." *Los Angeles Times*, November 3, 1987. https://www.latimes.com/archives/la-xpm-1987-11-03-fi-18333-story .html.

Gever, Martha. "The Spectacle of Crime, Digitized: *CSI: Crime Scene Investigation* and Social Anatomy." *European Journal of Cultural Studies* 8, no. 4 (2005): 445–463.

Gill, Rosalind. "Afterword: *Girls*: Notes on Authenticity, Ambivalence and Imperfection." In *Reading Lena Dunham's "Girls": Feminism, Postfeminism, Authenticity and Gendered Performance in Contemporary Television*, edited by Meredith Nash and Imelda Whelehan, 225–242. Basingstoke, UK: Palgrave Macmillan, 2017.

224

Glynn, Kevin. *Tabloid Culture: Trash Taste, Popular Power, and the Transformation of American Television*. Durham, NC: Duke University Press, 2000.

Goldberg, Lesley. "Peak TV Update: Scripted Originals Hit Another High in 2018." *Hollywood Reporter*, December 13, 2018. https://www
.hollywoodreporter.com/live-feed/peak-tv-update-scripted-originals-hit
-high-2018–1169047.

Goldberg, Lesley. "Peak TV Update: Scripted Originals Top 500 in 2019, FX Says." *Hollywood Reporter*, January 9, 2020. https://www.hollywoodreporter.com
/live-feed/peak-tv-update-scripted-originals-set-record-2019–1266256.

Good Morning America. "When Does Passion Become a Problem?" May 29, 2008. http://abcnews.go.com/GMA/story?id=4949565&page=1.

Goode, Ian. "*CSI: Crime Scene Investigation*." In *Quality TV: Contemporary American Television and Beyond*, edited by Kim Akass and Janet McCabe, 118–128. London: I. B. Tauris, 2007.

Goodman, Tim. "When TV Brands Go off Brand." *Hollywood Reporter*, November 23, 2010. https://www.hollywoodreporter.com/news/tv-brands-brand
-47791.

Gournelos, Ted. "Puppets, Slaves, and Sex Changes: Mr. Garrison and *South Park*'s Performative Sexuality." *Television and New Media* 10, no. 3 (2009): 270–293.

Gray, Herman. *Watching Race: Television and the Struggle for Blackness*. Minneapolis: University of Minnesota Press, 1995.

Greenfield, Rebecca. "Netflix Is Making Both Cable and Internet Television Better." *Atlantic*, July 8, 2013. https://www.theatlantic.com/technology/archive
/2013/07/netflix-making-both-cable-and-internet-television-better/313544/.

Griffin, Hollis. *Feeling Normal: Sexuality and Media Criticism in the Digital Age*. Bloomington: Indiana University Press, 2016.

Grindstaff, Laura. *The Money Shot: Trash, Class, and the Making of TV Talk Shows*. New York: NYU Press, 2002

Grossberg, Lawrence. "Is There a Fan in the House?: The Affective Sensibility of Fandom." In *The Adoring Audience: Fan Culture and Popular Media*, edited by Lisa A. Lewis, 50–65. New York: Routledge, 1992.

Grossberg, Lawrence. *We Gotta Get Out of This Place: Popular Conservatism and Postmodern Culture*. New York: Routledge, 1992.

Grusin, Richard. "YouTube at the End of New Media." In *The YouTube Reader*, edited by Pelle Snickars and Patrick Vondereau, 60–67. Stockholm: National Library of Sweden, 2009.

Haggins, Bambi. *Laughing Mad: The Black Comic Persona in Post-soul America*. New Brunswick, NJ: Rutgers University Press, 2007.

Haggins, Bambi. "*Homicide*: Realism." In *How to Watch Television*, edited by Ethan Thompson and Jason Mittell, 13–21. New York: NYU Press, 2013.

Haglund, David. "Why 'Think Piece' Is Pejorative." *Slate*, May 7, 2014. http://www
.slate.com/blogs/browbeat/2014/05/07/think piece_definition_and_history
_roots_of_the_word_show_it_has_long_been.html.

225

Halberstam, Jack. "It Gets Worse." *Social Text*, November 20, 2010. http://socialtextjournal.org/periscope_article/it_gets_worse/.

Hall, Alice. "Reading Realism: Audiences' Evaluation of the Reality of Media Texts." *Journal of Communication* 53, no. 4 (2003): 624–641.

Hall, Stuart. "Encoding/Decoding." In *Culture, Media, Language: Working Papers in Cultural Studies, 1972–79*, edited by Stuart Hall et al., 128–138. London: Hutchinson, 1980.

Hallinan, Blake, and Ted Striphas. "Recommended for You: The Netflix Prize and the Production of Algorithmic Culture." *New Media and Society* 18, no. 1 (2014): 117–137.

Harkins, Gillian. *Everybody's Family Romance: Reading Incest in Neoliberal America*. Minneapolis: University of Minnesota Press, 2009.

Harris, Geraldine. "A Return to Form? Postmasculinist Tragic Drama and Tragic Heroes in the Wake of *The Sopranos*." *New Review of Film and Television Studies* 10, no. 4 (2012): 443–463.

Harvey, David. *A Brief History of Neoliberalism*. New York: Oxford University Press, 2005.

Havas, Julia, and Maria Sulimma. "Through the Gaps of My Fingers: Genre, Femininity, and Cringe Aesthetics in Dramedy Television." *Television and New Media* 21, no. 1 (2020): 75–94.

Hemmings, Clare. "Invoking Affect: Cultural Theory and the Ontological Turn." *Cultural Studies* 19, no. 5 (2005): 548–567.

Hendershot, Heather. *Saturday Morning Censors: Television Regulation before the V-Chip*. Durham, NC: Duke University Press, 1998.

Heyman, Gene M. *Addiction: A Disorder of Choice*. Cambridge, MA: Harvard University Press, 2009.

Hill, Annette. "Reality TV Experiences: Audiences, Fact, and Fiction." In *A Companion to Reality Television*, edited by Laurie Ouellette, 116–133. Norton, MA: Blackwell, 2014.

Hills, Matt. *Fan Cultures*. New York: Routledge, 2002.

Holmes, Anna. "White *Girls*." *New Yorker*, April 23, 2012. http://www.newyorker.com/culture/culture-desk/white-girls.

hooks, bell. *Black Looks: Race and Representation*. Boston: South End Press, 1988.

Humphrey, William Steven. "The Paradox of *Portlandia*." *Portland Mercury*, January 20, 2011.

Hutcheon, Linda. "Irony, Nostalgia and the Postmodern." 1998. *Methods for the Study of Literature as Cultural Memory, Studies in Comparative Literature* 30 (2000): 189–207.

Jagoda, Patrick. "Wired." *Critical Inquiry* 38 (2011): 189–199.

James, Andrea. "I F*cking Hate @RuPaul." *BoingBoing*, April 4, 2014. http://boingboing.net/2014/04/04/rupaul.html.

James, Kendra. "Dear Lena Dunham: I Exist." *Racialicious*, April 19, 2012. http://www.racialicious.com/2012/04/19/dear-lena-dunham-i-exist/.

Jameson, Fredric. "Periodizing the 60s." *Social Text* 9, no. 1 (1984): 178–209.

Jameson, Fredric. *Postmodernism, or, The Cultural Logic of Late Capitalism.* Durham, NC: Duke University Press, 1991.

Jameson, Fredric. "Realism and Utopia in *The Wire*." *Criticism* 52, nos. 3–4 (2010): 359–372.

Jenkins, Henry. *Convergence Culture: Where Old and New Media Collide.* New York: NYU Press, 2006.

Jenkins, Henry. *Fans, Bloggers, and Gamers: Exploring Participatory Culture.* New York: NYU Press, 2006.

Jenkins, Henry. "The Guiding Powers That Be: A Response to Suzanne Scott." In *The Participatory Cultures Handbook*, edited by Aaron Delwiche and Jennifer Jacobs Henderson, 53–58. New York: Routledge, 2012.

Jenkins, Henry. *Textual Poachers: Television Fans and Participatory Culture.* London: Routledge, 1992.

Jenzen, Olu. "A Queer Tension: The Difficult Comedy of *Hannah Gadsby: Nanette*." *Film Studies* 22 (2020): 30–46.

Johnson, Barbara. "Apostrophe, Animation, and Abortion." *diacritics* 16, no. 1 (Spring 1986): 29–47.

Johnston, Maura. "Introducing the Trollgaze Index with an Analysis of the Internet's 'Cocaine' Video." *Village Voice*, November 1, 2011. http://blogs.villagevoice.com/music/2011/11/the_internet_cocaine_odd_future_trollgaze.php.

Joyrich, Lynne. "Going through the E/Motions: Gender, Postmodernism, and Affect in Television Studies." *Discourse* 14, no. 1 (1991–1992): 23–40.

Joyrich, Lynne. *Re-viewing Reception: Television, Gender, and Postmodern Culture.* Bloomington: University of Indiana Press, 1996.

Joyrich, Lynne. "TV Trumps." In *Unwatchable*, edited by Nicholas Baer, Maggie Hennefeld, Laura Horak, and Gunnar Iversen, 293–298. New Brunswick, NJ: Rutgers University Press, 2019.

Jullier, Laurent. "Philistines and Cinephiles: The New Deal." *Framework* 50, nos. 1–2 (2009): 202–205.

Kavka, Misha. *Reality Television, Affect, and Intimacy: Reality Matters.* Basingstoke, UK: Palgrave Macmillan, 2008.

Kavka, Misha. *Reality TV.* Edinburgh: Edinburgh University Press, 2012.

Keeling, Kara. *The Witch's Flight: The Cinematic, the Black Femme, and the Image of Common Sense.* Durham, NC: Duke University Press, 2007.

Kelly, Nicholas M. "The Hacktivist Cultural Archive: From Science Fiction to Snowden, Worms to the Women's March." In *From Sit-Ins to #revolutions: Media and the Changing Nature of Protests*, edited by Olivia Guntarik and Victoria Grieve-Williams, 127–140. New York: Bloomsbury Academic, 2020.

King, Elizabeth. "Stressed? Blame the 2016 Election." *Time*, April 26, 2016. https://time.com/4299527/election-mental-health/.

King, Katie. "Historiography as Reenactment: Metaphors and Literalizations of TV Documentaries." *Criticism* 46, no. 3 (2004): 459–475.

King, Rob. "Powers of Comedy, or, The Abject Dialectics of *Louie*." In *Abjection Incorporated: Mediating the Politics of Pleasure*, edited by Maggie Hennefeld and Nicholas Sammond, 291–320. Durham, NC: Duke University Press, 2019.

King-Slutzky, Johannah. "The Internet Has a Problem(atic)." *The Awl*, September 25, 2014. http://www.theawl.com/2014/09/the-problem-with -problems.

Kirsch, Adam, and Mohsin Hamid. "Are the New 'Golden Age' TV Shows the New Novels?" *New York Times Sunday Book Review*, March 2, 2014, BR31.

Kois, Dan. "Everything You Were Afraid to Ask about *The Wire*." *Salon*, October 1, 2004. http://www.salon.com/2004/10/01/the_wire_2/.

Kompare, Derek. *CSI: Crime Scene Investigation*. Malden, MA: Wiley-Blackwell, 2010.

Kreisinger, Elisa. "Queer Video Remix and LGBTQ Online Communities." *Transformative Works and Cultures* 9 (2011): n. pag.

Kubey, Robert, and Mihaly Csikszentmihalyi. *Television and the Quality of Life: How Viewing Shapes Everyday Experience*. Hillsdale, NJ: Lawrence Erlbaum Associates, 1990.

Kubey, Robert, and Mihaly Csikszentmihalyi. "Television Addiction Is No Mere Metaphor." *Scientific American* 286, no. 2 (February 2002): 74–80.

Lacquer, Thomas. *Solitary Sex: A Cultural History of Masturbation*. Boston: Zone Books, 2004.

Laine, Tarja. *Feeling Cinema: Emotional Dynamics in Film Studies*. New York: Bloomsbury, 2011.

Landsberg, Alison. *Prosthetic Memory: The Transformation of American Remembrance in the Age of Mass Culture*. New York: Columbia University Press, 2004.

Lapin, Lisa A. "Barbie Takes Up Rock 'n' Roll to Match Rival Jem." *Los Angeles Times*, October 6, 1986. http://articles.latimes.com/1986-10-06/business/fi -4330_1_barbies.

Lee, Tony. "*Friday Night Lights* Tackles Abortion." *Atlantic*, July 10, 2010. http:// www.theatlantic.com/entertainment/archive/2010/07/friday-night-lights -tackles-abortion/59495/.

Leerhrsen, Charles. "Sex, Death, Drugs, and Geraldo." *Newsweek* 112, no. 20 (November 14, 1988), 76.

Lentz, Kirsten Marthe. "*Quality* versus *Relevance*: Feminism, Race, and the Politics of the Sign in 1970s Television." *Camera Obscura* 15, no. 1 (2000): 45–93.

Leonard, Andrew. "How Netflix Is Turning Its Viewers into Puppets." *Salon*, February 1, 2013. https://www.salon.com/2013/02/01/how_netflix_is_turning _viewers_into_puppets/.

Lessig, Lawrence. *Remix: Making Art and Commerce Thrive in the Hybrid Economy*. New York: Penguin, 2009.

Leverette, Marc, Brian Ott, and Cara Buckley, eds. *It's Not TV: Watching HBO in the Post-television Era*. New York: Routledge, 2008.

Leys, Ruth. "The Turn to Affect: A Critique." *Critical Inquiry* 37 (2011): 434–472.

bibliography

Lipsitz, George. *The Possessive Investment: How White People Profit from Identity Politics*. Philadelphia: Temple University Press, 1998.

Lipsitz, George. *How Racism Takes Place*. Philadelphia: Temple University Press, 2011.

Litwack, Michael. "Making Television Live: Mediating Biopolitics in Obesity Programming." *Camera Obscura* 30, no. 1 (2015): 41–69.

Lothian, Alexis. *Old Futures: Speculative Fiction and Queer Possibility*. New York: NYU Press, 2018.

Lott, Eric. *Black Mirror: The Cultural Contradictions of American Racism*. Cambridge, MA: Harvard University Press, 2017.

Lotz, Amanda. *Cable Guys: Television and Masculinities in the 21st Century*. New York: NYU Press, 2014.

Lovelock, Michael. *Reality TV and Queer Identities: Sexuality, Authenticity, Celebrity*. New York: Palgrave MacMillan, 2019.

Lowry, Brian. "*Onion News Network, Portlandia*." *Variety*, January 19, 2011.

Lynch, Joe. "How A&E Got Rich Off of Recovery." *The Fix*, March 25, 2011. http://www.thefix.com/content/affliction-network?page=all.

Maciak, Phillip. "Who's Afraid of Serial TV?" *Los Angeles Review of Books*, September 15, 2016. https://lareviewofbooks.org/article/whos-afraid-serial-tv/.

Manovich, Lev. "What Comes after Remix?" 2007. http://manovich.net/index.php/projects/what-comes-after-remix.

Marks, Laura U. *The Skin of the Film: Intercultural Cinema, Embodiment, and the Senses*. Durham, NC: Duke University Press, 2000.

Martin, Brett. *Difficult Men: Behind the Scenes of a Creative Revolution; From "The Sopranos" and "The Wire" to "Mad Men" and "Breaking Bad."* New York: Penguin, 2014.

Marx, Nick. "*Family Guy*: Undermining Satire." In *How to Watch Television*, edited by Ethan Thompson and Jason Mittell, 177–186. New York: NYU Press, 2013.

Massumi, Brian. *Parables for the Virtual: Movement, Affect, Sensation*. Durham, NC: Duke University Press, 2002.

McAllister, Marvin. *Whiting Up: Whiteface Minstrels and Stage Europeans in African American Performance*. Chapel Hill: University of North Carolina Press, 2011.

McCabe, Janet, and Kim Akass. "Sex, Swearing, and Respectability: Courting Controversy, HBO's Original Programming and Producing Quality TV." In *Quality TV: Contemporary American Television and Beyond*, edited by Janet McCabe and Kim Akass, 62–76. New York: Palgrave Macmillan, 2007.

McCann, Hannah. "'A Voice of *a* Generation': *Girls* and the Problem of Representation." In *Reading Lena Dunham's "Girls": Feminism, Postfeminism, Authenticity and Gendered Performance in Contemporary Television*, edited by Meredith Nash and Imelda Whelehan, 91–104. Basingstoke, UK: Palgrave Macmillan, 2017.

McCarthy, Anna. "Reality TV: A Theater of Neoliberal Suffering." *Social Text* 25, no. 3 (Fall 2007): 17–42.

McCracken, Grant. "From *Arrested Development* to *Dr. Who*, Binge Watching Is Changing Our Culture." *Wired*, May 24, 2013. http://www.wired.com /opinion/2013/05/beyond-arrested-development-how-binge-watching-is -changing-our-narrative-culture/.

McFarland, Melanie "On TV: 'Addiction' Takes Pains to Show Us Real Drug Abuse." *Seattle Post Intelligencer*, March 12, 2007, C1.

McGrath, Charles. "The Triumph of the Prime-Time Novel." *New York Times Magazine*, October 22, 1995, M52.

McNamara, Mary. "Critic's Notebook: The Pros and Cons of Binge TV Watching." *Los Angeles Times*, January 15, 2012, D1.

McNeil, Daniel. "Slimy Subjects and Neoliberal Goods: Obama and the Children of Fanon." *Journal of Critical Mixed Race Studies* 1, no. 1 (2014): 203–218.

Melamed, Jodi. "The Spirit of Neoliberalism: From Racial Liberalism to Neoliberal Multiculturalism." *Social Text* 24, no. 4 (2006): 1–24.

Mitchell, W. J. T. "There Are No Visual Media." *Journal of Visual Culture* 4, no. 2 (2005): 257–266.

Mittell, Jason. "The Cultural Power of an Anti-television Metaphor: Questioning the 'Plug-In Drug' and a TV-Free America." *Television and New Media* 1, no. 2 (2000): 215–238.

Mittell, Jason. "A Cultural Approach to Television Genre Theory." *Cinema Journal* 40, no. 3 (Spring 2001): 3–24.

Mittell, Jason. "Narrative Complexity in Contemporary American Television." *The Velvet Light Trap* 58 (Fall 2006): 29–40.

Mittell, Jason. *Complex TV: The Poetics of Contemporary Television Storytelling.* New York: NYU Press, 2015.

Modleski, Tania. "The Rhythms of Reception: Daytime Television and Women's Work." In *Regarding Television: Critical Approaches—An Anthology*, edited by E. Ann Kaplan, 67–75. Frederick, MD: University Publications of America, 1983.

Molloy, Tim. "'Atlanta': 9 Teddy Perkins-Michael Jackson Parallels That Aren't So Obvious." *The Wrap*, April 7, 2018. https://www.thewrap.com/atlanta-9 -teddy-perkins-michael-jackson-parallels-arent-obvious/.

Monk-Payton, Brandy. "#LaughingWhileBlack: Gender and the Comedy of Social Media Blackness." *Feminist Media Histories* 3, no. 2 (Spring 2017): 15–35.

Monk-Payton, Brandy. "Tele-visionary Blackness." *Public Books*, June 26, 2020. https://www.publicbooks.org/tele-visionary-blackness/.

Moore, Lorrie. "In the Life of *The Wire*." *New York Review of Books*, October 14, 2010.

Muñoz, José Esteban. *The Sense of Brown*. Durham, NC: Duke University Press, 2020.

Murray, Susan. "'I Think We Need a New Name for It': The Meeting of Documentary and Reality TV." In *Reality TV: Remaking Television Culture*, edited by Susan Murray and Laurie Ouellette, 65–81. 2nd ed. New York: NYU Press, 2008.

Murray, Susan, and Laurie Ouellette. "Introduction." In *Reality TV: Remaking Television Culture*, edited by Susan Murray and Laurie Ouellette, 1–20. 2nd ed. New York: NYU Press, 2008.

Nash, Meredith, and Imelda Whelehan, eds. *Reading Lena Dunham's "Girls": Feminism, Postfeminism, Authenticity and Gendered Performance in Contemporary Television*. Basingstoke, UK: Palgrave Macmillan, 2017.

Navas, Eduardo. *Remix Theory: The Aesthetics of Sampling*. Vienna: Springer, 2012.

Netflix. "Netflix Declares Binge Watching Is the New Normal." Cision PR Newswire, December 13, 2013. https://www.prnewswire.com/news-releases/netflix -declares-binge-watching-is-the-new-normal-235713431.html.

Neves, Joshua. *Underglobalization: Beijing's Media Urbanism and the Chimera of Legitimacy*. Durham, NC: Duke University Press, 2020.

Newman, Michael Z. "TV Binge." *Flow* 9, no. 5 (2009).

Newman, Michael Z., and Elana Levine. *Legitimating Television: Media Convergence and Cultural Status*. New York: Routledge, 2012.

Ngai, Sianne. *Ugly Feelings*. Cambridge, MA: Harvard University Press, 2005.

Ngai, Sianne. *Theory of the Gimmick: Aesthetic Judgment and Capitalist Form*. Cambridge, MA: Harvard University Press, 2020.

Nichols, Bill. *Introduction to Documentary*. 2nd ed. Bloomington: Indiana University Press, 2010.

North, Anna. "'Think Pieces Were Made for Millennials Who Majored in English.'" *New York Times*, November 13, 2014. http://op-talk.blogs.nytimes.com/2014/11 /13/think-pieces-were-made-for-millennials-who-majored-in-english/.

North, Anna. "Louis C.K.'s Self-Deprecating Comedy Let Him Control the Narrative—Until Now." *Vox*, November 10, 2017. https://www.vox.com /identities/2017/11/10/16630268/louis-ck-masturbation-jokes-comedy.

NPR. "Lena Dunham Addresses Criticism Aimed at *Girls*." *Fresh Air*, May 7, 2012.

Nussbaum, Emily. "When TV Became Art." *New York*, December 4, 2009. http:// nymag.com/arts/all/aughts/62513.

Nussbaum, Emily. "It's Different for *Girls*." *New York*, March 25, 2012. http:// nymag.com/arts/tv/features/girls-lena-dunham-2012-4/.

Nussbaum, Emily. "Hannah Barbaric: *Girls*, *Enlightened*, and the Comedy of Cruelty." *New Yorker*, February 11, 2013.

Nygaard, Taylor. "Girls Just Want to Be 'Quality': HBO, Lena Dunham, and *Girls'* Conflicting Brand Identity." *Feminist Media Studies* 13, no. 2 (2013): 370–374.

Nygaard, Taylor, and Jorie Lagerwey. *Horrible White People: Gender, Genre, and Television's Precarious Whiteness*. New York: NYU Press, 2020.

O'Dwyer, Rachel. "A Capital Remix." In *The Routledge Companion to Remix Studies*, edited by Eduardo Navas, Owen Gallagher, and xtine burrough, 323–332. New York: Routledge, 2015.

231

Organization of Transformative Works. "FAQs." Accessed April 21, 2022. http://transformativeworks.org/faq#t454n6.

O'Sullivan, Sean. "Broken on Purpose: Poetry, Serial Television, and the Screen." *StoryWorlds: A Journal of Narrative Studies* 2 (2010): 59–77.

Ouellette, Laurie, and James Hay. *Better Living through Reality TV: Television and Post-welfare Citizenship.* Malden, MA: Blackwell, 2008.

Oxford English Dictionary Online. Oxford: Oxford University Press, 2022. http://www.oed.com/.

Palmer, Gareth. "*Extreme Makeover: Home Edition:* An American Fairy Tale." In *Makeover Television: Realities Remodelled,* edited by Dana Heller, 165–176. New York: I. B. Tauris, 2007.

Parks, Lisa. "Flexible Microcasting: Gender, Generation, and Television-Internet Convergence." In *Television after TV: Essays on a Medium in Transition,* edited by Lynn Spigel and Jan Olsson, 133–161. Durham, NC: Duke University Press, 2004.

Pearson, Jesse. "David Simon." *Vice,* December 2, 2009. http://www.vice.com/read/david-simon-280-v16n12.

Peters, Jeremy W. "When Reality TV Gets Too Real." *New York Times,* October 8, 2007, C1.

Petruska, Karen. "The Recappables: Exploring a Feminist Approach to Criticism." *Communication, Culture, and Critique* 12, no. 2 (June 2019): 173–193.

Phoenix, Aisha. "From Text to Screen: Erasing Racialized Difference in *The Handmaid's Tale.*" *Communication, Culture and Critique* 11 (2018): 206–208.

Pierson, David P. "Evidential Bodies: The Forensic and Abject Gazes in *CSI: Crime Scene Investigation.*" *Journal of Communication Inquiry* 34, no. 2 (2010): 184–203.

Pitts-Taylor, Victoria. *Surgery Junkies: Wellness and Pathology in Cosmetic Culture.* New Brunswick, NJ: Rutgers University Press, 2007.

Poniewozik, James. "The Decency Police." *Time* 165, no. 13 (March 28, 2005): 24–31.

Poniewozik, James. "Forget Too Much TV: It's Too Big TV We Should Worry About." *New York Times,* April 25, 2016, C1.

Povinelli, Elizabeth. *Economies of Abandonment: Social Belonging and Endurance in Late Liberalism.* Durham, NC: Duke University Press, 2011.

Projansky, Sarah. *Watching Rape: Film and Television in Postfeminist Culture.* New York: NYU Press, 2001.

"Queer TV Style." *GLQ: A Journal of Lesbian and Gay Studies* 11, no. 1 (2005): 95–117.

Raferty, Brian. "What's the Best TV Drama of the Last 25 Years?" *Vulture,* March 5, 2012. http://www.vulture.com/2012/03/the-best-tv-drama-of-the-last-25-years.html.

Rajewsky, Irina O. "Intermediality, Intertextuality, and Remediation: A Literary Perspective on Intermediality." *Intermédialités* 6 (2005): 43–64.

Reinarman, Craig. "Addiction as Accomplishment: The Discursive Construction of Disease." *Addiction Research and Theory* 13, no. 4 (2005): 307–320.

Restivo, Angelo. *"Breaking Bad" and Cinematic Television.* Durham, NC: Duke University Press, 2019.

Richmond, Scott. *Cinema's Bodily Illusions: Flying, Floating, and Hallucinating.* Minneapolis: University of Minnesota Press, 2016.

Robinson, Joanna. "What on Earth Is Louis C.K. Trying to Say about Rape?" *Vanity Fair*, June 3, 2014. https://www.vanityfair.com/hollywood/2014/06/louis-ck-rape-scene-pamela-part-one.

Romano, Aja. "Hasbro Halts Production of Unauthorized *My Little Pony* Video Game." *Daily Dot*, February 13, 2013. http://www.dailydot.com/entertainment/hasbro-my-little-pony-fighting-magic-game/.

Romano, Aja. "A History of 'Wokeness.'" *Vox*, October 9, 2020. https://www.vox.com/culture/21437879/stay-woke-wokeness-history-origin-evolution-controversy.

Ronell, Avital. *Crack Wars: Literature, Addiction, Mania.* Lincoln: University of Nebraska Press, 1992.

Room, Robin. "The Cultural Framing of Addiction." *Janus Head* 6, no. 2 (2003): 221–234.

Rose, Lacey, and Marisa Guthrie. "FX Chief John Landgraf on Content Bubble: 'This Is Simply Too Much Television.'" *Hollywood Reporter*, August 7, 2015. https://www.hollywoodreporter.com/live-feed/fx-chief-john-landgraf-content-813914.

Russo, Julie Levin. "Many Copies: Cylon Television and Hybrid Video." In *New Media, Old Media: A History and Theory Reader*, edited by Wendy Hui Kyong Chun, Anna Watkins Fisher, and Thomas Keenan, 440–450. 2nd ed. New York: Routledge, 2016.

Russo, Julie Levin, and Francesca Coppa. "Fan/Remix Video (A Remix)." *Transformative Works and Cultures* 9 (2012). https://doi.org/10.3983/twc.2012.0431.

Ryzik, Melena, Cara Buckley, and Jodi Kantor. "Detailing Lewd Acts, 5 Women Accuse a Comic of Misconduct." *New York Times*, November 10, 2017, A1.

Said, Edward. *Culture and Imperialism.* New York: Vintage, 1994.

Salvato, Nick. *Television Scales.* Brooklyn: Punctum Books, 2019.

Sammond, Nicholas. *Birth of an Industry: Blackface Minstrelsy and the Rise of American Animation.* Durham, NC: Duke University Press, 2015.

Sanneh, Kelefa. "The Reality Principle." *New Yorker*, May 9, 2011. http://www.newyorker.com/arts/critics/atlarge/2011/05/09/110509crat_atlarge_sanneh.

Sanson, Kevin, and Gregory Steirer. "Hulu, Streaming, and the Contemporary Television Ecosystem." *Media, Culture and Society* 41, no. 8 (2019): 1210–1227.

Schneider, Rebecca. "Intermediality, Infelicity, and Scholarship on the Slip," *Theatre Survey* 47, no. 2 (2006): 253–260.

Schneider, Rebecca. *Performing Remains: Art and War in Times of Theatrical Reenactment.* New York: Routledge, 2011.

Sconce, Jeffrey. "What If: Charting Television's New Textual Boundaries." In *Television after TV: Essays on a Medium in Transition*, edited by Lynn Spigel and Jan Olsson, 93–112. Durham, NC: Duke University Press, 2004.

Scott, Suzanne. "Who's Steering the Mothership?: The Role of the Fanboy Auteur in Transmedia Storytelling." In *The Participatory Cultures Handbook*, edited by Aaron Delwiche and Jennifer Jacobs Henderson, 43–52. New York: Routledge, 2012.

Sedgwick, Eve Kosofsky. *Epistemology of the Closet*. Berkeley: University of California Press, 1990.

Sedgwick, Eve Kosofsky. "Epidemics of the Will." In *Tendencies*, 130–142. Durham, NC: Duke University Press, 1993.

Sedgwick, Eve Kosofsky. *Tendencies*. Durham, NC: Duke University Press, 1993.

Sedgwick, Eve Kosofsky. *Touching Feeling: Affect, Pedagogy, Performativity*. Durham, NC: Duke University Press, 2003.

Seitz, Matt Zoller. "The Greatest TV Drama of the Past 25 Years, the Finals: *The Wire* vs. *The Sopranos*." *Vulture*, March 26, 2012. https://www.vulture.com /2012/03/drama-derby-finals-the-wire-vs-the-sopranos.html.

Sepinwall, Alan, and Matt Zoller Seitz. *TV (The Book): Two Experts Pick the Greatest American Shows of All Time*. New York: Grand Central Publishing, 2016.

Seresin, Asa. "On Heteropessimism." *New Inquiry*, October 9, 2019. http://thenewinquiry.com/on-heteropessimism.

Sharpe, Christina. *In the Wake: On Blackness and Being*. Durham, NC: Duke University Press, 2016.

Shattuc, Jane. *The Talking Cure: TV Talk Shows and Women*. New York: Routledge, 1997.

Shaviro, Steven. *The Cinematic Body*. Minneapolis: University of Minnesota Press, 1993.

Shaviro, Steven. "The Cinematic Body REDUX." *Parallax* 14, no. 1 (2008): 48–54.

Silverman, Kaja. *The Threshold of the Visible World*. New York: Routledge, 1996.

Smith, Barbara Herrnstein. *Contingencies of Value: Alternative Perspectives for Critical Theory*. Cambridge, MA: Harvard University Press, 1988.

Snyder, Sharon L., and David T. Mitchell. "Body Genres: An Anatomy of Disability in Film." In *The Problem Body: Projecting Disability on Film*, edited by Sally Chivers and Nicole Markotic, 179–204. Columbus: The Ohio State University Press, 2010.

Sontag, Susan. *Against Interpretation*. New York: Farrar, Straus and Giroux, 1966.

Sperling, Nicole. "Is Peak TV Slowly Killing TV Critics?" *Vanity Fair*, May 4, 2018. https://www.vanityfair.com/hollywood/2018/05/is-peak-tv-slowly-killing-tv -critics.

Spigel, Lynn. "From Domestic Space to Outer Space: The 1960s Fantastic Family Sitcom." In *Close Encounters: Film, Feminism, and Science Fiction*, edited by Constance Penley, 205–235. Minneapolis: University of Minnesota Press, 1991.

Spigel, Lynn. *Make Room for TV: Television and the Family Ideal in Postwar America*. Chicago: University of Chicago Press, 1992.

234

Spigel, Lynn. "Introduction." In *Television after TV: Essays on a Medium in Transition*, edited by Lynn Spigel and Jan Olsson, 1–34. Durham, NC: Duke University Press, 2004.

Steinlight, Emily. "'Anti-*Bleak House*': Advertising and the Victorian Novel." *Narrative* 14, no. 2 (2006): 132–162.

Stelter, Brian. "Second Clinton-Trump Debate Sees Big Ratings Drop Compared to First." *CNN Business*, October 10, 2016. https://money.cnn.com/2016/10/10/media/clinton-trump-debate-nielsen-twitter-facebook/.

Stewart, Dodai. "Why We Need to Keep Talking about the White Girls on *Girls*." *Jezebel*, April 19, 2012. http://jezebel.com/5903382/why-we-need-to-keep-talking-about-the-white-girls-on-girls.

Stewart, Kathleen. *Ordinary Affects*. Durham, NC: Duke University Press, 2007.

Swindle, Monica. "Feeling Girl, Girling Feeling: An Examination of 'Girl' as Affect." *Rhizomes* 22 (2011). http://www.rhizomes.net/issue22/swindle.html.

Tartiglione, Nancy. "The Too-Much-TV Debate." *Deadline*, August 28, 2015. https://deadline.com/2015/08/fx-john-landgraf-too-much-television-crisis-paul-buccieri-edinburgh-1201508794/.

Television Academy. "73rd Primetime Emmy Awards: 2020–2021 Rules and Procedures." Version 3, January 28, 2021. https://www.emmys.com/sites/default/files/Downloads/2021-rules-procedures-v3.pdf.

Tennessee State Legislature, Senate Bill 0623 (June 1, 2021). http://wapp.capitol.tn.gov/app.BillInfo/Default.aspx?BillNumber=SB0623.

Thain, Alanna. *Bodies in Suspense: Time and Affect in Cinema*. Minneapolis: University of Minnesota Press, 2017.

Thompson, Robert J. *From "Hill Street Blues" to "ER": Television's Second Golden Age*. Syracuse, NY: Syracuse University Press, 1996.

Thorne, Will. "'30 Rock' Blackface Episodes Pulled from Streaming, Syndication at Tina Fey and NBCU's Request." *Variety*, June 22, 2020. https://variety.com/2020/tv/news/30-rock-blackface-episodes-removed-tina-fey-1234645607/.

Treichler, Paula. *How to Have Theory in an Epidemic: Cultural Chronicles of AIDS*. Durham, NC: Duke University Press, 1999.

Uricchio, William. "Television's Next Generation: Technology/Interface/Flow." In *Television after TV: Essays on a Medium in Transition*, edited by Lynn Spigel and Jan Olsson, 163–182. Durham, NC: Duke University Press, 2004.

VanDerWerff, Emily, "The Most Controversial Episode of Louis C.K.'s TV Show Now Plays as a Veiled Confession." *Vox*, November 10, 2017. https://www.vox.com/culture/2017/11/10/16631926/louis-ck-louie-episode-pamela.

Van Es, Karin. "Liveness Redux: On Media and Their Claim to Be Live." *Media, Culture and Society* 39, no. 8 (2017): 1245–1256.

Varone, Patrick. "Linda from *Intervention*: The Case of the Runaway Intervention." *IBBB*, December 1, 2009. http://www.imbringingbloggingback.com/2009/12/01/linda-from-intervention-the-case-of-the-runaway-intervention/.

Ventura, Patricia. *Neoliberal Culture: Living with American Neoliberalism.* New York: Routledge, 2012.

Vice, Sue, Matthew Campbell, and Tim Armstrong, eds. *Beyond the Pleasure Dome: Writing and Addiction from the Romantics.* Sheffield, UK: Sheffield Academic Press, 1994.

Villarejo, Amy. *Ethereal Queer: Television, Historicity, Desire.* Durham, NC: Duke University Press, 2014.

Wallace, Benjamin. "Diamond in the Mud: The Death of *Buckwild* Star Shain Gandee and the Search for Authenticity in Reality TV." *New York Magazine,* September 23, 2013.

Wanzo, Rebecca. "Precarious-Girl Comedy: Issa Rae, Lena Dunham, and Abjection Aesthetics." *Camera Obscura* 31, no. 2 (2016): 27–59.

Wark, McKenzie. "Spectacles of Disintegration." *Social Research* 78, no. 4 (2011): 1115–1132.

Warner, Kristen J. "In the Time of Plastic Representation," *Film Quarterly* 71, no. 2 (2017). https://filmquarterly.org/2017/12/04/in-the-time-of-plastic -representation/.

Weber, Brenda R. *Makeover TV: Selfhood, Citizenship, and Celebrity.* Durham, NC: Duke University Press, 2009.

Weber, Brenda R., ed. *Reality Gendervision: Sexuality and Gender on Transatlantic Reality Television.* Durham, NC: Duke University Press, 2014.

Weber, Brenda R.. "Torture Porn in Dystopic Feminism." *Communication, Culture and Critique* 11 (2018): 192–194.

Wegenstein, Bernadette, and Nora Ruck. "Physiognomy, Reality Television and the Cosmetic Gaze." *Body and Society* 17, no. 4 (2011): 27–55.

Whelehan, Imelda. "Hating Hannah: Or Learning to Love (Post)Feminist Entitlement." In *Reading Lena Dunham's "Girls": Feminism, Postfeminism, Authenticity and Gendered Performance in Contemporary Television,* edited by Meredith Nash and Imelda Whelehan, 31–44. Basingstoke, UK: Palgrave Macmillan, 2017.

White, Mimi. "Crossing Wavelengths: The Diegetic and Referential Imaginary of American Commercial Television." *Cinema Journal* 25, no. 2 (Winter 1986): 51–64.

White, Mimi. *Tele-advising: Therapeutic Discourses in American Television.* Chapel Hill: University of North Carolina Press, 1992.

Williams, Linda. "Film Bodies: Gender, Genre, and Excess." *Film Quaterly* 44, no. 4 (Summer 1991): 2–13.

Williams, Linda. *On "The Wire."* Durham, NC: Duke University Press, 2014.

Williams, Raymond. *Television: Technology as Cultural Form.* London: Fontana, 1974.

Williams, Raymond. *Marxism and Literature.* New York: Oxford University Press, 1977.

Wortham, Jenna. "Where (My) Girls At?" *The Hairpin,* April 16, 2012. http:// thehairpin.com/2012/04/where-my-girls-at.

Zehme, Bill. "Jerry & George & Kramer & Elaine." *Rolling Stone* 660–661 (July 8, 1993): 40–46. https://www.rollingstone.com/music/music-news/jerry -george-kramer-elaine-162060/.

Žižek, Slavoj. *The Year of Dreaming Dangerously*. New York: Verso, 2012.

Zook, Kristal Brent. *Color by Fox: The Fox Network and the Revolution in Black Television*. New York: Oxford University Press, 1999.

Television Series Episodes

Atlanta. "Teddy Perkins." Season 2, Episode 6. FX, original airdate: April 5, 2018.

CSI: Crime Scene Investigation. "King Baby." Season 5, Episode 15. CBS, original airdate: February 17, 2005.

"80's Jem Toy Commercial + Cassette Offer." Original airdate: sometime in 1986. Uploaded to YouTube: April 30, 2008. https://www.youtube.com/watch?v =fyrM8_FQykc.

Funny or Die. "*Intervention Intervention* with Fred Armisen." College Humor, original airdate: August 4, 2009. https://funnyordie.com/2009/08/04/16047 /intervention-intervention-with-fred-armisen/.

Girls. "I Get Ideas." Season 2, Episode 2. HBO, original airdate: January 20, 2013.

Girls. "Beach House." Season 3, Episode 7. HBO, original airdate: February 16, 2014.

Girls. "Goodbye Tour." Season 6, Episode 9. HBO, original airdate: April 9, 2017.

The Handmaid's Tale. "Night." Season 1, Episode 10. Hulu, original airdate: June 14, 2017.

Insecure. "Broken As Fuck." Season 1, Episode 8. HBO, original airdate: November 27, 2016.

Intervention. "Allison." Season 4, Episode 18. A&E, original airdate: August 11, 2008.

Intervention. "Linda." Season 7, Episode 1. A&E, original airdate: November 23, 2009.

Jem and the Holograms. "Adventures in China." Season 1, Episode 10. Syndicated, original airdate: August 23, 1986.

Jiz. "The Abortion Episode." Sienna D'Enema, original airdate: January 17, 2010. https://www.youtube.com/watch?v=xAK1o8u2xAs.

Jiz. "It Gets Worse." Sienna D'Enema, original airdate: November 27, 2010. Available online at https://www.youtube.com/watch?v=cfqO7zmdooA.

Jiz. "The *Jiz* Commercial." Sienna D'Enema, October 25, 2011. https://www .youtube.com/watch?v=epP—ZPC7xA.

Law & Order: Special Victims Unit. "Hooked." Season 6, Episode 15. NBC, original airdate: February 15, 2005.

Louie. "Come On, God." Season 2, Episode 8. FX, original airdate: August 11, 2011.

Portlandia. "One Moore Episode." Season 2, Episode 2. IFC, original airdate: January 13, 2012.

237

Queer Eye. "You Can't Fix Ugly." Season 1, Episode 1. Netflix, original airdate: February 7, 2018.

Queer Eye for the Straight Guy. "Hair Today, Art Tomorrow: Brian S." Season 1, Episode 1. Bravo, original airdate: July 15, 2003.

Saturday Night Live. "Kerry Washington/Eminem." Season 39, Episode 5. NBC, original airdate: November 3, 2013.

Seinfeld. "The Contest." Season 4, Episode 11. NBC, original airdate: November 18, 1992.

Sex and the Remix. "Seasons 3–6." Eliza Kreslinger, original airdate: May 26, 2010. https://www.youtube.com/watch?v=f1QfWRD7qfA&t=1s.

The Sopranos. "Made in America." Season 6, Episode 21. HBO, original airdate: June 10, 2007.

30 Rock. "Believe in the Stars." Season 3, Episode 2. NBC, original airdate: November 6, 2008.

The Wire. "The Dickensian Aspect." Season 5, Episode 6. HBO, original airdate: February 10, 2008.

The Wire. "-30-." Season 5, Episode 10. HBO, original airdate: March 9, 2008.

index

243

244

index